Raising My Voice

Raising My Voice

Selected Sermons and Writings

Rabbi Ellen Lippmann

For Hope

Ellen

Rabbis Press

Central Conference of American Rabbis

5778   NEW YORK   2018

Library of Congress Cataloging-in-Publication Data

Names: Lippmann, Ellen, author. | Wiener, Nancy H., 1958- writer of forward.
Title: Raising my voice : selected sermons and writings / Rabbi Ellen
    Lippmann ; foreword by Dr. Rabbi Nancy Wiener.
Description: New York : Rabbis Press ; Central Conference of American Rabbis,
    5778-2018. | "Some of the pieces in this book were previously published in
    Voices, which began as the weekly [congregation] Kolot Chayeinu newsletter
    and evolved into a journal publishing Kolot's many writers"--Preface.
Identifiers: LCCN 2018022285 (print) | LCCN 2018022826 (ebook) | ISBN
    9780881233308 (ebook) | ISBN 9780881233292 (pbk. : alk. paper)
Subjects: LCSH: Jewish sermons, English. | Judaism--Prayers and devotions.
Classification: LCC BM740.3 (ebook) | LCC BM740.3 .L57 2018 (print) | DDC
    296.4/7--dc23
LC record available at https://lccn.loc.gov/2018022285

10 9 8 7 6 5 4 3 2 1

CCAR Press, 355 Lexington Avenue, New York, NY 10017
(212) 972-3636

www.ccarpress.org

DEDICATION

Oh God, you have been so good to me!
Finally, for the first time in my life,
You gave me something I wanted. . . .

And indeed we have bloomed through the years.

—Merle Feld
"The first time we made Shabbos together"

Thirty-four years ago I met Kathryn Conroy and was struck by a thunderbolt. We have been together ever since, and every time we make Shabbos together I repeat to myself these words of prayer,

"Oh God, you have been so good to me. . . ."

Mentioned little in these pages, Kathryn's thought and care and attention are everywhere, for without her I might never have followed my dream to become a rabbi, nor been the speaker I have become, nor had the strength to found and sustain a growing community.

To her, and to the Holy One, source of the spark of inspiration, I dedicate this book.

CONTENTS

FOREWORD

Dr. Rabbi Nancy Wiener

Words that emerge from the heart enter the heart.
                              —Moses Ibn Ezra Shirat Yisrael

This collection of writings is an offering of the heart of one of the *g'dolei hador*, leading rabbis of this generation, Ellen Lippmann. Each word on these pages conveys her deeply held values and commitments. For when Ellen commits words to paper or shares her words aloud, she is exposing her heart—its loves, its joys, its brokenness, and its longings. This gift is rare and precious indeed.

In *The Art of Loving*, Erich Fromm explains that loving requires listening, full presence, faith in the potentialities of others, humility, and courage.

The messages Rabbi Lippmann offers arise from her unique way of listening to words—words she hears on the street, in class, at the bedside, on the train—while simultaneously hearing the voices of religious sages, philosophers, poets, political activists, and commentators. Each voice represents a world not to be missed. Each unique voice is part of a universe in which everything is connected and interdependent.

The layout of this collection reflects her respect for and dependence on the rabbis in whose footsteps she walks. The content reflects her respect for and dependence on lived experience: her ancestors', her contemporaries', and her own.

Rabbi Lippmann is always fully present in her writings—with her faith and doubts, her hopes and disappointments. Rare among public orators, when speaking about events or issues she readily acknowledges the range of responses her listeners might be experiencing and then clearly and courageously articulates her own ideas and values. She does so not to demand agreement, but rather to invite others to freely and honestly explore and share their own reactions and values. Boldly, she acts on her beliefs, while at the same time nurturing in others the human capacities to grow and change, to make positive contributions to the world, to be partners with God. These themes suffuse her writings, find expression in her professional and personal interactions, and fuel her abiding commitment to social justice. While others often excoriate, Rabbi Lippmann urges from a place of love and example. Her love "resides in the way she lives her values" (see Rosh HaShanah sermon 2013, "A Covenant of Care").

I have had the incomparable pleasure of being Rabbi Lippmann's *chevruta*, study partner, for nearly thirty years. I continue to learn from her and with her about life, about faith, and most importantly about the transformative power of giving and receiving love—for each individual and for the whole world.

Work your way slowly through this collection. Savor the words, digest the profound messages, and be energized by the values you uncover within yourself so that you can find your own ways to actualize them in the world.

Open your hearts and let Rabbi Lippmann's words enter.

PREFACE

The rabbi speaks in seven voices. I learned that from reading an address by the writer Anita Diamant to graduating rabbis at Hebrew Union College–Jewish Institute of Religion in Cincinnati in 2002. She said, "The rabbi speaks in seven voices, too. Not all of the rabbi's voices can be joyful, but all of them count. The rabbi's voice can heal and challenge, can soothe and provoke, can build and honor. The seven voices of the rabbi include the voice of celebration, and the voice of consolation. The voice of hilarity, and the voice of exhortation. The voice of the teacher, and the voice of imagination. And finally, the rabbi's own voice, his authentic voice, her authentic voice."

Her description speaks to me, and I think you will find my seven voices expressed in this wide-ranging selection of my words, including sermons, *divrei Torah*, articles, op-eds, letters, and blessings gathered from hundreds of pages accumulated over the twenty-five years since my small idea of connecting eating and community became a reality, growing far past its origins to become a full-fledged synagogue comprising *beit t'filah*—the house of prayer, *beit midrash*—the house of study, and *k'hilah k'doshah*—sacred, loud, boisterous, loving, irking community.

There is humor here, certainly, and strong urging and outrage, explanation, suggestion, flights of fancy, and textually grounded midrashim. Consolation is here, for our community has weathered tragedy and accident more than we would ever have wished. So yes, my tears are clear here too, as is my laughter and I hope my love for the community that has been the locus of so many aspects of my life.

You will see the changes in twenty-five years of speaking and writing. I hope my growth is clear, and so is a kind of through-line of consistency. Organizations named and admired may have gone out of business, opinions once clear have almost certainly evolved, and I know you will recognize the dates and their distance from today. Even so, I pray my voice is clear.

Diamant wrote, "Finding your own voice isn't so much about being 'original,' as it as about being true to yourself and trusting the notion that we are all created in God's image."

In a *d'var Torah* that you'll find in these pages (*Vayeishev*, December 2016), I wrote about finding my way to that understanding via an understanding of the ways clothing, exemplified by Joseph's coat, both covers and uncovers us:

> *When I first put on my rabbi robe, I was as though a child dressing up in a father's clothing. I say "father" deliberately. The night I received a letter of acceptance to rabbinical school, I dreamed I grew a long white beard. How else should a rabbi look? Twenty-five years later, the robe is gone, and so is the idea of the beard. I know a woman can be a rabbi, and lots of other people know it too. The interweaving lines between Ellen and rabbi are not always so clear. . . .*
>
> *How can you be a rabbi without being arrogant? the prospective rabbis ask. My answer? Know you are naked underneath your clothes, and know too that God can see you. Walk in the world enrobed, but do not for one second imagine that you of all people will escape God's notice. My Hebrew name is not Esther—hidden one—for nothing.*

For related reasons, we are presenting these writings in six groupings, drawn from the words of Simon the Just and Rabbi Shimon, son of Gamliel, in *Pirkei Avot* 1:2 and 1:18: On three things the world stands: on *Torah* (learning), *avodah* (service and prayer), *g'milut chasadim* (mutual communal care), *din* (justice), *emet* (truth), and *shalom* (peace). I am grateful for this idea and for the lion's share of the work that went into this book in a very short timeframe, to Trisha Arlin, Kolot member, friend, sister-wrestler, and editor beyond compare.

More than anything else, I hope, these words I send out into the world will reveal me, my gathered wisdom, uncertain truth, Torah-wrestling, fear, sorrow, and the deep abiding joy of having planted a seed that became a mighty oak, the strong, powerful, spreading, leafy tree that is Kolot Chayeinu/Voices of Our Lives.

It is the voices of all the lives of the people of Kolot Chayeinu that keep it growing, keep it strong. I was the first but thankfully I am not the last. For that I am deeply grateful.

Editor's note: Some of the pieces in this book were previously published in *Voices*, which began as the weekly Kolot Chayeinu newsletter and evolved into a journal publishing Kolot's many writers and edited by Trisha Arlin. There was usually an annual overarching theme, with sub-themes for each issue. The rabbi's essay was always published on page 2.

Part One

Torah

Learning, *D'Rashot*

Learning

Seeing the Moon Eclipse

December 25, 2010

I went out in the middle of the night Monday night to see the eclipse of the moon. It was freezing cold, but we stayed out for over an hour as the shadow passed slowly over the face of the moon. We have seen lunar eclipses before, but this is the first time there has been one at the time of the solstice since 1554, 456 years ago. This was the chance of a lifetime. And it was wondrous. Standing on a street in Brooklyn, I saw God's shadow. Wow! Wow! is a seed of faith, the response that led Abraham to say, "There is more here than just us."

The seed of science is "Why?" A small answer: An eclipse of the moon (or lunar eclipse) can only occur at full moon, and only if the moon passes through some portion of earth's shadow. That shadow is actually composed of two cone-shaped components, one nested inside the other. The outer or penumbral shadow is a zone where the earth blocks part but not all of the sun's rays from reaching the moon. In contrast, the inner or umbral shadow is a region where the earth blocks all direct sunlight from reaching the moon.

The wow and the why can go together—no reason why not. Faith and science in our time can't possibly be separated or live in separate spheres. They are two great lights that illuminate our world.

God said, "Let there be lights in the expanse of the sky to separate day from night; they shall serve as signs for the set times—the

3

days and the years; and they shall serve as lights in the expanse of the sky to shine upon the earth." And it was so. God made the two great lights, the greater light to dominate the day and the lesser light to dominate the night, and the stars. And God set them in the expanse of the sky to shine upon the earth, to dominate the day and night, and to separate light from darkness. And God saw that this was good. And there was evening and there was morning, a fourth day. (Genesis 1:14–19)

The Rabbis asked, "Torah says there were two great lights. Why did God make the moon smaller than the sun?" One answer is that the moon had to be made smaller because it encroached on the sun by being visible during the day sometimes. Another is that it complained about having to share space with the sun, so God made it smaller. And a third answer is that the moon is like us, the people Israel: it is small but active, waxing and waning and waxing again, just as—they hoped—Israel would always renew itself.

The Rabbis asked, "Why did God create the moon instead of allowing the sun to light the evening sky?" Their answer: God knew that people would worship celestial bodies. Rather than have them regard the sun as an all-powerful god—as they did in Egypt, perhaps?—God created the moon to lessen sun's influence.

Moon worship was strong in Mesopotamia; in Haran, where Abraham came from, there was a great temple dedicated to the moon god, Sin. Can we hear its echo in the place God will choose to reveal Torah, Sinai?

During our trip to Israel and Palestine in October, we stayed for two nights in Beit Sahour, a town next door to Bethlehem. Beit Sahour means "house of the moon-watchers." It is the home of the fields where, they say, those certain poor shepherds lay and saw the special star that indicated Jesus's birth. They saw it because they were looking at the moon.

This week's was the first eclipse on the solstice since 1554; some say since 1638. The year 1554 was not a great time for the Jews. On May 29, after an appeal by Jews in Catholic countries, the pope agreed to allow the burning only of the Talmud, but not of "harmless rabbinical writings." On September 4, in Rome, Cornelio da Montalcino—a Franciscian friar who converted to Judaism—was burned alive.

Does this explain why an eclipse of the moon was seen as an evil omen for Israel? It is also true that the moon was seen as representing Jacob, Moses, Joshua, and Esther. Eclipsing it in shadow may have been seen as though covering these important ancestors, who shaped us as a people and ensured our survival.

The sixteenth century was also the time of the early kabbalists, who saw in the moon's monthly disappearance the exile of the *Shechinah*, God's indwelling presence. So they created Yom Kippur Katan, a "little day of atonement," a fast day of sorrow and yearning.

If the last eclipse on the winter solstice was in 1638, then let's note that in 1638, in Baghdad, the Ottoman sultan Murad IV conquered Baghdad. The day was celebrated by Jews as a day of miracles (*yom neis*). In general, when the Ottomans ruled the city, life for its Jewish residents improved.

The year 1638 was 372 years ago. Not much to do with 372, gematria-wise. But 1554 was 456 years ago. From the number 456 we get the letters ונת, *tav-nun-vav*. This can be the command for "give," as in *t'nu chavod laTorah*, "give honor to the Torah." Or it can be "they taught," as in a familiar Talmudic phrase, *Tanu rabboteinu*, "Our rabbis taught. . . ."

T'nu chavod laTorah: Give honor to the Torah because its stories are so incredibly great. We begin reading now the story of our people being formed, a people born in slavery and pain, but pain that caused crying out to God, which caused God in turn to look for a liberator. Moses is born and lives in two worlds, shows bravery and compassion, and is chosen just when he seeks to escape. I think he'll get us out. We are on our way to Sinai (see-nai), place of the moon god and of receiving the Torah.

Tanu rabboteinu: Our rabbis taught us to look up at the sky and note its inhabitants, sun and moon and stars, not to worship, but as a sign of God's power. Our rabbis taught that there was a shadow side: a need for atonement, for guarding against moon worship, for fear of abandonment. To see that shadow pass across the moon at the solstice, a time of change, an unsettled time, a dark time, was wondrous and scary and needed explanation. We escaped slavery and pain time and again and became a people of faith and science.

Give honor and teach: To look at the moon in eclipse in the middle of *erev* solstice is to see the seeds of both faith and science:

Wow!

Why?

The Rabbi's Robe

December 24, 2016 / 24 Kislev 5777 / Erev Chanukah

I have had several conversations lately with people who are exploring becoming rabbis. One question that came up several times was a version of "How do you become a rabbi and not become arrogant?" Whew! A good question, and a pertinent one today, as we begin the story of Joseph, the young prince of arrogance whose favored status is best exemplified by that coat of many colors his father gives him.

When I was ordained, my parents bought me a rabbinic robe of an old-school type: black, poofy sleeves, big cuffs. I put it on and laughed. At that time and for years later, putting on my title or that robe made me feel like an imposter. Rabbi? Me? Really?

Well, really. I have not worn the robe in years except for occasional ceremonial occasions. It still feels like putting on a costume, and in fact I have worn it for Purim more than once. I don't need it to tell me I am a rabbi, though for many women rabbis in the early days, a robe kept away unwanted comments about their clothing or even their bodies. A robe, a coat, can cover or uncover, offer protection or masking. For me, as my comfort with the title and role have grown through the years, my need to hide inside that "robe" has shrunk. How does its presence or absence tell me whether I am more humble or less than when I began?

As I said to our former student rabbi, Daniel Reiser, at his installation at Westchester Reform Temple, "There are many ways you can get a swelled head as a rabbi." The best way to avoid it is probably to follow Joseph in his growing recognition that his abilities are not entirely his own. "Not me," he will say much later on, after his original robe is long gone and he has changed clothes and names and roles many times. "Not me, but God." "Israel loved Joseph best of all his sons . . . and he made for him a *k'tonet pasim*" (Genesis 37:3). That coat looms so large in our childhood memories and popular imagination. Many colors! Technicolor! A dream coat. A favoritism coat. A reminder of his status. A reminder he has no status yet. An object of aspiration? Derision? Prophecy? Wonder?

A series of midrashim and commentaries link Joseph's coat to clothing worn long before and long after—a sartorial lineage my rabbi robe could only yearn for. It starts with Adam and Eve: Once they ate of the Tree, they perceived that they were naked; and they sewed together leaves—or was it fur?—and made clothing. "How did you know you were naked?" asked God (Genesis 3:11), and the jig was up. We are all naked underneath, and certainly in God's eyes, but we don't always know it.

Then there's Esther's robe—another kind of covering. Is she a Persian queen or just a Jewish girl trying to have it all? Her uncle Mordecai warns her: "Do not imagine in your soul that you, of all the Jews, will escape because you are in the king's house" (Esther 4:13). You won't escape your Jewishness and you won't escape the king and you won't escape God. We are all naked underneath. God knows it. And if we are smart, we will know it too.

Finally in the lineage of Joseph's coat, there is the High Priest and his layers of linen garments, designed especially to cover his genitals, his deepest nakedness. Only the High Priest wears underwear! And layer upon layer over it, changed in elaborate ritual aided by attendants. Hadassah disappears and Esther emerges enrobed. Aaron disappears and the *Kohein Gadol*, the High Priest, emerges enrobed. Bratty little brother disappears and Joseph emerges, wrapped in his striped, colored, attention-grabbing coat. Later he'll take on the robes of the chief deputy to Pharaoh. But that is many years in the future. Today, he is just receiving the coat given with love, we hope, by his already aging father. His father who himself put on skins to impersonate his brother and steal his blessing. Put on skins, or leaves, or a royal robe, or linen underwear, or a coat of many colors. Who do you become? What are you hiding? What shows more clearly? Who is watching?

When I first put on my rabbi robe, I was as though a child dressing up in a father's clothing. I say "father" deliberately. The night I received a letter of acceptance to rabbinical school, I dreamed I grew a long white beard. How else should a rabbi look? Twenty-five years later, the robe is gone, and so is the idea of the beard. I know a woman can be a rabbi, and lots of other people know it too. The interweaving lines between Ellen and rabbi are not always so clear. As all rabbis do, I cover and reveal, reveal and cover in an ever-changing dance. So Joseph, reputed to have worn makeup and curled his hair, and continually covering and revealing, is a fair model. When does Joseph's arrogance disappear? Even before he acknowledges God, I think, when he weeps as he recognizes his brothers, though they do not know him in his Egyptian royal finery. His sorrow at their treatment of him and his of them, his deep connections to his home and family, his recognition of his journey and who his bratty young self has come to be, are all there in his unstoppable tears. He sends everyone out. He cries in private, uncovered. Arrogance melts. Human heart emerges.

How can you be a rabbi without being arrogant? the prospective rabbis ask. My answer? Know you are naked underneath your clothes, and know too that God can see you. Walk in the world enrobed, but do not for one second imagine that you of all people will escape God's notice. My Hebrew name is not Esther—hidden one—for nothing. And I bid my brother Joseph welcome, as we enter his story and he ours.

Teach us, Joseph. Teach us what you learned. When is taking off a coat the best idea? When will putting on a robe add confidence, not arrogance? Did you know your first coat was woven with history? Did you ever see it again? Would you want to wear it now?

Lech L'cha

Voices, November 2005

It is an astonishing and particular pleasure to find that Kolot Chayeinu has arrived at its bar/bat mitzvah year. When one is the founder, the next day is often a mystery, so how much more so the realization that thirteen years have passed! I reflect a bit these days on the early days and years, the Shabbatot of five or fifteen people praying and studying Torah in someone's living room, the learning program of seven children in a member's basement, the High Holy Days of seventy-five—a huge crowd at the time—in a church basement. As I note the prevalence of basements in our history, I wonder if in fact Kolot's journey has been one of ascents, an *aliyah*, a going up of growth and creativity and hard work and hope.

We now worship in a sanctuary that seats 250 officially and 400 for some children's or adults' *b'nei mitzvah*. Our learning program involves 70 children this year and is housed at the Brooklyn New School, another growing venture that began with small steps—my daughter was in the first class there! And on the High Holy Days we worship in a sanctuary that seats 400, but we add chairs and use the side room and the balconies and join 700 strong to hear *Kol Nidrei* or sing *Avinu Malkeinu*. Our growth in numbers is clear. I hope our growth as people who struggle to answer God's call is clearer. Then we can truly call ourselves bar/bat mitzvah, people who try to understand what *mitzvah* means and strive to respond with seriousness of purpose, open doubts, creative understanding, and curious seeking.

Lech l'cha, God says to Abraham, the first Jewish community founder. "Get going," or maybe "go for yourself," or "to yourself"—all these have been suggested by later commentators as translations of this enigmatic phrase. And all are possible for a founder, who has to get things moving, will surely find incredible rewards, and must engage in self-reflection. Abraham's life was not easy, and he had to deal with well-documented family strife and other challenges, as well as try to keep his infant community on its right path. My way has been easier, and I feel blessed. "I will make of you a great nation," God promises Abraham, "and I will bless you; I will make your name great and you shall be a blessing" (Genesis 12:2). Samson Raphael Hirsch says this is a command, not a promise: "To merit the promised reward, you must so live as to be a blessing to the world." Isn't this our hope? Surely it is mine, to be a blessing to the world.

Yet being a founder is not just about the founder, it is about what is begun. *Etz Hayim: Torah and Commentary* notes that in asking (or is it telling?) Abraham to *lech l'cha*, "God seeks to create a community, a people, descendants of a God-fearing couple, in the hope that the members of that community would sustain and reinforce each other. In that way, ordinary people would be capable of displaying extraordinary behavior."[1] There could not be any better description of Kolot Chayeinu, latest in a long line of Jewish communities to enable ordinary people to display extraordinary behavior.

For me, the people of Kolot are my inspiration, along with my striving to hear God's voice. When Abram and Sarai, not yet renamed Abraham and Sarah, leave Haran to follow God's instruction, they take with them with "the persons that they had

---

1. David L. Lieber, ed., *Etz Hayim: Torah and Commentary* (New York: Rabbinical Assembly, 2001), 69.

acquired in Haran" (Genesis 12:5). The Rabbis of the midrash *Genesis Rabbah* understand this to mean converts, people whom they led to belief in God. We are taught in the Talmud (BT *Sanhedrin* 99a) that "one who brings a person to the Torah is regarded as having given birth to that person." It may be that every rabbi is a bit of a parent. Surely I have thrilled over the years as Kolot members, many formerly unschooled in Judaism, learn Hebrew, learn to chant Torah and haftarah, start celebrating Shabbat regularly, read Jewish newspapers or magazines, become *b'nei mitzvah*, and bring their new learning to bear on life's decisions.

And now here we all are, becoming *b'nei mitzvah* together. We are studying Torah all year in *Voices*, as in life. We have restarted Shabbat morning Torah study, along with weeknight intergenerational study and study of prayer. Shabbat services upstairs (main service) and downstairs (children's services) complement one another as the music of both intertwines. Our learning program hums with excitement and activity. We are growing up. Yet as with all *b'nei mitzvah*, we are not yet grown-ups. Rather, we have tried for thirteen years to heed God's words: "Go . . . to the land I will show you" (Genesis 12:1). Thirteen years later, after a long journey, we stand in that place in time and take a minute to look around in awe. Is this the place God is showing us? *Mah nora hamakom hazeh*, "How awesome is this place" (Genesis 28:17).

Vayeitzei

Kristallnacht

November 9, 2013

"Jacob left Beer Sheva and set out for Haran. He came into a Place and stayed there, because the sun was coming down, and he took from the stones of the Place and placed them around his head and lay down in that Place" (Genesis 28:10–11).

That's Torah.

Here is poet Rosemarie Waldrop: "Place there is none, he quotes. Not even to hang up our archetypes. . . . We go forward and backward, and there is no place. Therefore it is a name for God."[2]

I went to visit my father this week. Before I left I learned of the death of nine-year-old Lucien Merryweather, hit by an SUV in Fort Greene, his mother a close friend of a distraught Kolot member. When I returned, I learned of the death of Jerry Sager, beloved life partner of founding Kolot member Judith Kane, fifteen years after their later in life love story began. And today is Kristallnacht, the night of broken glass. "Broken windows, empty hallways, a pale dead moon in a sky streaked with grey. Human kindness is overflowing, and I think it's gonna rain today." That is Randy Newman, and everybody else.

2. https://www.poetryfoundation.org/poems/53465/conversation-4-on-place.

Death is everywhere this season, and yes, human kindness overflowing is often the only thing that helps. But where is God?

After Sammy Cohen Eckstein's death, I talked with our *b'nei mitzvah* students. One said something like this: "Well, you know, I don't, you know, really believe in God, but you know, if I did, well, where is God?"

I said that they would never hear from me that God had a plan for this death or that it was for the good, even if we did not understand it. We surely don't understand it, but it is not for the good, not Sammy's death or Lucien's or Jerry's. So where is God? Gone, as the Psalmist suspected? Watching us from a distance? Enfeebled? Horrified at what people will do to each other, like the God who knew Noah? Poet Rosemarie Waldrop asks, "And when I say your name, do I draw water, a portrait, curtain, bridge, or conclusion?" What conclusion are we to draw in a season like this one, overfull of deaths so near us? A day to remember how the Holocaust began, a day to remember a peace-seeker shot down, a Shabbat to ask, "So where is God?"

And then along comes Jacob, leaving the familiar and even the light of day to lie down among the stony reality of the Place that is God, and to—as Aviva Zornberg puts it—"move into the world of the night. Here, nothing is clear, all is shifting, phantasm, illusion. And here, paradoxically," she tells us, "Jacob finds his ground of truth." Jacob, Zornberg posits, intended to pray in the daylight, "but God put out the lights and Jacob discovers a new possibility— almost an impossibility . . . —called the Evening Prayer."[3]

Jacob lies down and dreams: angels on a ladder, a ladder firmly standing on the ground, and God, firmly standing beside him, telling him, "Remember, I am with you" (Genesis 28:15). Zornberg says that as God stands over Jacob to protect him, Jacob reaches "a still point in the turning world." It is as much Jacob as the angels

---

3. Aviva Zornberg, *The Beginning of Desire: Reflections on Genesis* (New York: Schocken Books, 1995), 188.

who go up and down that ladder. "But God provides reassurance
. . . by allowing him to experience" all the ups and downs, and by
promising stability and protection. "To sleep in a holy place," says
Zornberg, "is to betray an ideal of heroic stability and consciousness. But God wants this sleep. . . . Darkness too is a way of knowing God."[4]

It has been hard for me to pray these weeks and months,
feeling a lot like [congregant] Lisa Zbar said when we looked at
texts together at Kabbalat Shabbat services last month: "I'm not
talking to You anymore!" But not talking is too hard for me, too.

So maybe for me, and maybe for you, Jacob opens a window
on the night, teaching us that darkness too is a way of knowing
God. If we can know that, we can remember with Jacob that God
is with us. We are the children of Israel, the ancestor Jacob is
becoming. May we each be able in the darkest times to sleep and
dream and understand, even in shock, that "surely God is present
in this place, and until I entered the dream, the *Anochi*, the God-
ness of the Place that is God, I did not know" (Genesis 28:16).

---

4. Ibid., 192, 195.

Divrei Torah

Vayeishev

November 27, 2010 / 20 Kislev 5771

Every week when we say the blessing of thanks here at Kolot Chayeinu—*hatov v'hameitiv*—we have a moment before the end of the translation in which different ones of you insert your own take on what it means that God is good and . . . sometimes, often, on average, or *always* makes good things happen. I thought of this practice of ours when reading chapter 39 of Genesis, the middle of *Parashat Vayeishev*, the beginning of the story of Joseph. Joseph is born, is favored by his father (who gives him that famous coat), has dreams that anger his brothers, is sold by them into slavery, and begins his time in Egypt as an increasingly trusted servant in the home of Potiphar, an official in Pharaoh's government.

But what struck me when I read the chapter was that it tells us so often that God is with Joseph; meaning usually *Yod-Hei-Vav-Hei*, the unpronounceable "was-is-and-will-be" Eternal Presence that we call *Adonai*. Potiphar is referred to as *adonav*—his lord—yet even "his lord," the *parashah* tells us, recognizes that *Adonai* is with Joseph. Before that, though, we see that God is with him because he is a successful man. Or are the two parts of the sentence separate? *Adonai* was with Joseph. Joseph was a successful man.

Several Chasidic commentators, who were often speaking to very poor people, comment on this connection between God's presence with Joseph and his success. Rabbi Mordechai from

Chernobyl notes that the text did not need to include God's presence; it could have just said, "He was a successful man in the house of his Egyptian master." The inclusion of God here, he says, is to remind us that success can take you one of two ways with regard to God: (1) you may serve God when you are dirt poor, but when you get really successful you abandon God; or (2) your poverty puts God out of your mind, and when you get successful, you change your ways for the good. Joseph, who was sold into slavery and then became successful, took both situations in stride and, says Reb Mordechai, in slavery or in success Joseph's heart was faithful with God. This quality of Joseph's as he matures—this possibility to sense God's presence in adversity or success—may be why our text reminds us so often that God was with Joseph. Rashi understands these mentions to mean that for Joseph, God's name was fluent in his mouth. I was originally skeptical of Rashi's answer, reading "fluent" as "overly facile," seeing Joseph as his brothers must have seen him, the pretty boy who never has to struggle yet to whom good things always seem to come.

Since I was in the car yesterday afternoon, coming back from our Thanksgiving dinner upstate, I asked Kathryn how she would understand Rashi's comment. She said that for her, fluency means something far beyond a surface understanding, that in language, say, fluency means not only that you know the words, but that you know the culture, the nuance, the deeper meaning of what you are hearing and seeing. Let Kathryn be our tzaddik today: It must be that Rashi was so fluent in Torah that when he saw fluency in Joseph—the fluency of God's name—he recognized a kindred spirit, a man who knew God so deeply that he called God's name often, invoked God's name often, prayed often, and felt God's presence with him often. Joseph may have been a braggart child and a bit of a dandy, but Rashi sees deep into his heart and reminds us not to scoff.

So, for us: Why not thank God for *always* making good things happen? It does not mean that bad things don't happen or that we don't stick with God when they do. But honest, expressed gratitude may open our hearts and remind us in many situations not to scoff. Rabbi Cheryl Peretz wrote this week that "the Talmud teaches that each time we benefit from something in this world, it should be preceded by the recitation of a blessing—lest we be labeled a thief, stealing from God and/or from the society in which we live. Intentional gratitude transfers ownership from God to the one who says the blessing. So, we bring to the words of the blessing formula the feeling of thanks, and that changes our experience; it changes us." כן יהי רצון, *Kein y'hi ratzon.*

Mikeitz

Seeing Clearly

December 23, 2006 / 2 Tevet 5767

My father recently had cataract surgery, first on one eye and then on the other. Afterward, he has been able to stop wearing glasses—for the first time in more than seventy years! I haven't seen him yet without them and am wondering whether I will recognize him and whether he will see me more clearly.

I think about this as I read *Mikeitz*, the second of four *parashiyot* about Joseph and his father and brothers. Jacob sends his sons down to Egypt to get food during a famine in Canaan. There they find the vizier—in Hebrew, the *shalit*, the supervisor of food distribution—who is none other than their brother Joseph. The Torah says, "When Joseph saw his brothers, he recognized them; but he played the stranger toward them. . . . Though Joseph recognized his brothers, they did not recognize him" (Genesis 42:7–8). How could they not recognize him? He used to wear that incredibly show-offy coat, and they must have seen his face as he sat at the bottom of the pit they threw him in. A Chasidic commentary says he looked just like Jacob, from whom they have just come. But several factors intervene: One, they think he is dead so don't expect to see him. Two, he is wearing a disguise—he is dressed as an Egyptian official. Three, they are hungry! They have come to get food for survival. And four, "he played the stranger toward them."

How often do we not recognize even the people we love because of any number of intervening factors? How often do we "play the stranger," avoid revealing what we think of as our true selves, often due—as with Joseph—to past hurts? How often are important changes we make in ourselves not seen by those we most hope will notice? And how often do we do what Jacob castigates his sons for doing: *Lamah titra-u*? "Why are you looking at yourselves?" (Genesis 42:1). Why are you contemplating your own navel? we might ask. How can you truly see another—your brother, your sister—if you are focused within? The verb can also mean "fearful." Aren't we sometimes fearful to see someone clearly, to know their heart? What will we find there? Pain we cannot assuage? Anger that may be directed at us? An intensity we may not be able to match?

I love my father and we speak often, yet I am not sure we truly see one another. I am not sure if his new 20-20 vision will help that. I fear that I often play the stranger toward him, a loving, daughterly stranger. And for me, he too often *titrah*—is looking into himself—and cannot see me clearly as other than a reflection. Like Jacob and Joseph, we look very much alike. But we do not see eye to eye or—too often—face to face. Joseph reminds me.

Divrei Torah

Sh'mot

Voices, January 2006

I became bat mitzvah at the age of thirteen. I got a new turquoise blue dress and patent leather pumps with heels! I read from Torah and, I guess, haftarah too, and I made a speech. My portion was about Moses, but from the Book of Numbers, a later *parashah* than the one we are focused on in this issue. What I didn't do for my bat mitzvah was learn Hebrew. Really. I essentially memorized my portion and then sort of pretended to read it. Such was the state of Hebrew school in a Reform synagogue in Virginia in the early 1960s. We would never let our Kolot students do it that way.

I learned some Hebrew in the year before I began rabbinical school, and I really learned Hebrew during my year in Israel with Hebrew Union College–Jewish Institute of Religion. After a few months, I was reading slowly with my teacher: *U'Mosheh hayah ro-eh et tzon Yitro chot'no kohein Midyan* . . . , "Now Moses, tending the flock of his father-in-law Jethro, the priest of Midian . . ." (Exodus 3:1). I kept reading and suddenly realized what I was reading: "It's the story of the Burning Bush!" I cried in delight. And Hebrew came alive. Ever since, the Burning Bush has been my story in a deep, important way. It was there that I, like Moses, really decided to take on this role of rabbi.

The January before last, while I was on retreat at the monastery I now go to each year for space and time and reflection, I walked through that high desert country of New Mexico, stopping from time to time to sit and drink in the beauty. One morning, the sun was so strong that trees and bushes seemed lit from within, and I understood how a story about a burning bush would appeal to our ancestors and would show them an indication of God's presence. That high desert does that for me, never more so than on a day that lights the place up. A day or two later, as I did my required work helping out in the monastery gift shop, I noticed that they were selling oval silver pins that drew my eye. Engraved on the pin was what appeared to be a tree labeled "Burning Bush." It is the emblem of that monastery. I am wearing my Burning Bush pin as I write.

Last spring, I was invited to a women's seder and asked to write about "The Gates" installation in Central Park, or the tsunami, or the Pesach story. Kathryn and I wrote together about "The Gates" as lines in the sand, me looking at Moses and she at Harriet Tubman and later "Moseses" who work to help people get free, in her case battered women seeking shelter and liberation.

I pictured the Burning Bush in that context and saw it as the place we draw our line in the sand or cross a line that has seemed impassable. The early Rabbis noted "there is no early or late in the Torah." I feel free, then, to draw lessons from the future and bring them back into the past, and vice versa. You should too. This is a story of a story, a midrash that looks to hope and acknowledges pain, a tale of coming to maturity as we each do, as Kolot is, as anyone who becomes bar or bat mitzvah must. Faced with Moses's choice, how would you choose?

Exodus 3:1: "Now Moses, tending the flock of his father-in law, Jethro, the priest of Midian, drove the flock into the wilderness and came to Horeb, the mountain of God." Moses is married now, to Zipporah, Jethro's daughter, and has a son. His life is pleasant, comparatively easy: he has love, work, food, shelter. And thus he arrives at the mountain of God. There he sees a flame, which causes him to turn aside from his usual path. As he draws closer, amazed, he sees that it is no flame, but rather a gate of bright orange, shining in the desert sun. As he approaches, he hears a voice, speaking to him from between its poles, above the swaying curtain. The Voice says, "Moses, Moses, walk through this gate. But before you do so, you must know: If you walk through, your life and the world's life will be forever changed. No more for you the good simple life of Jethro's tent, the easy pleasures of life with Zipporah. No, the path through the gate is rocky and hard, full of fear and hatred. Those you must face have great power, and those you will lead are drowning in misery, unable to see the path at all. All will condemn you, spit at you, revile you. But at the end of the path lies hope. There is no greater gift. If you walk through this gate you will lead your people to hope. It is a great promise. But you must know the risks."

Moses draws back, shaken. He vaguely remembers his mother telling him a story about his great-great-great-grandfather Jacob who had a dream . . . oh, yes, now he remembers! A dream of a ladder planted on the ground and its top reached to heaven. When Jacob awoke from his sleep, he said, "Surely God is in this place and I did not know. How awesome is this place! This is none other than the house of God, and this is the gate of heaven" (Genesis 28:16–17). "Is this, too, the gate of heaven?" Moses wonders. "This is an awesome place, and this gate looks very real. This is no dream. But what am I to do? Do I want to take that hard, rocky path? Why me?

"Life is so good now, so easy, so pleasant to spend an evening by the fire with Jethro, and Zipporah, and little Gershom, talking, singing, preparing to sleep. If I take that path, will I know life's pleasures again? If I take that path, will I succeed in leading my people? Couldn't I just send a check and let other, younger people lead? Why me?" The Voice speaks, startling Moses from his thoughts: "Moses, you drew your line in the sand back there in Egypt. You are already on the path. Can you really rest here in Midian while your people are groaning in slavery there?" The Voice tells Moses a story:

"Many years from now there will live a woman named Ruth, daughter-in-law to Naomi. Naomi will also have another daughter-in-law, Orpah will be her name. Naomi will live in their land during a time of great sorrow for her and great suffering for her people at home. She will decide to return home and will tell her daughters-in-law to go back to their own families. They will refuse and travel with her some distance. But then I will make this gate to appear, and will speak to them as I speak to you, telling them of the harsh path that awaits them if they move forward, and of the hope at the end. Orpah will decide to stay, returning as Naomi will suggest to her own home and family. But Ruth will walk through the gate, telling Naomi, 'Where you go, I will go.' They will be linked forever. Through Ruth I will create a line that leads to the *Mashiach* [Messiah], symbol of hope.

"So, Moses," the Voice asks, "will you be Ruth, or will you be Orpah? The choice is yours."

Moses walked through the gate.

For me, starting Kolot was to walk through that gate. It was to leave behind the ordered world of rabbinic placement, the work at MAZON that drew so much praise, and to take a chance on a dream and a handful of dreamers. We were reviled at first as upstarts encroaching on the territory of the more organized Jewish community in this part of Brooklyn. Thirteen years later there are several new minyans here, and we have to laugh as we look a bit askance at them—are they here to encroach on us? If so, good for them. We are old enough to need some shaking up, young enough to feel insecure, established enough to forget the gate we walked through to get here. If there are only one or two lessons I hope we learn, they are: to keep walking through the gate, taking the "road less traveled," facing fears and taking risks, *and* to remember to see the hope beyond the fear.

Long before I had that moment of joyous recognition as I read the story of the Burning Bush in Hebrew, I arrived in Israel alone, for my first visit, which was to last a year. I unpacked at the YMCA on King David Street in Jerusalem, my early temporary home, and walked out to see what I could see. I was overcome by the realization of what I had just done: packed up and left friends and family to live for a year in what was still a strange land so that I could fulfill the dream that just wouldn't let me alone. Was I crazy? Could I do this nutty thing at an age when many other rabbis were deep into their careers? Why had I thought this was a good idea? Those thoughts plagued me for months; each Friday I would cry and say, "I can't do it, I can't do it." And then came the story of the Burning Bush: "He gazed and there was a bush all aflame, yet the bush was not consumed" (Genesis 3:2). Miracles come to us at odd moments, unexpected. The story of the Burning Bush and my first reading of it in Hebrew was one, and Kolot's growth and vitality is another. May we always face the risks, walk through the gate, and find the hope we work for.

D'var Dikduk: Va-eira

January 1, 2011 / 25 Tevet 5771

This is a brief *d'var dikduk*: a word about grammar. The grammatical form I want to talk about is the *vav hahipuch*, the reversing *vav*. In Torah, we often get a verb that appears to be in the past or future tense, but it is preceded by a *vav* that changes the tense.

Our Torah potion begins with three such forms: **Vay'dabeir** *Elohim el Mosheh* **vayomer** *eilav*, "*Ani Adonai*. **Va-eira** *el Avraham . . .*" (Exodus 6:2–3).

In his reading of Torah, Rashi establishes a fundamental principle as to the difference between two narrative forms, with and without the *vav hahipuch*. When the narrative tells an event with the *vav hahipuch* (such as *vay'dabeir*), the given event occurred at this point in the narrative. When, however, the event is described without the *vav hahipuch*, the event occurred prior to the previously recorded event. Time is fluid in Torah; our ancient Rabbis said there is no early and late in Torah.

Dr. Joseph Lowin writes, "There is something akin to magic in what is popularly called (if anything in grammar may be deemed popular) the [*vav hahipuch*], the 'conversive vav.' This is a letter that turns the past into the future and the future into the past. For example, when the Torah wishes to say 'Moses spoke,' it takes the future form, e.g., the phrase [*yidabeir Mosheh*], 'Moses shall speak,' adds the [*vav hahipuch*], and 'Presto Changeo!' we have [*vay'dabeir Mosheh*], 'Moses spoke.'"

Va-eira means "I appeared." Without the reversing *vav*, it would be *eira*, "I will appear." I am reminded of an earlier *parashah* that we know well, since it includes the story of the *Akeidah*, the Binding of Isaac: *Vayeira*, "God appeared." Same reversing *vav*, different grammatical person. There the tale is told in third person: "God appeared." Here, today, we see God speaking in first person: "I appeared." And we learn a little lesson about the difference between Abraham and Moses, perhaps, both beloved of God, both in direct communication with God, but Moses may have a slight edge: God speaks more personally here about God's self, as God introduces the deepest self to Moses. Saving Isaac was a crucial act. Saving the people of Israel is even more urgent. God digs deep here.

Another brief comparison: Our *parashah* begins with *Vay'dabeir Elohim*, unusual in a book that more often reads *Vay'dabeir Adonai*. The first time Torah says *Vay'dabeir Elohim*, it tells of God speaking to Noah. Noah, the guy who will save some people and some animals in a boat on the water—an ark, a *teivah*. Moses, the guy who is saved in a vessel on the water—an ark, a *teivah*—and will save many others, millions, it seems. *Elohim* is the God of justice, *Adonai*—*Yod-Hei-Vav-Hei*—is the God of mercy. It is *Elohim* who appears to Abraham when Abraham has just circumcised himself and is sitting and recovering. It is *Elohim* who speaks to Noah about the ark. It is *Elohim* who speaks today to Moses about saving the enslaved people. But it is *Adonai* who saves Isaac and *Adonai* who gives Moses and Aaron the resources to get the people out of slavery.

Back to the question of past and future, future and past. Wouldn't it be nice to have a device that could change our past to future, allowing us more time to work on the things that were wrong or enjoy those that delighted us? How would it be to change our future into our past, taking what we cannot yet know and make it finished, known and done? On this New Year's Day, the first Shabbat of 2011, what are you taking from the past that you hope to bring into the future? What hopes or fears do you harbor for the future that can be tempered or enlivened by events of the past?

Right before our portion, at the end of the portion *Sh'mot*—and remember the Torah has no demarcation of portions or even sentences ending—we read, "Then *Adonai* said to Moses, 'You shall soon see what I will do to Pharaoh: he shall let them go because of a greater might; indeed because of a greater might he shall drive them from his land'" (Exodus 6:1). The past shows us the future. Our portion ends in mid-story: "Pharaoh's heart stiffened [*vaye-chezak*] and he would not let the Israelites go, just as *Adonai* had foretold through Moses" (Exodus 9:35). It happened as foretold. Past and earlier past. It may have been foretold, but we, like Moses, have to make it happen. *Vay'dabeir Adonai. Vay'dabeir Elohim.* May God's presence appear to each of you in a perfect balance of justice and mercy, from day 1 to day 365; 365 in *g'matria*, my favorite end-of-year activity, is *shin-nun-hei, shinah* = repetition or teaching. Like the Mishnah. Our days pass in repetition, but we can learn. And we can find our way to *shinui*, to change. May it be so.

Divrei Torah

Mishpatim

Strict Justice or Compassionate Compromise?

February 16, 2007 / 29 Sh'vat 5767

Our Torah portion for this week, *Mishpatim*, begins with God saying to Moses, "And these are the laws that you should place before them" (Exodus 21:1). What or who is the "them" that these laws are placed before?

A Chasidic commentator who hides behind the appellation "Robe of Light" insists that it is Israel—that is, us—who is the "them." That seems obvious to us: the people are still standing at Mount Sinai, and this is part of God's revelation or its follow-up. But this Robe of Light brings in a line from Psalm 72: "God, give Your laws to the king, Your justice to the son of the king" (v. 1). The king, represented in this midrash by Moses or Solomon, knows the law so deeply and so well that he knows who is innocent and who guilty without need of proof or witness. The son of the king, though—that is us. And we lower-level humans must compromise, must interpret to arrive at true justice from the given law. Moses is one thing, we—Israel—are another.

I thought of this midrash while I was preparing the wedding ceremony for the couple we will honor in a little while. Because when they exchange their rings on Sunday, they will say the words that have been handed down in Jewish tradition: *Harei at m'kudeshet li b'tabaat zo k'dat Mosheh v'Yisrael*, "Look! With this ring, you are consecrated to me according to the law of Moses and Israel."

We have just learned that the law of Moses and the law of Israel may be different, one strictly understood, one more lenient, allowing for interpretation and compromise. So what can we mean by marrying "according to the law of Moses and Israel"? What would Moses think about this wedding, or mine? He himself was married to the daughter of a priest of Midian. Would he remember that when seeing Brett and Paula under the chuppah? Or would he be the one sticking strictly to established understanding, which might look askance at this chuppah?

This is where it is so good that we are Israel in this pair, Israel who is urged to interpret and compromise; in fact, says the Baal Turim, Israel *must* interpret and compromise before making a judgment. So I, the *m'saderet kiddushin*—the one who creates the order of the wedding ceremony—take up my charge: I interpret **k'dat Mosheh v'Yisrael**, the law of Moses and Israel, to mean the law of the Moses who was called *rabbeinu* by the ancient Rabbis—"our teacher," the one from whom we learned to make change. And **k'dat Mosheh v'Yisrael**—the law of Israel who must compromise in every time and every place where we find ourselves.

This is why in my time and place, or more specifically, in Queens on Sunday, I will happily watch while this Jewish man from Texas and so many other places around the world puts a ring on the finger of this Jamaican woman from Kingston who absorbed the culture of Rastafarianism, which is often so similar to ours, and says, "With this ring you are consecrated to me, according to the law of Moses and Israel."

Ki Tisa

February 23, 2008 / 17 Adar I 5768

The people are restless, Moses is late, they ask Aaron to make them a god, he collects their jewelry and creates what is known forever after as the Golden Calf. The making of the Golden Calf is referred to in most of ancient Rabbinic literature as "that deed," implying it is the worst thing the people of Israel could ever do, a deed that requires no modifier. They turned against God, they created an idol, they broke the covenant and betrayed their promises made at Sinai. Yet Aaron, who engineered the making of the Golden Calf, is referred to in that same literature as a peacemaker, and he retains that reputation through the centuries. I have been curious about why Aaron can be known as the great peacemaker for his role in the same incident that is known as "that deed."

So let me tell you the story of the Golden Calf in a new way, as I am understanding it this year, a retelling that may help answer my questions, and maybe yours.

For two and a half weeks, as it were—though it has been forty days or more in the Torah—we have been reading about God's plans for the *Mishkan*, as told to Moses. God tells Moses in great detail the materials, measurements, dimensions, and adornment that are to make up the *Mishkan*, the place God will dwell among the people. Everyone whose heart is moved is to bring all of these things. Because we are reading these words—hearing God tell it, in a way—we assume the people of Israel are also hearing them.

But they are not. The portions of two weeks ago, of last week, and even part of the way into this week's are God telling Moses these specifications. God and Moses are up on the mountain, away from the people, who see only Moses's absence.

God understands this people and knows that after years of slavery, and the huge effort to walk through the sea into freedom, they are going to need something shiny and beautiful around which to create a cohesive community. So God is ready to tell them how to make that shiny, beautiful central gathering place—the *Mishkan*, the *mikdash*, that holy place. The people know from shiny and beautiful; they have been witness to Egypt's treasures all their lives. They are ready for God's *Mishkan*, ready to bring their offerings to create it. Except they do not yet know that God intends them to do so.

And Moses is late. No cell phone call. No e-mail to say he is coming, hang on. So, the Torah tells us, "When the people saw that Moses was so long in coming down from the mountain, the people gathered against Aaron and said to him"—and here I translate differently than do our commentaries—"'Come, make us God [*aseih lanu Elohim*] who will walk before us, for that man Moses . . . we do not know what has happened to him'" (Exodus 32:1). Now watch Aaron. He says, "Take all your jewelry and bring it to me"; he casts it in a mold and creates the Golden Calf, a shiny beautiful thing, probably very small, around which the people can gather.

I submit that Aaron stands in for God here, saying to the people a version of what God is asking Moses to say to them. Like the people, he does not know God has told Moses to make the *Mishkan*. Like God, he understands that these former slaves—restive now, almost on the verge of becoming an out-of-control mob— need something shiny and lovely to gather around. And the people look at the Golden Calf and say, "This is your god, Israel, who brought you out of the land of Egypt" (Exodus 32:4). What is their tone? Mocking? Angry? Vengeful? Aaron seems to think they are sincere, or near it, and he builds an altar and announces a festival of *Yod-Hei-Vav-Hei*—the God of Israel.

The people are happy and apparently noisy, because God, Moses, and even Joshua hear their voice . . . and understand it differently, seeing it as the sound of a rabble, warlike, anti-God. Moses hurries back, carrying the tablets of the commandments he has received, and smashing them in his anger at the people he perceives to have turned against God. Later God will give Moses a new set of tablets, and the old ones will be carried in the Ark, symbol of that deed that almost broke the covenant with God. But did it? Did the people reject God in their fear and confusion at Moses's absence? Did Aaron, soon to be the High Priest in the *Mishkan* God wants the people to build, really ask the people to reject God and all he and his brother have worked for? I don't think so.

With Moses gone, and God's intentions not known, Aaron kept the people together, avoiding chaos and the possibility of escalation to violence. It is Moses who kills thousands of the people in his rage at their supposed betrayal. But Aaron? He saw into the people's willing hearts and built them a shiny, beautiful symbol of their connection to God, thus keeping them connected to God, to each other, and even to him and to Moses. Hence we read in *Pirkei Avot* that Hillel urged, "Be of the disciples of Aaron, loving peace and pursuing peace; love your fellow creatures and draw them near to Torah" (1:12).

As to the people, the Jerusalem Talmud says it best: "What a peculiar people! When asked to give to build the *Mishkan*, they give generously. When asked to give to build an idol, they give equally generously." These former slaves have some difficulty telling the difference, and truth be told, sometimes so do we. Ultimately, we are asked to be of the disciples of Moses, not of Aaron, trying to imagine the unimaginable and connect to God without anything shiny and beautiful but our minds and hearts.

Divrei Torah

Sh'mini

April 1, 2016 / 23 Adar II 5776

Menachem Mendel of Kotzk notices that at the beginning of this week's *parashah, Sh'mini,* Moses tells Aaron and his sons and the elders to bring to the just completed *Mishkan* a variety of sacrifices. When they do, Moses says, *Zeh hadavar asher tzivah Adonai taasu,* "This is the thing that *Adonai* commanded you to do" (Leviticus 9:6).

What thing? They've already been commanded to bring the sacrifices; does Moses have to say it again? No, says the Kotzker, drawing on earlier translations, this *davar* is something else. This commandment is to "remove the *yetzer hara* from your hearts, and immediately the glory of God's *Shechinah* will be revealed to you."

My translation? A mitzvah has several parts: First come the hands—doing the physical part, like lighting candles for Shabbat or cleaning your house before Pesach. Next comes the head—starting to do what the Kotzker calls arranging your mind to be ready for a connection with God. And then comes the heart, opened by the act and the arranged mind so it is ready to stand before God, as our *parashah* says the people did with their sacrifices.

So when we approach a mitzvah, we want to remember what we are doing, what we think about it, and how it can create in us a greater opening for the spiritual potential. Let's try it together as we prepare to light Shabbat candles.

Divrei Torah

Tazria-M'tzora

April 17, 2010 / 3 Iyar 5770

I went to see the play *Next Fall*, this week. It is about a young gay man who is also a fundamentalist Christian. He wants to be gay and he wants to be a good Christian, and so he moves in with his lover and in one particularly painful scene, it turns out that he prays for forgiveness every time he and his partner have sex. We are deep into Leviticus now. Next week comes the *parashah Acharei Mot*, when we will read again the Torah's injunction to men not to lie with a man as one lies with a woman. But I am not here to talk about the Torah's primary anti-gay law, which has been d'rashed and parsed in all kinds of horrifying and important ways in recent years.

Instead, I want to talk about redeeming this idea of sin as it applies to any one of the most joyful, loving, connected things one can do as a human being. Making love, say, or having a baby.

In *Tazria*, the first *parashah* in this week's double portion *Tazria-M'tzora*, a mother gives birth, undergoes a period of purification after giving birth, and then, we read: "On the completion of her period of purification, for either son or daughter, she shall bring to the priest at the entrance of the Tent of Meeting, a lamb in its first year for a burnt offering and a pigeon or turtledove for a sin offering. The priest shall offer it before God and make atonement on her behalf; *she shall then be pure from her flow of blood*" (Leviticus 12:6–7).

35

What has this woman done wrong? She has had a baby. And yes, she has some blood flow, similar, the Torah recognizes, to menstrual blood. But a sin offering—for what?! Some say it is because when she was in the pain of labor she might have shouted things she wouldn't have said otherwise, like "I am never going near my husband again!" "I am never doing this again!" Perhaps in childbirth, as during sex, we are most like animals, and our ancestors thought we needed to bring an offering, a ritual, to bring us back to full humanity, understood as the uniting of the animal and the divine within.

Blood is the stuff of life, a flow that shows we are alive, the newborn baby is alive, the mother is still alive—*L'chayim*! we ought to shout. In fact a new mother often benches *Gomeil*, says the prayer that thanks God for having brought this person through a life-threatening situation. But a sin offering?!

Blood is the flow of life, and so is water, the flow of water that cleanses the blood and sustains us all in life. So after the sin offering and the ritual, the Torah portion tells us, *V'taharah mim'kor dameha*, "She will be pure from her flow of blood." But wait. The translation skipped something. It should read, "She will be pure from the source of her blood."

So there is a third flow I want to mention here and that is the flow of *shefa*, God's divine flow that takes blood and water, skin and bones and organs, and makes us human. That is our source, as it flows over and around us and returns to God in a never-ending stream, not unlike the way blood flows from and to the heart. It is why we thank God for our having gotten up in the morning or for having created us as a pretty damn good machine that works for us, most of the time.

So now this woman who just a sentence ago was in a state of sin, is cleansed, but in a different way. Now her blood, instead of being scary and threatening and foreign, is life-giving, divine, the core of hers and the new human life she created.

So too for Luke, the young man in the play. My wish for him is that he can learn to pray in thanksgiving for great sex, not in atonement. His animal nature too unites with the divine to create a human being engaged in human love, human warmth.

Dam Yah. Adam.

I am interested in birth today because today is my birthday. My mother was twenty-three when I was born, too young and too filled with her own fears and the seeds of future depression to be a fully loving mother, but she grew into it, and on this day I want to dedicate my words to her, the mother who gave me life, who became the loving mother I still miss eleven years after her death.

I became a mother in a whole other way: by falling in love with someone who came into my life with a three-year-old. I never gave her birth, though I am grateful to the woman who did. And I have struggled with the role of stepmother for many years, while my daughter struggles with having five mothers who love her and want to help her and sometimes suffocate her. I want to dedicate these words to her too, the three-year-old who became a loving, thoughtful adult and who helped me become a loving mother.

And I dedicate these words to that long-ago mother in the Torah, the one who brought a sin offering because that was how she could feel God's presence in her life, know that the blood that would be cleansed in water would lead her to the flow of *shefa*. Her blood would become *dam Yah*, divine flow within the "adam," the human being that would be silent without blood or *shefa*, a silent *alef* joined to blood to form a human being, shaped by God.

Chukat

June 28, 2014 / 1 Tammuz 5774

Earlier this year, a Kolot staff person realized that things would go a lot smoother on certain Shabbat mornings if the Torah study group met in the balcony. So up we went, some of us entering the balcony for the first time, others the first time in many years. If you've been around Kolot for a while, you've probably heard about *the balcony*. There are a bunch—not more than twenty—Kolot folks who hold strong and loving memories about the balcony. For them, it is the locus of the glory days of Kolot, where prayer and community flourished, and all present loved each other easily. So I was eager to see the balcony again, to see if that latter-day Eden was still in evidence.

The place is a pit. It is dirty, shabby, filled with junk and old machines, and barely big enough to fit our growing Torah study group. As much as I tried, I could not evoke there even one fond memory of the long-ago gathering.

You can't get the same water out of that same old rock any more.

Miriam died, and the people had no water. That is how the commentators read two separate sentences in our *parashah, Chukat*, cause and effect. Miriam, always tied to water—the Nile, the Sea of Reeds—is said to have brought a mystical well along with the people on their journey from the land of slavery to the land of freedom. But the people have already been sentenced to die in the desert for their lack of faith, and now Miriam is dead, and with her the life-giving water.

Moses's response is to yell at the people and bang angrily on the rock to get water. Moses, who has sometimes asked for the help of others leading the people, and who has already seen what magic can happen when others than he prophesy, is now too worn out by threats to his authority to recognize when he needs help.

Moses is also in mourning. His sister has died, and she brought *him* water too. She saved his life early on, and walked with him out of slavery, and danced and sang with him at the sea. But she too has lately been complaining about him, and while God punished her for it, perhaps her complaints were valid and Moses knew it. So he mourns her death and maybe he mourns his own weakening. How hard to know you do not have the confidence of the people as you did when you were the hero of the liberation! So in one rash, unthinking, desperate act, he bangs the rock when he should have prayed or asked for help or acknowledged that he did not know what to do. And he yells, "Listen, you rebels, shall we get water for you out of this rock?" (Numbers 20:10). He called the people rebels. *Morim*. But if he had had his wits about him, he might have realized what he was saying: *Morim*. It also means "teachers." If only he had turned to the people to learn from them, to see them as his teachers, to realize what extraordinary lessons they might teach him.

You can't get new water from an old rock. But you do get water. Moses yells and bangs and water gushes out. So the people get to drink. Why isn't that okay? Any old water is okay when you're desperate. But God holds Moses—and us—to a higher standard. Moses—and we—are not supposed to yell at thirsty, needy people. And even more, we are to acknowledge the divine possibility of water, what we might call water-drawing that aligns with our values. Any old water does not do that.

So what's next? Let's go back to the balcony. It *is* a pit. But I recognize that it holds some very precious memories, and we need to hold onto them. When Miriam dies, the people spend little time mourning her. They needed more. Moses needed more. And we need more: we need to find a way to speak those memories, maybe write them, and then find a place to keep them, so that we can move on. Moses did that with the Ark, taking the old broken tablets and the new ones and Joseph's bones along on the journey. Let's take our old tablets and bones and move on. That balcony, that old prayer book, those old ways: it was sometimes lovely, but it was never Eden and ahead there lies no Promised Land.

But as [congregant] Rachel Feldman taught us recently about community organizing: If we can imagine it, we can build it. We can look at the old and use it to help us find the new. In that way we *can* get new water from some old rocks.

It is of course always wise for rabbis to remember we are not Moses. Sometimes we are not as humble or wise as Moses. But today, maybe I am glad not to be as stubborn as Moses. I am very grateful to you, my teachers. Sometimes you teach through rebellion, sometimes by imagination, sometimes with love.

May we be blessed to travel together through an unknown wilderness, full of possibility *and* danger. May we think and provoke and ask and argue and reckon with each other and with God as we head to the place we do not know.

Part Two

Avodah

Service, Prayer

Kavanah before *Un'taneh Tokef*

Rosh HaShanah 2012 / 5773

Baruch atah, Adonai Eloheinu, Melech haolam, yotzeir or uvorei choshech, oseh shalom uvorei et hakol.

Blessed are You, Adonai our God, Your Presence fills creation. You shape light and create darkness, make peace and create everything.

We sang this a short while ago, mostly unaware that those words come from the prophet Isaiah, whose version was different in a small but crucial way. Isaiah said, speaking of God, *oseh shalom uvorei et hara*, "You make peace and create evil" (Isaiah 45:7). Marc Brettler, an editor of *The Jewish Study Bible*, says we might better translate Isaiah as "you make peace and create trouble."

With trouble in mind, we come to the *Un'taneh Tokef*: "We are given the power of the holiness of this day, for it is awe-full and dread-full."

The rabbis who put together our liturgy gave us "you make peace and create everything," rather than attribute evil or even trouble specifically to God.

But what do you think when someone you love dies? When a terrible murder happens far away? When floods or fires take hundreds of thousands of lives in India or Colorado? I'd say many of us are quite ready to attribute trouble specifically to God.

43

Last week the Children of Abraham Peace Walk[5] stopped at Christ Church in Cobble Hill to gaze on the broken steeple, which broke when it was hit by lightning and a piece fell to the ground, killing a passerby. That passerby was Richard Schwartz, a sixty-one-year-old prosecutor. As a sixty-one-year-old rabbi, this hit me hard.

During the Peace Walk, we spent a moment at the church in silence, filled with thoughts of the unimaginable, the power of the holiness of a day, awe-full, dread-full. But God did not cause centuries of stress cracks in that steeple nor cause Mr. Schwartz to be walking by at that exact moment.

What then can we attribute to God? Why do we reach out in prayer? Is it all coincidence, accident, random, unknowable?

A friend calls to say, "I know my loved one's cancer was not caused by God. But I do not know how to think about God because of the cancer."

I said, "Do you think God is all good?" I don't. I find myself comforted by Isaiah's words: "You, God, make peace"—though it is not always clear where or when—"and create trouble." Oh, yeah. I am even comforted by our early liturgists' change: "You make peace and create everything." Everything! Not church steeples but maybe lightning, fires when the land is too dry, floods when human-caused global warming begins to take hold or when rivers that have always burst their bounds do it again. The power of the holiness of this day.

I don't think God is all good. I think God is all: the holy power that undergirds the universe in which we find ourselves, unimaginably tiny and so often powerless, great as we think we are. That power too can sometimes be unbound, burst its banks.

Those of you for whom I have officiated at funerals know that when we get to the moment of *k'riah*, cutting clothing or ribbons

---

5. An interfaith walk in Brooklyn (and now Manhattan), begun by Rabbi Lippmann, Debbie Almontaser, and Rev. Tom Martinez, in 2004.

to symbolize broken hearts, I remind us of the words, "*Baruch Dayan ha-emet*: Blessed is the truthful Judge." And then I say, "My translation is: We don't understand anything."

That is the truth, and for me is at the heart of the power of the holiness today: We don't understand, we don't like it, we wish we did, we can't, we have to bow before that recognition. It is full of awe and dread.

Who will die this year by fire or floods, by stoning or plague? I have no idea and neither do you. Is God really writing it down today and sealing it next week? Nah. But that is a whole lot easier to imagine than that there is a force underlying all we are and all we do, and we cannot grasp more than a handful of its hem nor understand anything of where it is headed. The secret God has that we cannot know is the future.

I speak often in traditional terms about God because I love the imagery and even the anthropomorphism. I like to think that there is in some way a God who cares about me. That is lovely for evening or morning prayers, or even Shabbat.

But the power of this day lies elsewhere, in the reality of what we cannot understand. Today we face the un-faceable. It is holy, awe-full and full of dread.

Sermon in a Dream

Yom Kippur 2003 / 5764

Astonishing things happened on my summer vacation. A hawk flew right by our porch, close enough to touch, and moved me to tears. I saw a coyote for the first time, thrilling and terrifying. I saw the first blue heron I'd seen in several years, just as the summer ended. And I had a strange dream that has stayed with me. In this dream I said, and clearly it was I speaking, "This is the year I stopped thinking about politics and started thinking about death."

I put some stock in what happens in my dreams. We are, after all, descendants of both Freud and Jacob, Jacob who dreamed those angels going up and down a ladder that was planted on the ground, and heard God reassuring him. This dream seemed more in the Jacob line than in Freud's, so I paid attention. But what did it mean? I had been taking a break from the news, which was and is so often filled with the violence of our world. For some weeks, beginning in the spring and continuing even now, I read and listened to much less. I bought the paper regularly while on vacation only so I could follow the Tour de France and the tennis matches at Wimbledon. So in a way, like many of you, perhaps, I had stopped thinking about politics, if by politics I meant the actions of governments and armies, large and small. News fatigue, someone called it. Violence fatigue is more like it. But had I started thinking about death this year? I decided I had, though immediately after the dream I understood that somehow death in that phrase actually meant life.

This was the year I started thinking about life.

Death is what defines life, after all; life's end point is what provides our intensity, our drive, our need to do what we call really living. Leon R. Kass, in an article called "L'Chaim and Its Limits," outlines four reasons that our mortality is good for us. First, as I just suggested, he says life's limit enhances our interest and engagement in life's joys and sorrows. Second, he says that we develop seriousness and aspiration as a result of being mortal; he quotes the Psalmist, "Teach us to number our days that we may get a heart of wisdom." When our days are numbered, they count more. Third, Kass says, beauty and love are deepened and enhanced by the fact of their death, and fourth, he tells us that the human possibility for virtue and moral excellence are due to mortality: we rise above what he calls "our mere creatureliness to attain courage, generosity, devotion to justice." And finally, Kass speaks of the soul and its deep truth: "The human soul yearns for, longs for, aspires to some condition, some state, some goal toward which our earthly activities are directed but which cannot be attained in earthly life. Our soul's reach exceeds our grasp."[6]

My soul has been yearning. Hasn't yours? This is the year my soul was yearning; maybe that's what my dream self meant. It yearned to fly with the hawk, run with the coyote, break out of its confines. Last week as we walked to *Tashlich*, two very active members of this community said, "We've had enough of organized religion." I knew exactly what they meant. Yet here we are in the belly of the beast, as it were: the Yom Kippur service, which owes so much to the highly structured sacrificial service conducted by the High Priest of old. My soul yearns for that too, for the chance to give up something important to get something crucial, the chance to spill a little blood to avoid major bloodshed.

---

6. Leon R. Kass, "L'Chaim and Its Limits: Why Not Immortality?" in *Best Spiritual Writing 2002*, ed. Philip Zaleski (New York: HarperOne, 2002).

Sacrifice too is death, meaning life; it's death to get life, to rid life of its hindering baggage, the fear, bitterness, cynicism that prevent us from living. All that the ancient priest would place on a goat, and then send the goat into the wilderness to a mysterious place called Azazel, where perhaps some demonic being lived and gathered up human impurities. This was the wilderness, a place barren of life; life's garbage heap, if you will. And there went our goat, the one with all our sins on it, trotting out to wander or die, but it took our sins with it. This is the year my soul was yearning for a way to take our sins away and be done with them. Yet I know that life is not so simple, that ridding of sin requires engagement in life, not just a reluctant goat. "See, I set before you this day life and good, death and evil. . . . Choose life so that you and your children may live." Those are the brilliant words our Reform ancestors chose to replace the goat and Azazel on Yom Kippur. Choose life.

A Chasidic commentator called Ohel Yaakov reminds me that the intention of the desire for life is not just physical life, but rather the love of and service of God. Be engaged with life and its source. This is why we beseech God during these High Holy Days, *Zochreinu l'chayim, Melech chafeitz bachayim, v'chotveinu b'sefer hachayim, l'maancha Elohim chayim*, "Remember us for life, O King who delights in life, and write us in the Book of Life, for the sake of the God of life." *This is the year I started thinking about life, because I was thinking about death.*

Kathryn's mother had an accident during our vacation that sent her to the hospital and it became clear that she was no longer able to live alone in her home of fifty-two years. We were luckily able to find an assisted living facility nearby that had a vacancy, and she moved there right from the hospital. She loves it, feels cared for in a way we hadn't realized she needed, eats well, has company and activities of all sorts. And we, mostly Kathryn, have been cleaning out her house of those fifty-two years of life's accruals. It is a death of sorts, though we are in fact lucky to be doing this before her death: death of the way life was, death of home and family, death of independence, death of her children being children in any way. Choose life that you and your children may live.

Yehuda Nachshoni, in a traditional commentary on our portion, says, "Forefathers are possibly not able to saddle their descendants with an obligation, but they can certainly take a positive step to benefit their descendants."

My father moved this year into a continuum of care facility, long before he needed to, a step I admire and am deeply grateful for. The result of all this caring about our parents, which I know so many of you have and are experiencing, is that Kathryn and I are planning our own demise. We have told our daughter that we will try never to be a burden to her, though she sees that this is something that may be expected of her. My friend Judith says one honors one's parents by being good parents, not by being good children. Choose life, that you and your children may live.

This is the year I started thinking about death. The writer Michael Ventura, in an essay called "Fifty-Two," says, "For most of human history, to be old has been a mark of honor. Today it's a source of fear, even shame. . . . One difference between being young and no-longer-young is: the young don't know they are going to die, not really; the no-longer-young know." But there is help: there is an Old One inside that helps with this. Says Ventura, "One of the tragedies of America today is that it ignores and shames this Old One. . . . The Young One seems the only part of you that our commercial culture takes seriously . . . the most insidious result of our buying into this cult of the Young One is that we insult and shame the Old One," though "the Old One has been in us from the beginning, just like the Young One." "When I turned fifty-two," says Ventura, "my Old One came to me. . . . He bade me to respect him, feed him, sing to him, speak to him, listen to him, walk with him . . . to make a place for him to occupy, so he can do his job, when it's time. For time doesn't kid around. It will come soon enough, the day when I'll awake and be very lonely and frightened if the Old One isn't there or isn't able."[7]

This is the year I started thinking about death. And it stopped me thinking about politics as usual, because thinking about death meant thinking about people and their humanity. So the two American soldiers who died Wednesday in Iraq are real kids, including one young woman, who for many reasons put themselves in harm's way. Their death is about politics, but if it is only about politics we are lost. If candidates to be president of the United States can't see beyond the competition of the next debate to the needs of elderly people like Kathryn's mother, who spends $1,600 per month on prescription drugs, why would I want one of them to be president? If they can't see that there are real children living in real poverty who cry real tears when they are hungry, why wouldn't I stop thinking about politics? The writer Annie Dillard describes spending time in the obstetrics ward of a city hospital and seeing the newborn babies being washed, one after another, each handled with the greatest of care. "There might well be a rough angel guarding this ward," she writes, "or a dragon, or an upswelling current that dashes boats on rocks. There might well be an old stone cairn in the hall by the elevators, or a well, or a ruined shrine where people still hear bells. Should we not remove our shoes, drink potions, take baths? For this is surely the wildest deep-sea vent on earth: This is where the people come out."[8]

There was a pregnant Israelite woman slave in Egypt, after Pharaoh's harsh decree to kill all male Israelite newborns. When she felt her time of delivery was near, she went outside and delivered her child on a dung heap. Immediately the *Kadosh Baruch Hu* (the Holy One of Blessing) came down and bathed [the baby] and

7. Michael Ventura, "Fifty-Two," in *Best Spiritual Writing 1999*, ed. Philip Zaleski (New York: HarperOne, 1999).
8. Annie Dillard, "Acts of God," in *Best Spiritual Writing 1999*, ed. Philip Zaleski (New York: HarperOne, 1999).

nursed it and clothed it, as it is written, "I bathed you in water and washed the blood off you and anointed you with oil. . . . Your food was choice flour, honey, and oil" (Ezekiel 16:9, 16:13, in *P'sikta Rabbati* 48:2). God shows us how to care for a baby, just as it was God who, visiting Abraham in his elderly infirmity, showed us how to visit the sick. What do we learn? First, how to care for immediate needs: to bathe and nurse and clothe and feed. Stepping back, though, we realize that we also learn that we are to care for the child of someone unable to do so herself. The Israelite slave, trapped in the desperation of slavery, can see no other alternative than to give birth outside, away from family as well as the prying eyes of the Egyptians. And because she is a slave living in slave quarters, what she finds outside is a dung heap, from which God lifts her child. Why God, and no one else?

It is written, "When you were born, your navel cord was not cut, and you were not bathed in water to smooth you; you were not rubbed with salt, nor were you swaddled. No one pitied you enough to do any of these things for you out of compassion for you" (Ezekiel 16:4–5). The worst part of the story of this Israelite slave and her baby is not that she gave birth alone, desperate, on a dung heap, though all of that is terrible enough. No, the worst part is that only God came along to help and to rescue the baby. No passerby, no relative, no neighbor took any notice of this desperate woman and her child. A human need was left to God to fulfill—this is an indictment. Thinking about humanity and not about politics, I hope that it will no longer be an indictment of us.

I set before you today life and good, or death and evil. Choose life that you and your children may live.

Time doesn't kid around, so we have to engage in life. Annie Dillard says the newborn babies, washed already and not yet washed, "are keenly interested. None cries. They look about slowly, moving their eyes. They do not speak, as trees do not speak. They do seem wise, as though they understood that their new world, however strange, was only another shade in a streaming marvel they had known from the beginning." If we stop thinking about politics and start thinking about death and life, we will see that we live in a streaming marvel of a world. The God we pray to daily and on this Yom Kippur is *nora t'hilot, oseh fele*, "awesome in splendors, doing marvels." It is marvelous to see a wild hawk fly by the window as though we could fly together. It is marvelous to imagine a world where newborn babies would get care as good as God's. It is marvelous, as Kathryn's mother described it, that there is a place where a woman who made a home for her mother, and raised three children, and created a long and happy marriage can get care and good food and companionship late in life. And it is marvelous to be able to join together to get rid of our sins in this organized religion we somehow still love.

This is the year I stopped thinking about politics and started thinking about death.

Changing Text, Changing Life

Yom Kippur 2008 / 5769

What is it about sacrifice and the Days of Awe? On Rosh HaShanah, as I protested then, the long-standing tradition is to read the story of the *Akeidah*, the binding or potential sacrifice of Isaac. On Yom Kippur, the traditional text is of a different sort of sacrifice: the sacrifice of a goat and a bull, while another goat (often called the scapegoat, possibly because he escapes) is sent off into the wilderness carrying all the people's sins to a place or a demon called Azazel. What do these sacrifices have to do with each other?

Poet Alicia Ostriker links them, asking,

> who shall live and who shall die
> which goat will have his throat cut
> like an unlucky isaac
> spitting a red thread and which goat
> will be sent alive to the pit where the crazies are
> thread tied lightly around its neck[9]

Another link is Leviticus 16, the beginning of the section traditionally read on Yom Kippur. Here is how it begins: "The Eternal One spoke to Moses after the death of the two sons of Aaron who died when they drew too close to the presence of the Eternal." Aaron's sons died when they offered "strange fire" before God,

---

9. Alicia Ostriker, *The Volcano Sequence* (Pittsburgh, PA: University of Pittsburgh Press, 2002), 82.

which God had not commanded. In response to their death, the Torah tells us, "Aaron was silent" (Leviticus 10:1–3). Silent, we can imagine, in the face of inexplicable, confounding power.

Here there is no command from God to submit or respond to, no chance to say *Hineini*. Here there is only stunning death. And death, more than any experience I know, brings us close to God's power. It is that power that we recall in the memory of sacrifice that leads us into the heart of Yom Kippur.

We had two deaths in the larger Kolot community this summer, both stunning in their loss. At the cemetery for one of them, I learned about a custom I had never known: that in some Jewish communities they take off their shoes at the cemetery, to walk in bare feet on the ground that will soon or just has covered the dead. Why? To recall Moses at the Burning Bush: "Take your shoes from off your feet, for the place you are standing on is holy ground" (Exodus 3:5). I was stunned into silence to learn of it.

One of the most powerful Jewish rituals surrounding death is the reading or speaking of the final *Vidui*, the deathbed confession. It echoes Yom Kippur's confessions, the words we speak or sing at many times throughout Yom Kippur's hours. In part, it reads, "O my God and God of my ancestors. Let my prayer come before You, and disregard not my supplication. O forgive all the sins I have committed from my birth until this day . . . may my death expiate all my sins, iniquities, and transgressions that I have committed before You. . . . Into Your hand I commit my spirit."

Yom Kippur is practice for death: we confess, we wear white, we don't eat, we don't bathe, we move past our bodies into the realm of the spirit. Yom Kippur lets us taste death without dying. The sacrifices show us the irrational, destructive, animal side of death—and they bring us close to God in a way nothing else can. How? By connecting us literally or figuratively to the stuff of life. Real, animal sacrifice involved blood and guts, fat, sinews, bone. We meat eaters often prefer to ignore this reality in the slaughtering process, but the description of the Yom Kippur sacrifices leaves us no out. Aaron takes the blood of the bull and the blood of the goat, sprinkles it around the altar, and later the hides, flesh, and dung are taken outside and burned. It's real.

Spiritual sacrifice—our task on Yom Kippur—should also get close to the bone, should push us to dig deep into the painful truths we so often want to hide from, stripping away layers of denial and artifice like stripping flesh from bone. It is painful and scary, sometimes, and can suggest a death of the old self, of the old protections. The word for sacrifice in Hebrew is *korban*, from the root "to be close, to bring close." Our ancestors offered sacrifices to get close to God. The Latin root for sacrifice means "sacred work," a good translation of the Hebrew *avodah*, which variously means sacrificial service, prayer service, service of any kind, work. Our sacred work on Yom Kippur is to try to get close to God, in part by digging deep and stripping away, in part by recognizing that we are mortal and may die at any moment, in part by bringing to life the memory of the sacrifices.

So for the second time in ten days, I want to suggest a change in text. In the nineteenth century in Germany, in the early days of Reform Judaism, the rabbis decided to replace the traditional texts of Yom Kippur that were too archaic, too bloody, too emotional for their rationalist ways. They replaced Leviticus 16, with its reminder of Aaron's dead sons and its description of the Yom Kippur sacrifices, with *Nitzavim*, a democratic text about all of us standing to enter into covenant with God, a covenant and teaching that are accessible to all. We will hear that text tomorrow morning. For the afternoon of Yom Kippur, those German rabbis replaced a list of prohibited sexual activity—some I think we'd still want to prohibit and some we dearly love—with the Leviticus 19 Holiness Code, reminding us of the greatest of Torah's social legislation. We'll read that tomorrow afternoon. I want to keep the Holiness Code, with its aspirations for generosity, communal connection, and just relationships. But I want to bring back Leviticus 16 and the sacrifices in the morning.

I love *Nitzavim*, with its evocative description of how readily accessible the Torah teaching can be for us, and its choice to do good or evil. I think it offers us a chance to stand before God without intermediaries, just us, no priest. But I think that in gaining a good example of all of us standing, attentive, ready to enter into covenant with God, we lose the reminder of and the practice for death that are so crucial to Yom Kippur. Some of you are now going to be asking, "Is she suggesting the opposite of what she urged last week?" I don't think so. The *Akeidah* is about God's command to Abraham to offer his son as a sacrifice, not a tale of the power of death nor a reminder of it via descriptions of blood and guts. Abraham had a choice about his son's death. Aaron had no choice. The goat, the bull of Yom Kippur have no choice.

I don't advocate killing, but I deeply believe that staring death in the face is at the heart of Yom Kippur. Rabbi Leon Morris wrote recently that "the language of the Temple and sacrifice, which could have lent itself so easily to metaphor, art, and poetry, disappeared, and the vast number of sources that were rooted in such language were cut off. We need these sources today, particularly during Yom Kippur. . . . The language of these sources expresses vital ideas about relationship, closeness and distance, gift-giving, and the connection between human behavior and God's willingness to abide among us."[10] In the deathbed *Vidui*, the dying person can say, "*Modeh ani l'fanecha*," which we sing every day or each Shabbat morning at Kolot as "I give thanks before You." Here, in confession, it means "I acknowledge You."

The line between life and death, between gratitude and confession, is very thin. If you have seen someone, person or animal, die, you know that line. There is breath one moment, and no breath the next. When we sing *Modeh ani l'fanecha*, we also thank God *she-hechezarta bi nishmati, b'chemlah, rabbah emunatekca*— God "who returned my breath, my soul to me overnight, in mercy.

10. Leon Morris, "The Imaginative Power of Sacrifice," in *Sh'ma*, August 1, 2013.

What great faith You have in me." Yom Kippur is our time to acknowledge God's faith in us and to try once again to find our faith in God. We need a *korban*, or the memory of a *korban*, a gift that brings us close, to help us do so. To hold that memory close, and vivid, we need, as Rabbi Morris suggested, new approaches to reclaim our difficult texts.

Although the Temple and sacrifice have long ceased to exist, Rabbi Morris says, the imaginative, interpretive, and linguistic influence of these texts can indeed last forever. A few years ago I heard a rabbi speak about what had happened at his synagogue one Yom Kippur. He lived in small town in Oklahoma and had become friendly with someone who raised birds—doves, or pigeons. On this Yom Kippur, the bird man came to the synagogue with a truckload of birds, and the whole congregation went outside to meet him. Each person there got to hold a bird, stroke it, speak to it, tell of that person's sins. After everyone had had a chance to bond with the bird in this way, they all—at once—let the birds go. Up and up they flew, carrying the people's sins and hopes and touch. The rabbi said, "I wanted to fall on my knees; it was the most stunning thing I had ever seen."

On Yom Kippur, as at a gravesite, we are standing on holy ground. Take off your shoes, and feel the dirt underneath, the blood underneath, the holiness that links the animal and the angel in you. *Hamakom asher atah omeid alav admat kodesh hu.*

Blessings

Mi Shebeirach: Blessing for the Sick

*Mi shebeirach avoteinu Avraham, Yitzchak, v'Yaakov,
v'imoteinu Sarah, Rivkah, Lei-ah v'Rachel, hu yivareich et
kol hacholim ha-eileh.*

May the One who blessed our ancestors Abraham, Isaac, and
Jacob, Sarah, Rebecca, Leah and Rachel, also bless all these
who have been named as well as others whose names we may
not know. Grant their doctors, nurses, other caregivers great
measures of wisdom and skill. Grant their loved ones, their
family, friends, neighbors, colleagues, all of you who care for
them at home or from afar, additional measures of hope and
strength. And grant to them all a *r'fuah sh'leimah*, whether
we understand that to be a complete recovery or a cessation
of their pain. Amen.

Aliyah Blessing for Those Who Have a Sense of Something Curled or Condensed Within, Ready to Expand at Some Propitious Time

You stand here with the sense of something condensed
within. Let's remember that Joseph met that man, that *ish*,
who directed him toward his brothers and thus the rest of
his life. When Jacob wrestled with an *ish*, he said he had
struggled with a being divine and human. And so too, this

ish Joseph encounters seems to be divine and human. I hope you are able to encounter someone who points you toward the future you are meant or hope to have. But if you never have that encounter, what you can have is the question the man asks Joseph: "What are you looking for?" My blessing for you is that you take that question in so that it becomes your own, and keep asking it whether you encounter an *ish* or not. "What are you looking for?" Amen.

Blessing for Recent Graduates

May the One who blessed our ancestors Abraham and Sarah, Jacob, and Joseph when they left home and began new lives also bless these young people of our community as they move on to new adventures, new learning, new challenges.

Bless their parents who stay behind, missing them and sending them off in one moment, a brave and difficult thing to do.

May the hearts of the parents and the hearts of the children be often turned to one another, even as years and distance separate them.

May they ever prosper.

Help them remember with affection their years at Kolot Chayeinu.

Enable them always to stand up for peoples in trouble and to continue to engage in the questions of what it means to be a Jew.

Blessed are You, who listens to prayer. Amen.

On Prayer

Voices, May 2009 / Sivan 5769

How can any siddur—any written prayer book—encompass all that we want prayer to do? Any prayer or song or ritual moment or word of Torah or outstretched hand may be deeply moving to any person sitting in the sanctuary at any time during any Shabbat service. I smile to look out at the congregation and see the faces—many kinds of people, some deep in thought, some worn with care, some alive in love or friendship, some seeking comfort or wisdom or connection or a new thought, some bored, some sleepy, some knowing what our next word will be and some awash in confusion.

When Kolot began, we did not have any formal prayer. We had monthly meetings that included Torah study and planning for what we would eventually do. When we began to meet as a fledgling community, we started with Shabbat dinner, which included the Shabbat blessings, songs and music and stories. In September of that year (1993), we opened a tiny Children's Learning Program. I was frankly more enamored of Torah study than of prayer, believing with Dr. Louis Finkelstein that "when you pray, you speak to God. When you study, God speaks to you." I was also hoping to develop a community of nonformal Jewish learning and strong community connections, based in a Kolot-owned and operated café. We spoke of prayer services happening informally in that dreamed-of café but did not place much emphasis on them.

But soon we began holding Shabbat morning Torah study, and it felt wrong to do that without some prayers surrounding our learning. The prayer grew as people wanted blessings that addressed their lives, joys, and fears and then as the Mourner's *Kaddish* seemed necessary. Then it began to seem odd not to begin with some morning prayers after our customary blessing for food. (We always began with food and still do, and I remain convinced that there are few better ways to make a transition from the workaday world to the world of intentional community, prayer, and study.)

So it was that the first of several Kolot cut-and-paste siddurim were born, along with holiday celebration booklets and song sheets. Some longtime members are still nostalgic for those booklets, remembering, I think, the joy of a small circle of prayer in which there were no strangers for long and prayers and blessings really were directed at each individual. Those booklets seem overly sparse to me now—in need of greater choice, more tradition, prayers for many occasions, and songs. And though the smaller gathering is still a joy at Kabbalat Shabbat, Shabbat morning services have grown too large to fit in a circle. This larger and more diverse congregation expresses many needs: different God language, clear introductions for newcomers to Jewish prayer, enough tradition and Hebrew for those with background and skill, and notes for everyone to enrich our understanding.

A few years ago, Kolot graduated from cut-and-paste siddurim when we were invited to be one of many draft-using sites for the Reform Movement's siddur-in-development, *Mishkan T'filah*. A group of us met to give feedback to those who created what is now the finished siddur. It was a good step up for our congregation, but two things made it clear that we needed to evolve yet again: The books began to fall apart! And they too began to seem a bit skimpy. Why didn't it have songs? Some versions included the full *Sh'ma* and others did not; ditto for the full haftarah blessings. It was time to explore our next step.

And so we find ourselves in the spring of 2009 (5769). After analyzing five siddurim that had potential to meet Kolot's many needs, the Siddur Selection Committee chose three siddurim to explore in more depth. Each Shabbatot, for two months each, whenever there is not a bar/bat mitzvah, we are using each "candidate" siddur. We have recruited a large feedback team that has volunteered to pay special attention and fill out feedback forms. After their feedback and more mulling by the congregation as a whole, we hope to arrive at consensus about which book to select.

This is a major step for Kolot Chayeinu. For the first time we will be purchasing a new, hardcover siddur for our community. We hope it will enhance and enrich our prayer and last for many years. But none of us have any illusion that a prayer book creates prayer on its own, especially not the deeply felt prayer and song we strive to create.

Communal prayer is a complex dance or play or opera, involving many participants, many words, a lot of music, strong and subtle symbols, and in the background the unfolding story of the congregation. The siddur—any siddur—can only be what its name implies: an order, the structure that holds us all in the dance that is our prayer. It helps to know what prayer may come next, but no book can say how I will feel saying that prayer on that Shabbat, or how it will be sung, or whether we will stand or sit or dance or stamp our feet or hold a hand as we do it. The siddur is not a script, it is an outline and *aleinu*—it is up to us—each of us—to fill that outline in every week. If we do it the same way every time, we will quickly grow bored. But if it is too different each time, we will be confused, unmoored. This dance, as all dances, needs balance, and it is the prayer leaders' job to provide it.

I am excited at the chance to try out three new siddurim, three new kinds of outlines with new prayer and song and meditation offerings. We all need some help to renew what we have done for many years, and this process offers one such help. Rachael Bregman suggests that prayer is like climbing a mountain. She is a mountain climber, I am a cave dweller, as I hope to go inward deeper and deeper, not up and out, as I enter into prayer.

As we explore these siddurim, I try to read under the familiar and unfamiliar words, to hear the voices of those who prepared this particular book and those who will be using it. In the prayer called the *Yotzeir*, which leads us toward the *Sh'ma*, and which focuses on God's creation of the natural world, of light and darkness, we are allowed the chance to hear the voices of angels singing God's praises. In a note in the siddur *Kol HaNeshamah*, the first of the three we are trying out, Rabbi Sheila Peltz Weinberg wrote:

> Who are holy beings?
> They are beloved, clear of mind and courageous.
> Their will and God's are one.
> Raising their voices in constant gratitude they marvel at
>   every detail of life,
> Granting each other loving permission to be exactly who
>   they are.
> When we listen for their sweet voices, we can hear the
>   echo within our own souls.

With the angels' voices echoing, I am still sure that God speaks to me when I study. But Shabbat after Shabbat, weekday after weekday, holy day after holy day, as I pray in this community I can also—from time to time—hear God speak to me.

We eventually chose *Kol HaNeshamah*, the siddur of the Reconstructionist Movement. To read about our siddur selection, please take a look at "Choosing a Siddur in a Pluralistic Congregation" by Rabbi Ellen Lippmann and Trisha Arlin, in *Studies in Judaism and Pluralism*, edited by Leonard Levin (Teaneck, NJ: Ben Yehuda Press, 2016).

Shabbatasana

October 19, 2012 / 3 Cheshvan 5773

I am thinking about Shabbat rest. Shabbat *m'nuchah.* Anyone else
for a bit of rest?

I do yoga, as some of you know, and my favorite pose since
my first class, is shavassana: the deep lying down, fully spent,
flat out rest that comes at the end of a class. It is waking rest,
though sometimes people fall asleep, and our breath eases,
our minds are clear, we are truly at rest for however many
minutes are allowed us. I think of Shabbat rest like that, fully
spent, flat out after a week of hard work of many kinds. Shab-
batasana.

> *There was evening and there was morning, a sixth day. The heavens
> and earth and all their hosts were completed. God completed by the
> seventh day all God's work that God had done. Vayishbot Elohim:
> Then God had a Shabbat on the seventh day from all the work that
> God had done. And God blessed the seventh day and made it holy,
> for on it God rested—shavat—from all the work that God had cre-
> ated to be done. (Genesis 1:31–2:3)*

Rabbi Adin Steinsaltz, the great Talmud scholar, writes,
"The basic view of the Sabbath as a day of rest appears very
simple. . . . But Shabbat is not merely a day when one refrains
from work, nor is it merely a day when it is customary to attend

public prayer. It is a day when one enters a completely different sphere."[11]

What is that sphere? "On the seventh day there is a cessation of all work and a heavenly delight is manifested. The week is thus devoted to an awakening process from below; it is as though the Shabbat is the hidden purpose of labor—a purpose that is revealed only on the seventh day. . . . Shabbat means putting aside creative activity in order to concern oneself completely with personal reflection and matters of the spirit, free of struggle and tension."[12]

A couple of summers ago I had the pleasure of visiting with Rabbi Sami Barth and his family in Gloucester, Massachusetts. Their son, Yishai, was expounding on an ongoing argument he had with his father. Sami wanted their home and each of their lives on Shabbat to be, as Steinsaltz says, putting aside creative activity. Yishai was mad! He wanted to create, to write, I think. And he asked, "Isn't that a Shabbat thing to do?" I tended to agree with him: certain kinds of writing seem especially fruitful on Shabbat when other work recedes. But Sami asked, "Maybe Shabbat is the time to reflect on what you have written and will write. Isn't some non-writing or non-painting time necessary for the creative process?" Point taken, though Yishai went on arguing.

Yes, the *non*-time is necessary for creation and for renewal, and just so we need the rest that comes after creating and the rest that leads to it. I had a wonderful talk on Wednesday with my spiritual director about this non-time, which she reminded me might link to the *ayin*—the nothingness or no-thingness that the Chasidim understand as a necessary state in which to receive divine input.

11. Adin Steinsaltz, *The Miracle of the Seventh Day: A Guide to the Spiritual Meaning, Significance, and Weekly Practice of the Jewish Sabbath* (New Jersey: Jossey-Bass, a division of John Wiley & Sons, 2003), 1.
12. Ibid., 2.

I was struck by three meanings of *ayin*, even though they have slightly different spellings:

- *Ayin* אין one is the nothingness, like *ein*. Its opposite is *yeish*: there is something, tangible.
- *Ayin* עין two is an eye. So if we enter a state of *ayin*, maybe we begin by looking around, rather than listening, especially if we listen to a lot of talk most of the time.
- *Ayin* עין three is a spring, just like in Spanish, where *ojo* means both "eye" and "water source." But this *ayin* may also be an internal spring, or perhaps both: once we have looked around the empty no-thingness within, we may find wellsprings of possibility that can receive the input that Chasidic wisdom says always flows from the Divine and is only waiting to be received.

So enter the space of no-thingness. Look around. Find the spring welling up within, answered by the flow from God. That is a nice rest, right?

Now let's hear from Noah. It's his *parashah* this week. But why may we want to hear from Noah on the subject of Shabbat rest? Noach was born at the end of last week's *parashah*: "Lamech lived 182 years and he sired a son. He called his name Noach, saying, 'This one will comfort us in our work and the toil of our hands'" (Genesis 5:28–29). Like Shabbat rest, right? But no: Rashi comments, "It is not that he will comfort us. It is that he will give us rest from the toil of our hands." And he adds, "Until Noah came they had no tools for plowing, and he prepared for them these tools. . . . This is what it means to say—not that he will comfort us—but that he will give us rest. His name is Noach, not Menachem." Comfort is nice, Rashi says, but one who can give rest by seeing what is needed and providing it is surely one who will save us when the flood comes.

On this Shabbat, let us all be blessed with deep, renewing, re-souling *shavat vayinafash* rest. And when our time of work resumes, let us remember our time in the no-thingness, look around, and see what needs bubble up in a spring that we can attend to. Let us give Noach a little extra *kavod* this week, just for offering the rest that can come with a new tool or a new recognition.

T'shuvah

Sh'ma Koleinu

Hear Our Voices

Yom Kippur 2011 / 5772

Sh'ma koleinu: hear our voice. *Sh'ma koloteinu*: hear our voices. We call out to You, O God, longing to know that someone is listening, yearning to have an ear attend to all we wish to say. In the loud public sphere many voices are heard, but not always ours, and not always the ones we wish to be heard. We hear the voice of Timothy Geithner, and the voice of bank CEOs, but not the voices of those who have no jobs.

Hear our voice. We hear the voice of Dominique Strauss Kahn, but not the voices of women attacked in hotel rooms or the streets and subways of Park Slope and Windsor Terrace.

Hear our voice. We hear the voice of the U.S. drone seeking out its target, but not the voices of children too often killed in war.

Hear our voice. We hear the voice of standardized tests, but not the voice of equitable quality education.

Hear our voice. We hear the voice of an aspiring prosecutor, but not the voice of a murder victims' relatives in pain or the voice of a wrongly convicted prisoner being put to death.

Hear our voice. We hear the voice of angry anti-immigration bills, but not the voice of the huddled masses yearning to breathe free, desperate now to get away.

Hear our voice. We hear the voice of vast fields of corn and soy being harvested, but not the voice of the small farmer and the small store.

Hear our voice. We hear the voice of foreclosures and still-overpriced mortgages, but not the voice of the middle-class home-owner.

Hear our voice. We hear the voices raised against Islam and Muslims, but not the voice of Muslims driven by their faith to work tirelessly for interfaith connections.

Hear our voice. We hear the murmurings of antisemitism in a bad economy, but not the voices of Jewish leaders striving vigorously for understanding and recognition.

Hear our voice. We hear the voice of religious exclusion and self-righteousness, but not enough the voice of godly justice.

Hear our voice. Hear our voice, Eternal our God, and accept our prayer with compassion and with will. Compassion alone is not enough, for us or for You. We ask that You will Your ear to really hear, to really attend, to really respond. We understand that we too must have the will to listen, and not just the compassion. Teach us to listen, to heed, to do, and by doing, deepen our hearing.

Hear our voices, O God, all our voices.

Picture this scene: eighteen years ago, twenty or so originators of Kolot are gathered, trying to come up with a name that sounds a little more aspirational than "Ellen's place." We are thinking of a café, remember, and the names we imagine have to do with feasting and celebrating and gathering in joy. "Never-imagined-she'd-be-a-cantor" Lisa B. Segal suggests the use of the word "voice," and then we came up with "the voice of joy, the voice of celebration." And then Michael Forman, *z"l*, said, "We are many voices. And life is not all about joy and celebration. We want to acknowledge all our lives in all their fullness." And voila! Kolot—many voices—Chayeinu—of our lives.

Last week at the 6:00 p.m. service for Rosh HaShanah, I suggested to everyone that they might take a leaf from our ancestors' book and write an actual ledger of their deeds and results and changes. I spoke of the wrongdoings we commit and how a ledger might help us to arrive at *t'shuvah*. After the service, Debra Everett-Lane came up to ask, "If we are making a ledger of our lives, shouldn't it include all our lives, the joy too, and not just the bad stuff?" Not just the joy. Not just the hard stuff. All our voices. *Sh'ma kolot chayeinu*. O God, hear, we pray, the voices of our lives.

I have often quoted the unknown sage who said that all Jewish prayer can be characterized as "Please. Thank you. Oops. And wow." [Congregant] Melanie Holcomb suggests that we add lamentation, a crucial addition for ancient days and now, the prayer of *Eichah* and of the lamenting women who weep for all. I would add anger, another crucial Jewish mode, the prayer of Levi Yitzchak of Berditchev and Elie Wiesel and countless ones of us. Please, thank you, oops, wow, lamentation, anger. What is your one prayer on this night of nights?

Please, God, do not cast us away when we are old, as our strength diminishes, do not abandon us. We are older and vibrant, grown and sexy, a little more forgetful, a little more tired at night. No reason to cast us off. Please? And do not ignore us because we are young; we are creative and smart and ready to serve You in our way. Please?

Thank You, God, for the small joys, the simple pleasures, the slanted sunlight, the leaves of red and gold, the child's smile in a painful time, an unexpected hug. What a gift!

Oops! I forgot to call her, I meant to write him. I knew there was something I was supposed to do yesterday besides getting food for the break-fast. I know I can't ask You for forgiveness if I have not asked other people. But, maybe now? Hear my prayer with compassion on my busy life? Oops?

Wow, God, when I saw the sun on the lake in the park I had to say a prayer. When that hawk flew by the porch on its way to break-fast and took my breath away, my tears were for You. When I heard that extraordinary *d'rash* last week, sitting on the edge of my seat, in awe at one of our own, my astonishment was Yours. Wow!

I lament, God, at the loss of life, the life of our friend, the life of so many young soldiers, the lives of starving refugees. *Eichah*, how can it be, the breathing heart of so many stopped before their time. *Eiyecha*, where are You then?

I am angry! How could You?! Over and over I have pleaded with You, others have made probably foolish vows to get Your attention, but You hide Your face, I only see the results of Your power smashing us under the force of hurricane or tsunami, earthquake and lightning, fire in dry trees, flooding from rains. How long do You think people will keep praying to You when their house is crushed, their beloveds dead beneath the weight, or drowned with no hope. Give us some hope, dammit.

I wonder if God ever says, *Sh'ma koli*, "Hear *My* voice." Ancient writers saw the creation of the universe as the act of a lonely God, they saw God's distress at Cain's murderous impulse and the corruption surrounding Noah and imagined that the one thing God sought was a connection to the people God sometimes wished had never been created. After Moses died, did God cry out to Joshua, "Hear My voice"? And now, when humans treat one another far worse than Noah or Joshua could ever imagine, can *we* hear God? Can we accept that voice?

Hear My voice, God says.
I know that you still reach for Me,
you know Me by many names.
My voice is the power of the thunder and the still small
   voice within,
the rush of the waters, the crash of the heavens,
the prayer of the heart, the outstretched hand,
the unexpected smile, the welcoming embrace,
and yes, the unexpected death, even the painful illness.

Listen, hear My voice
urging respect, pursuing justice,
wishing for you to turn, seeking your finest self.
You know Me, say God,
you see Me,
inside and out.
Hakartani:
explore Me, reach for Me,
yell at Me, accuse Me.
But do not hide your face from Me,
do not turn your ear from Me.

Hear My voice! *N'um Adonai*—**so says God.**

So . . . Can we listen? Can we hear? Can we *forgive*? Can we
forgive God the tsunami, the hurricane, the awful death? Wars,
murder, rape, genocide are human acts, hard, maybe impossible to
forgive. I imagine God weeping at what we have wrought. Let us
try to forgive God and ask if it is at all possible for God to forgive us.

Sh'ma koleinu. **Have compassion on us, accept our prayer
with compassion and will. Hear our voice. And we, with our
human weakness and human ear, will try to hear Yours.**

T'shuvah

Elul Teachings

Elul 4: The End and the Beginning

And now the month begins to draw to a close. September 13 is its last day, as we enter the new year that night. This month that spread out before us when we began: Have we used it well? Done what we needed to do? What remains?

I learn from Simon Jacobson of the Meaningful Life Center (in his book and online teachings *60 Days: A Spiritual Guide to the High Holidays*) that one possible acronym of the name Elul comes from the Book of Esther, our Purim story. Chapter 9, verse 22, tells of a month that was turned from sorrow to joy and ends by saying we should celebrate by sending sweets to one another and gifts to the poor. That ending phrase is the acronym: *ish l'rei-eihu u'matanot la-evyonim*. The *i-l-u-l* of its first letters in Hebrew are *alef-lamed-vav-lamed*, or Elul.

I am reminded that Yom Kippur is sometimes called Yom Ki-Purim, "a day like Purim," its obverse: solemn versus hilarious, fasting versus feasting, simple white clothing versus costumes galore. Yet both days, the solemn and the hilarious, urge us to care for one another and for our society.

T'shuvah, t'filah, tzedakah: the three sets of acts that may, as our central *Un'taneh Tokef* prayer tells us, mitigate the harshness of what divine decree is meant for us. Many of us do not take this literally. But we know the randomness of this world and its great and terrible surprises. And we can imagine, I hope, that the combination of turning to our finest selves (*t'shuvah*), praying in ways that elevate and inspire us (*t'filah*), and giving of our selves and our resources to help balance our society (*tzedakah*) *may* in fact sustain us in times of tragedy and keep us resilient in times of challenge.

This is the time. May all our journeys through the next month, the month chock full of holidays, take us to new heights and new inward exploration, to clear decisions and renewed hope.

Hashiveinu Adonai eilecha v'nashuvah, chadeish yameinu k'kedem. Turn us to You, and we will turn. Please renew our days from the past and turn them toward the future.

Elul 3: Give It Up to Where You Want to Be

Elul is in full bloom, and many are taking advantage of its push to do self-assessment, repair relationships, change course. As someone I know said to me, "Elul is kicking my ass this year!"

As I write, I have just returned from marching with the NAACP and a bunch of rabbis on one leg of American's Journey for Justice, a march from Selma to Washington, DC, August 1 to September 16, when a big Washington rally will culminate this extraordinary effort. I walked miles in the blazing South Carolina sun because, as a white Ashkenazi Jew, I felt the need to be an active ally and an actor in the push for justice and because we had just read in a recent Torah portion, "Justice, justice you shall pursue" (Deuteronomy 16:20). So I went in pursuit of justice; my Judaism demands it. One of my prayers for this Elul is that the march is a success in that its recommendations in Washington are heard and enacted or strengthened, as with the Voting Rights Act, which turned fifty this summer. (See more at naacp.org.)

Just before I left, someone sent me this deeply important quote by James Baldwin: "I imagine one of the reasons people cling to their hates so stubbornly is because they sense, once hate is gone, they will be forced to deal with pain."

Wow.

If you give up hate right now, or rage, or even judgment, what may you find? Pain? Fear? Deep sorrow? Can you recognize that possibility and still take a step toward change in this Elul time? I find that sometimes it is the smallest steps that open the biggest doors.

A midrash on the Song of Songs teaches, "The Holy One said, 'Open up for me an opening like the eye of a needle and in turn I will enlarge it to be an opening through which wagons can enter (Song of Songs *Rabbah* 5:2).'" The midrash is on this verse, Song of Songs 5:2, about a different sort of opening: "I sleep, but my heart is awake. Hark! My beloved is knocking: Open for me, my sister, my beloved, my dove, my perfect one, for my head is full of dew, my locks with the drops of the night." Can you imagine opening to the new, the unexpected, the delightful, the awesome, this Elul? And what would happen if you did? What do you have to give up or turn away from to be able to do so?

Right now, take one small step. Elul might kick your ass, but hopefully it'll be a kick in the direction of more openness.

Elul 2: You're Invited—Visit God's House

One of the mystical concepts I love about Elul is the idea that in this month "the King is in the field."

Okay. You may know that some of Rosh HaShanah's imagery is of God as a King on a throne; we respond with awe to this display of majesty. I know King imagery is hard to swallow for many, certainly for many feminists. That said, whatever transcendent metaphor we use, there is an understanding that after Rosh HaShanah, God travels. By the following Elul, God has returned to a spot near the divine palace but has not yet entered it. Instead, God lingers in the field, the front yard of the palace (maybe we Brooklynites can imagine God on the palace stoop); in this setting, God is more accessible and more immediate. God is less distant and there is no throne. For some, this may seem too anthropomorphic, but I love the idea that somehow the Divine Presence—the *Shechinah*—is much more available to us at this season, in this special month. What can that mean? During Elul, some people read Psalm 27 daily. At Kolot, we sing from it every Shabbat.

The words we usually choose to sing: "One thing I ask of You, Eternal One, that is the thing I seek: To dwell in Your house all the days of my life, and to envision the pleasantness there, and to visit Your palace" (Psalm 27:4). So one question is: What is the one thing you desire from God? What is a more precious hope to you than any other? And what would dwelling in God's house feel like? Another note: The word for "visit" in the psalm—*l'vakeir*—can also mean "to criticize." Hmmm. So while I may want to dwell in God's house and find it pleasant, I may not be able to relax there unless I can also offer some well-placed criticism. Certainly our world, which is one understanding of "God's house," offers plenty of opportunity for criticism.

Either way, whether you want to make your most precious request or offer some criticism on the state of "God's palace," this is the time when the King is in the field, and you can do your asking and offer your criticism quite directly. Don't wait. Soon enough it will be Rosh HaShanah, and the King will have ascended the distant throne. There is awe then, and turning inward, finding ourselves again in the new year, 5776. But now, the Presence is very close at hand, waiting to meet us.

Will you accept the invitation?

Elul 1

The Jewish month of Elul began last night, August 15. Until the night of Sunday, September 12, when Rosh HaShanah begins, we have a month to prepare for the High Holy Days—the Awesome Days—and the Ten Days of Repentance from Rosh HaShanah until Yom Kippur. What will each of us do in this month? How will we prepare? What can preparing mean? How will you search within, how will you offer and receive forgiveness? How can you get back to the "you" you mean to be? We will be sending a teaching each week of Elul, which we hope will help in your preparations.

Today we look at the word *Elul*, the name of this month, likely borrowed from an ancient Akkadian and/or Aramaic word meaning "search." This month we can ideally spend some time searching inwardly, trying to be honest with ourselves about the ways we have missed the mark, or strayed from the way we know we want to behave. The Hebrew word for "sin"—*cheit*—seems to mean "missing the mark." It is something we all do if we are human beings, a comforting realization, and easier to acknowledge than "sin." Some say *Elul* is an acronym, the letters formed from the Hebrew words *Ani l'dodi v'dodi li*, "I am my beloved's and my beloved is mine" (from the Song of Songs 6:3). In this month, the beloved is The Beloved, a way to understand God's presence that is said to draw closer to us now in a nonformal and intimate way.

So we are given a month to search within, to find a newly close connection to the Divine, to explore what the life of the spirit feels like now. One practice for the entire month feels especially important: we are asked not to come before God with repentance until we have repaired the breaches that may have opened between us and other people. So we may want to take up a long-standing practice: Say to loved ones, friends, and relatives this month, "If I have offended you in any way, I hope you will forgive me." And when asked, try hard to offer forgiveness too. It is not always easy, and sometimes all we can do is seek to start a process of forgiveness and reconciliation. But starting is good!

Part Three

G'milut Chasidim

Communal Care

The Kolot Chayeinu Café

Yom Kippur 1994 / 5755

Kolot Chayeinu is a developing progressive Jewish community dedicated to the understanding that prayer, study, and *tzedakah* can only be engaged in meaningfully if the members of the community first get to know one another and spend time together; Jews and our families and friends get to know one another best when we eat together; therefore, eating together is at the center of our community's life; and therefore, Kolot Chayeinu's long-term vision is of a café, which will also be our congregation's home.

There won't be a real menu; a café isn't a restaurant. A long time ago, I decided to agree with Vincent Urward, who runs Café LaFortuna, where John Lennon used to hang out. He says a café serves coffee and desserts, period. I add bread, knowing we can't live on bread alone, knowing the rest comes from someplace else than the food. In fact, I don't really care all that much about the food. I'm interested in the feeding.

You know, someone once asked the food writer M. F. K. Fisher, may her memory be for a blessing, why do you write about food and eating and drinking? Why don't you write about the struggle for power and security, and about love, the way others do? Her answer? "The easiest answer is to say that, like most humans, I am hungry. But there is more than that. It seems to me that our three basic needs, for food and security and love, are so mixed and mingled and entwined that we cannot think of one without the others, so when I write of hunger, I am really writing about love and the hunger for it, and warmth and the love of it and the hunger for it."[13]

Welcome to the Kolot Chayeinu Café.

"What am I interested in," you want to know, "if not the food?" I'll tell you, if you've got the time.

I'm interested in what food can do. Like Judy Wicks says—she runs the White Dog Café in Philly—"By using good food as a common ground, you can break down the walls that separate people."[14] I want to break down those walls. I'm interested in seeing you come in the door, and reading your eyes, and wondering if you'll want to talk about it, or celebrate, or spend a little time alone. I'm interested in what makes you tick, and how you'll say so after sharing a lingering cup of coffee; and I want to know what makes him weep, and what makes her think she doesn't believe in God. I'm interested in hearing what you'll have to say about a Torah text after you've eaten your bagel, and I want to give you a chance to pray for a friend who's ill or to mourn a grandparent or a colleague or a spouse. And what I'm really interested in is hospitality, sharing our table, sharing our bread with the hungry, sharing our souls along with our bread, as the prophet Isaiah urges (58:10). I love the Passover seder, the rebbe's *tisch*, the wedding banquet where the poor ate first.

At the Whistlestop Café, it wasn't the fried green tomatoes that made it a hospitable place, it was Idgie's taking Smokey Lonesome outside for a little hair of the dog that bit him when the DTs made his hands shake too much to lift a fork. And it wasn't even her taking him outside to spare him shame; it was having the bottle ready for him, and putting her arm around his shoulder, and telling him that crazy story—about the lake that froze with the ducks on it,

13. M. F. K. Fisher, *The Gastronomical Me* (New York: North Point Press, an imprint of Farrar, Straus & Giroux, 1989), ix.
14. *Ms. Magazine*, vol. V, no. 1 (July/August 1994), 39.

and the ducks carried the lake off to Georgia—that just had to make him laugh. That's hospitality.

At the Women's Lunch Place in Boston, there are fresh flowers on the tables every day, to warm the hearts of the desperately poor women who eat their meals there and spend the day. Jane and Amy and the other tzaddikim who run the place built a huge kitchen counter so people could come in and hang out in the kitchen while meals are being cooked, just like people do in every kitchen I've ever been in. They bring each woman's lunch to wherever she wants to eat it: on a bench just inside the door, if she can't face coming in; to a table for one in a corner, if she wants to eat privately and in peace; or to a table full of other women, where she can talk, joke, or just relax in the buzz around her. I thought of them last week at Rosh HaShanah lunch, when someone pulled a chair over to the little table by the wall, saying, "I don't do so well with laps."

But the most amazing thing they do at the Women's Lunch Place is provide a small screened-off corner where one fearful woman can make her nightly preparations for going out alone into the scary world. They know a little about why she is afraid, and they know she has good reason, and they know the world is even scarier than she may know. But they don't try to get her to change or to live in a shelter when she doesn't want to. They merely give her the space to get ready. That's hospitality, and it's what we all need.

Bailey, whose name isn't Bailey, but who some of you know runs Bailey's Cafe, says it like this: "Even though this planet is round, there are just too many spots where you can find yourself hanging onto the edge . . . and unless there's some space, some place, to take a breather for a while, the edge of the world—frightening as it is— could be the end of the world, which would be quite a pity."[15]

---

15. Gloria Naylor, *Bailey's Cafe* (New York: Open Road Intergrated Media, 2017).

Ellyn Rosenthal and the people at the Food and Hunger Hotline have just opened the One City Café on 14th Street in Manhattan. It's a café for people who can afford to pay for a very good lunch, and for people who need a discount for a family dinner, and for people who will pay with food stamps. When they were planning their café, they asked a lot of people living in nearby shelters what they would want most in a café. Their answer: white tablecloths and fresh salad. What would you say, if asked? At the One City Café, they have white tablecloths and fresh salad.

In Laurie Colwin's book *Happy All the Time*, a character whose name I've forgotten seems to spend most of her time making things beautiful. Eating at her table meant there would be flowers and beautiful place settings and the loveliest fruits and the best-chosen wine. When I first read the book, I thought she was silly, and a little trivial. I don't anymore. Now I think of her when I hear a phrase about God's grace—*chein vachesed v'rachamim*, say, or any number of others.

Adding beauty to an ugly world, making people feel special in a time when we often feel anonymous, remembering to remember the crucial small things—these are the things that set a place apart. *Kadosh*—it means "set apart." Sometimes we call that holy.

Welcome to the Kolot Chayeinu Café. Want another cup of coffee?

Now, where was I? Oh, yes, talking about the grace of welcome, offering haven, making people feel special. We learned that from Abraham. Yes, that Abraham. It starts here: One day, "[Abraham] was sitting at the entrance of the tent as the day grew hot. Lifting up his eyes, he saw three men standing near him. As soon as he saw them, he ran from the entrance of the tent to greet them and, bowing to the ground, he said, 'My lords, if it please you, do not go on past your servant. Let a little water be brought; bathe your feet and recline under the tree. And let me fetch a morsel of bread that you may refresh yourselves; then go on—seeing that you have come your servant's way'" (Genesis 18:1–5).

Now, Abraham is a complicated, difficult human being, and some of us know other stories about him that are not so sympathetic. But let's just look at this story right now, because this story gave Abraham the reputation he still has for hospitality, rushing about on a hot day soon after he'd had surgery to make sure his unexpected guests had food and water and a brief time of comfort. From this little story, the Rabbis taught us a big lesson: Bread is the comfort of the heart (*Genesis Rabbah* 48).

They also told us more. Abraham's tent was always open on all four sides, so people passing from any direction would be greeted as these guests were greeted. And Abraham greeted warmly all who passed, whether they were of his people or not, whether they worshiped other gods or not, without knowing whether they were friendly or not. He asked them to thank his God for the food, according to his beliefs. Some decided to stay with him and Sarah, joining their destinies to theirs. Some just ate, rested, and traveled on. Either way, apparently, those who had known it told others of the hospitality at Maison Abraham. The memory of it echoes through the generations.

Listen: Many years after his death, when his descendants were suffering in slavery to Pharaoh in Egypt, that Pharaoh dreamed up the most evil of decrees. He instructed the Egyptian midwives, Shifra and Puah among them: "When you deliver the Hebrew women, look at the birthstool; if it is a boy, kill him" (Exodus 1:15–16). A midrash tells us:

> *The king used all sorts of devices to render the midwives amenable to his wishes. He approached them with amorous proposals, which they both repelled, and then he threatened them with death by fire. But they said [to themselves]: ". . . Abraham opened an inn, that he might feed the wayfarers . . . and we should neglect the children, nay, kill them?! No, we shall . . . keep them alive." Thus they failed to execute what Pharaoh had commanded. Instead of murdering the babes, they supplied all their needs. If a mother that had given birth to a child lacked food and drink, the midwives went to well-to-do*

*women, and took up a collection, that the infant might not suffer
want. They did still more for the little ones.*[16]

At a moment of life-and-death choice, Shifra and Puah remembered Abraham's hospitality. They did not know Abraham, they were not of his people. But they knew of the welcome he provided for those who were also not of his people, and they could not bring themselves to kill his descendants. They were midwives, charged with bringing life into the world; they resisted the decree of death and chose life.

I want to walk in Shifra and Puah's footsteps, and I want you to join me in making the Kolot Chayeinu Café a place of such welcome, such a haven, that those who spend an hour or a day with us there will walk with them, as well. I want you to join me in resisting any decree, from any quarter, that tells us we must not care, must exclude, must see "other-in-a-different-category" when we should see a human face.

We must resist. I want us to resist attempts to make us think that famine, warfare, disease, and the sight of refugees fleeing everywhere are as distant from us in heart and mind as the biblical stories these sights evoke are distant from us in time. We know these stories: Abraham and Isaac and Jacob were refugees who fled their homes during famine, in search of food. Our people loaded onto boats were refused entry at this country's shores while the Statue of Liberty wept. We must remember.

And we know now how it can feel, how it must have felt once, to sit together over coffee and say, "What a horrific situation it is over there—in Sarajevo, in Rwanda, in Auschwitz . . ." and to feel helpless to do anything. That, too, we must remember.

And we must argue. I want us to argue about refugees, and political quagmires, and helplessness, and much more. I want

16. Louis Ginzberg, *Legends of the Jews,* vol. 2 (Philadelphia: Jewish Publication Society, 1969), 52.

great, loud arguments to rise from our café's tables along with the scent of good coffee. I want our arguments to rival those of Hillel and Shammai, and I want to learn from them. I want to hear from you about Israel's place in your lives, and I want to argue about giving away the Golan, or whether Assad can be trusted, or whether Arafat can, or Rabin. I want to argue over who should be governor of New York, and who attorney general, and I want to try and understand together what happens in Crown Heights or in Hebron. I want to study Talmud in our café, and to hear within its walls the voices of Yochanan ben Zakkai and Beruria and all the Gamliels and the voices of our lives, and I want us to make tough decisions after listening to them all.

I want to mourn with you. I want to say *Kaddish* for our parents and for the parents of babies living too long in New York City hospitals, for lack of any other home. I want to say *Kaddish* for victims of violence in Bosnia and Rwanda and Haiti and East New York, and for those who boarded an ill-fated airplane, and for those too many thousands who've died of AIDS, and for Jessica Tandy, and for Jackie Kennedy Onassis. And I want us to celebrate—in traditional ways and ways we have not yet invented. I want to welcome baby girls into this world on equal ground, and maybe Kurt Vonnegut's welcome to babies will echo alongside the ancient Rabbis' blessings. I want to celebrate first days of school and graduations and new jobs and the first day of spring. I want to sing with joy at the life-joinings of women with women, women with men, men with men. I want to celebrate the changes of midlife and old age, greeting wrinkles and new freedom and wisdom as the gifts they are.

I want to hear the sounds of every kind of music spilling out of the doors and windows of our café, and the softer, urgent sounds of poetry, and the laughter and tears that flow freely at the end of a story. I want to see our children's art and the art of recognized artists mingling on our walls, and I want to see our children thrive against all odds like the tree that still grows in Brooklyn.

I want us to sit in our sukkah and celebrate the vegetables and the relationships and the chutzpah that we harvest in our city, and I want to remember Shifra and Puah every year at Passover. I want to dedicate new two-room apartments and first-time houses, and fifty-year homes that have never been dedicated in this way.

And most of all, I want to hammer a mezuzah onto the doorpost of our café, saying, this place is set apart, it is holy, here we remember to remember and remember to resist and remember to create and remember to argue, and here we give thanks to the One who gives us daily the chance to remember:

> *Baruch atah Adonai* / Blessed are You, *Adonai*, Source of all life, ultimate Source of coffee and bread. As we refrain from eating on this holy day, give us the wisdom to know how to respond to many kinds of hunger. As we pause amid life's joys and challenges, give us the creativity to live life to the fullest. As we contemplate Your unknowable face, give us the grace to recognize the hint of Your image in all who enter our door. As we listen to and speak the words of our ancestors, give us full voice to add our own words to Your great ongoing conversation. And as we end this day's reflections with food and celebration, give us cause for celebration, and enable us to eat and drink always with joy, compassion, and warm camaraderie.
> Amen.

Kolot Chayeinu

Kesher

Connection

Voices, February 2007

I want to tell you about a conversation and a letter I read recently that make me think about Kolot and *kesher*—the connections that are both the necessary foundation for and a significant goal of our Jewish community, which, after all, is called the Voices of Our Lives. The first conversation was with many Kolot members on Shabbat afternoon when we gathered for the first of several discussions about possible affiliation with a Jewish denominational movement. There were many great questions asked and a lot of good discussion. But one question really grabbed me: "What would we have to do to get kicked out?" This grabbed me not because I hope we will be kicked out of any movement we might choose to affiliate with, but because it was the "edge" question, the one that teaches us by saying what is in and what is out. I think of it now because writing about *kesher*—the web of connections at Kolot—is for me really a way to say what is in and what is out; what is bottom line necessary and what not. I would love to know what is bottom line for you as member or friend of our community. For me, it's these two things more than anything else:

1. That there is something called Kolot Chayeinu to which all
   members belong, whether they come to family services or

Shabbat morning services or the Children's Learning Program or join Eitz Kehilla to work on social justice issues or come to a fundraising event or a concert. That entity must be the center from which all other activities flow, and we must each feel responsible to it and it to all of us. Right now, the Internet—mostly e-mail—is the only place we all connect and it is not enough. My early and continuing dream of a café is for me the symbol of this center, a non-religious space where any Kolot member and friend can come, eat, talk, argue, see art, hear music, and yes, sometimes find prayer and Jewish study too. We need a center that is not the school and not the sanctuary—the two primary centers in Kolot now—where all members can enter and know they are home. This idea is bottom line for me, and I continue to think of the café as a symbol and potential fulfillment of the dream. But the idea—that there is a Kolot to which all belong and are responsible—that is the bottom line. For generations, that idea/center was Judaism, first the Temple, then Rabbinic Judaism. One member recently suggested to me that it still is, that it is Judaism that links all of us at Kolot, no matter our background. But I think Judaism without connections, without the *kesher* of a smaller community within the larger whole, will not sustain most of us in this day and age. Kolot Chayeinu was always meant to be that smaller connector, in both idea and tangible café form.

2. That because we all belong to one entity, we are responsible to each other. Our tradition teaches, *Kol Yisrael areivim zeh lazeh*, "All Jews are mixed up with each other." This too, I want to condense into "all Kolot members—not all of whom are Jews, remember—are mixed up with each other." To me, that means that any Kolot member can be a help, a comfort, a sharer of joy with any other, whether you know them at all, beyond knowing that you are both Kolot members. In practice, this means that all members should try hard to be present when a young Kolot member becomes bar or bat mitzvah. All members should call

someone in mourning or send a card, or come to shivah. These are not things that can be delegated to a committee. Kolot's Gemilut Chasadim Committee can learn what is happening and contact the rest of us and make the arrangements, but they can never substitute for personal connections—for *kesher.* Having condensed the mutual responsibility we have for each other, I would now expand it in two ways. I think there cannot be an authentically Jewish community that does not reach out into the world to try to repair some part of the damage we find there. Kolot's Eitz Kehilla group or the fledgling family justice group can gather us and urge and suggest, but we have to do it. I hope we do it together, and together with those whose lives are different from ours. But we have to do it. We can't read our prayers or the prophetic texts, say, if we are not doing some of that repair.

We need to look inward: Kolot has always been a place where people seen as on the fringe in other Jewish communities can find home. It is our responsibility to ensure that this remains true. I look at my tallit when I put it on every Shabbat morning and realize that the fringes are the important part, the reminder of how to live. People on the fringe remind us that a community is not a community without that *kesher*—that connection to people within who may be different from you or me. Difference is good, it shakes us up, it makes us think, it acts like the fringe on the tallit. In practice, this means that each of us says hello to whoever walks into any Kolot door, whether it is the basement door to our *b'nei mitzvah* classes or the front door to services or the basement door to monthly Shabbat Café lunch and learning or the Park Slope Jewish Center door where our younger students learn or the door to someone's home where a meeting is being held or yes, a café door where some Kolot members are gathering. Our designated *shamasses* are there on a Friday night or Shabbat mornings to greet people and show them where we are in the siddur at that moment. But neither they nor anyone else can stand in for each of us taking on the obligation, as we sing each Shabbat morning, to love our neighbor as ourself. In this case, this means greeting anyone as you would want to be greeted. Or, adapting Hillel's formation in the negative, do not ignore someone as you would not want to be ignored.

Now for the letter I read, Rabbi Eric Yoffie's "Dear Reader" letter in the Winter 2006 issue of *Reform Judaism* magazine. Rabbi Yoffie writes about the desire to make one's congregation "a community of warmth and intimacy, where members and visitors alike are welcomed and embraced." Many of you know that I dislike the word "welcoming" when it refers to a specific group of people, because it sets up an "us" and "them" situation, in which the "us" is welcoming the "them." But I believe deeply in creating a congregation that is welcoming to all. And Rabbi Yoffie supports this, saying, "This much is clear: Spiritual communities are not built with more adult ed lectures, better brochures, and efficient administrations. They are built with caring relationships and very large doses of personal attention."

Kein y'hi ratzon. May it be God's will that we at Kolot Chayeinu are able to create a community with a real sense of itself, in which anyone who walks in the door is greeted as warmly and kindly as anyone else. For Jews leaving slavery in Egypt, the way they treated the stranger they encountered later was a symbol of their depth of understanding and loving-kindness. This is no less true today.

On the Ordination of
Cantor Lisa B. Segal

May 2011

I had the honor this past week of being present for the ordination of Kolot Chayeinu's *chazan*, Lisa B. Segal, who received *s'michah* as cantor at the Academy for Jewish Religion.

For Lisa's ordination, where I served as her presenter, the first to announce her to the world as cantor, I wrote these words, which were published in the ordination journal opposite Lisa's own autobiography:

I knew Lisa B. Segal for at least two years before I knew she could sing! She was an earliest member of Kolot Chayeinu/Voices of Our Lives, the community I founded, and I knew she was a passionate Jew and a hilariously funny mimic and a hard worker and a beloved partner to Arthur and a warm and engaging friend. But it took her a long time to admit that she could sing and, more, that she wanted to sing Jewish music and, more, the music of prayer.

It turns out she had sung for years, in teen choirs and on the streets of Paris, but not as the leader of prayer. Eighteen years after our meeting, I think that the prospect of singing prayer was so deeply important that it took Lisa significant internal struggle to be able to say out loud that this is what she wanted to do. Now we all know that her song and her prayer are worthy of struggle, are deep and rich and important.

So Lisa began. First as a sort of backup singer at High Holy Day services, then as the primary *chazan* for the *Yamim Noraim*, then as a leader on Shabbat. And as she sang, she gained confidence and skill such that I finally asked if she might consider studying to become a cantor. "Oh, no," she replied. "I don't think I want to be clergy." Another moment of struggle, for it was clear to her that becoming a cantor was deep and important and needed all her heart and all her soul and all her might. She wasn't ready. But bit by bit, as her singing became prayer and her song became psalm, as she reached out as a pastor and a teacher and a community leader, the idea of becoming a cantor grew from within.

We see the result today. Six hard years of study have been matched by six years of increasingly joyful prayer and increasingly deep song and mastery of the pastoral and the envisioning that is reflected in the name *"chazan."* Six years that seemed endless at times, to her and to her beloved husband and to her community, have resulted in this high moment, a mountain peak of celebration.

Lisa has become among other things a master of ritual. What would she have us do now, we who burst with pride and love and gratitude as our *chazan*—our visionary singer—becomes a fully ordained cantor? I think she would want us to join hands first, remembering the chain of teaching and inspiration and support that has brought her through. Then, a moment of prayer: let's say a prayer of gratitude to *HaBocher b'shirei zimrah*, the "God of wonders who delights in song." Let's join in song then, a psalm for her who brings so much song to so many of us: *Ashrei yoshvei veitecha, od y'hal'lucha, selah.* We are so happy to be dwelling in this moment in this place, that we just must keep on praising You; so be it. And finally, a moment of silence, a time to stop and take a breath and just be.

Can you feel it?

Several years ago, Lisa's father, who shows up annually for Rosh HaShanah or Yom Kippur, said to me, "I think you are making my daughter into half a cantor." Was he complaining? Hoping? I was not sure. But today, I say to him, and to all of Lisa's parents: That was half. This is whole. We have arrived, with Lisa, at a place of *sh'leimut. Hal'luyah.* Cantor Segal remains at Kolot Chayeinu as our beautiful, inspirational leader of prayer and song, as well as my clergy partner, offering pastoral care, planning of life-cycle events, tutoring, etc.

What a blessing!

A Covenant of Care

Rosh HaShanah 2013 / 5774

I have been thinking about the sacred *schmatta*. For those who may not know this evocative word, it means a rag, or it can mean "this old thing?"

For several years I was honored to be part of the long-running women's seder originated by the late great writer and ritual maker Esther Broner. At the end of every seder, we wrapped ourselves and all of us together in the sacred *schmatta*: a long collection of pink scarves that had grown pretty shabby by the time I came along, but which had a glorious history and still holds in its fraying threads the possibility of a kind of covenant. Not the lofty commandments Moses got or wrote on Sinai and brought to the people, but an earthbound, human, connective understanding that we are all bound as were the women at the seder. As writer Debra Nussbaum Cohen noted there, it is at once a little silly, and holy.

I love that in 1984 filmmaker Lilly Rivlin and Esther took the *schmatta* to Mount Sinai, somehow joining our ancient covenant and this new one, the one we need now more than ever. They were there as part of an interfaith pilgrimage, and Rivlin says, "I was sure that given the types of people who were there, an imam, a great Sufi teacher, Rabbi Marshall Meyer, Reb Zalman Schachter-Shalomi, and more, when we took out this pink chiffon *schmatta* they must have thought we were nuts, but we wove the *schmatta* between and around this august body, telling them that this is how we did it at the Feminist Seder."

I am thinking about the sacred *schmatta* because I am thinking about new ways to look at covenant, especially a covenant of care.

Before I go further let's take a step back to think about what a covenant is and what it is not. I sometimes say, in a shorthand way, a covenant is a holy agreement sealed by a physical symbol. Not bad. It covers the covenant of circumcision, the *b'rit bat* for new daughters, covenant of the rainbow, the covenant of Torah at Sinai, the implied covenant of putting up a mezuzah, and I want to say the covenant of the pink chiffon *schmatta*.

The significant word here is "holy." What makes a covenant differ from a contract? As Britain's chief rabbi Sir Jonathan Sacks wrote in 2010, "In a contract, two or more individuals, each pursuing their own interest, come together to make an exchange for mutual benefit. . . . In a covenant, two or more individuals, each respecting the dignity and integrity of the other, come together in a bond of love and trust, to share their interests, sometimes their lives, by pledging their faithfulness to one another, to do together what neither can achieve alone. . . . Contracts benefit, but covenants transform. . . . In covenant as the Bible understands it, each individual has significance, dignity, moral worth, the right to be heard, a *voice*."[17]

We at Voices of Our Lives can and must look at covenant in large ways and small. Writ large, we may sometimes call it the public good or civil society; a city, say, in which all are bound to one another in respect, mutual concern, and responsibility. Something to be thinking about in the primary week ahead. What kind of city do you want to live in? What is not all right? What is all right? How do we join in bonds of empathy across vast differences? And given this new year, what would you or I sacrifice to make it happen?

---

17. Jonathan Sacks, *Future Tense: Jews, Judaism, and Israel in the Twenty-First Century* (New York: Schocken Books, 2009), 163.

When I first talked to a few friends about the idea of speaking about covenant, and a covenant of care, they said it sounded sappy, oversweet. It is a little sappy, I guess, like a pink chiffon *schmatta*, maybe. Yet why do we think it is sappy, this idea of people bound together by trust and respect? Why is cynicism more popular? I think we yearn for the sappy ideals but have seen them literally shot down way too often to believe without protecting ourselves, binding ourselves instead in cynical coverings.

Yet just last week we thrilled again as we heard, and some remembered, the dream of a great, inspiring, idealistic leader. Dr. King's dream has lost its grandeur coming through. We mourned and raged at the death of Trayvon Martin and later the verdict for George Zimmerman; we were shocked by the lack of congressional action on gun control and the Supreme Court decision on voting rights. But even now we see bright spots, the light at the end of the tunnel that is not after all an oncoming train but rather a small victory that lets our imaginations fly. As the president reminded us last week, "The arc of the moral universe may bend toward justice, but it doesn't bend on its own."

I see a lot of bright spots brought about by human action, your action: Fast-food workers gaining strength across the country! Stop-and-frisk defeated! Participatory budgeting spreading to more council districts. Domestic workers' rights gaining. Paid sick leave for one million working New Yorkers. The Defense of Marriage Act defeated. More recognition of the needs of transgender people. A real push for immigration reform. And more. Somebody is out there bending that arc!

Most of those things are not specifically about me, so why should I care?

There are a lot of reasons to care. I was on a phone call last Friday with a thousand rabbis and President Obama, and some rabbis asked about the growing gap in our country between rich and poor. The president said that a solution will not work if it is "a charitable effort toward the poor; it must be a common effort for all of us." That is where the sacred *schmatta* comes in, binding us together in need and opportunity, in empathy and hope. The sacred *schmatta*: that is a covenantal symbol I can get behind, God in pink chiffon.

Now let's bring it closer to home. That might mean thinking about landlord and tenant relations, or your bank and your mortgage, or your roommates and division of space and labor. I am guessing that at least some of us gathered here employ someone who works in our home or the home of a loved one; some of us work in others' homes. My uncle Bob, whose funeral was just this past Sunday, was lucky to be attended for a short time by a kind, sensitive, open-hearted aide named Mohammed, hired by my cousin to help her father. What fate would have brought together a ninety-one-year-old, nominally Jewish, white, well-to-do Upper West Sider with a young, black, poor, Bronx resident aide? Yet to watch them together, as I got to do briefly, was magic.

It is not always true. Sometimes badly paid aides and lonely old people fight and misunderstand one another. Sometimes a nanny harms children. Sometimes an employer abuses a worker. But more often, astoundingly, employers and the employees who work in their homes are bound by an agreement that is at least a contract and at most a covenant, linked by trust and respect and often love. It can be a tricky business. So often a person or a family who does not have quite enough money to do so hires a worker who needs to be paid more. And then, the employer asks, "You also want me to buy health insurance and pay for vacations and overtime? All alone? Just me, just us?" And then the employee says, "I can't work all year without a vacation, and I can't afford to take it without pay. I need health care, and if it is expensive for you, it is even more so for me."

In a truly covenantal society there would be communal care for children and old people and people with disabilities. Each individual household would not have to figure out alone how to

manage this quandary: I need to work, to be able to work I need
to hire an aide or nanny, to be able to pay that person I need to
work more, now what?! Yet in our imperfect society we still need
to remind ourselves that if we are hiring someone, we are becoming an employer and need to abide by the laws—the contract—of
that hiring. My hope is that having a covenant we can look to as
Jewish employers or employees can help, can remind us of what
our sacrifice is worth, can remind us that each of us is created in
God's image.

In 2010, New York made history by becoming the first state
in the nation to pass a Domestic Workers' Bill of Rights. This
historic law granted basic labor protections to workers that had
been excluded from labor laws since the 1930s. The Jewish community—including Kolot—played a pivotal role in this campaign.
This year a group of dedicated people—Jewish parents, seniors,
people with disabilities, family caregivers, neighbors, members
of this community—are working to build on the Bill of Rights
victory and move to establish fair community standards that go
beyond the law and benefit workers and employers alike. They
ask us to enter into a *b'rit*, a covenant of care for our whole
community. The covenant reminds us that true *sh'lom bayit*—
peace in the home—comes from ensuring dignity for all those
who work *and* reside in our homes. The covenant of care standards will establish a trusting partnership, with clear expectations for us as employers as we establish clear expectations for
our employees. Those who decide to embrace this covenant will
sign our name to make a commitment to abide by basic just
standards.

You received the *b'rit* itself and a commitment form when you
came in. It will be so great if you can take them home. Read them.
Reflect during these Days of Awe. Ask yourself: "Am I prepared to
sign this pledge and commit to implementing these standards in
my home? If I feel that I can't do so, what further support would

I need?" Everyone knows these questions are hard to think about and wrestle with. So we are joining with others: During these Holy Days, Rabbi Marc Katz of Congregation Beth Elohim and Rabbi Carie Carter of the Park Slope Jewish Center are speaking about this covenant as it is launched in Park Slope. In Manhattan, our friends at Bnai Jeshurun and Central Synagogue are developing a covenant of care specifically devoted to eldercare, which will also be launched this year.

To give us all time to think, we will come back to the covenant in three weeks; we'll be talking about it a bit at the Kolot Children's Learning Program parents and kids dinner in the sukkah on September 23. If you won't be there, we can figure out other times to talk.

The main thing is: When it works, it works. Robin Vickers Batzdorf's family hired a nanny some years ago. Here is what a covenantal relationship looks like to him. Listen (Robin, age ten, spoke these words):

Rosa started looking after me when I was just six months old . . . . She looked after me, my brother and my sister for nearly ten years, two afternoons a week. . . . Rosa was born in Mexico and is Hispanic. We didn't talk about it much, because it didn't matter to me. The only thing that matters is that she was nice and treated me well, so I respected that and treated her well back. That is how you should treat your nanny. Rabbi Lippmann taught me that Jewish people believe, like Hillel taught us, that you should not treat others in a way that you would not like to be treated yourself. If you hire a nanny, you have to treat her nicely. This doesn't mean just being polite, or paying well, it also means respect, and treating the nanny as a part of your family. Rosa is important in our lives. I miss her every week.

Sir Jonathan Sacks wrote, "The first philosophers of civil society were the prophets. Unlike the priests, who spoke in terms of holy and profane, permitted and forbidden, pure and impure, the prophets spoke the language of the covenantal virtues: righteousness (*tzedek*), justice (*mishpat*), loving-kindness (*chessed*) and compassion (*rachamim*)."[18]

When Rabbi Menachem Creditor's new daughter was born, he wrote her a song, taking these covenantal values and giving her and all of us a lesson we can sing and learn together: "Olam Chesed Yibaneh"—"We will build this world with love." As we sing it, I will be hearing the words of David Novack's mother, Lee, who passed away last week. In her dying days, she said to her grandchildren, not "I love you," but "I hope I taught you values." That is where the love resides, in the ways we live our lives, and the values that undergird our decisions, and the bonds we form not only with those like us, but those as unlike us as can be. For me, those values infuse that pink chiffon *schmatta*, the most earthbound covenant I can imagine. Imagine it wound around you and the three people on either side of you. That is how we will build this world of *chesed*, loving-kindness: *Olam chesed yibaneh*.

18. Ibid., 175.

Leadership

Voices, Korach issue, May 2006

I was talking at a conference in January to a young rabbi who was about to start his own congregation. Several people had told him to talk to me, and he had therefore sought me out to ask his questions about this new venture. We had a lively conversation, and I was caught up in what we had been able to do here at Kolot Chayeinu. Suddenly another young rabbi, listening in, asked about my starting Kolot, "What did ego have to do with it?" I stopped for a moment, surprised by the question and yet not surprised. "Some," I answered.

I answered, but I have thought about his question since then. And now along comes our editor asking me to write about *Korach*, and this raises for me more questions about ego and its positive and negative potential. When I speak of ego here, I am not talking about pure psychological definitions. No, I mean what my questioner meant: How proud are you of yourself for doing this? How gratifying is it to have a lot of people praise you? How good does it make you feel about yourself?

"Now Korach . . . betook himself . . . to rise up against Moses, together with 250 Israelites, chieftains of the community, chosen in the assembly, men of repute. They combined against Moses and Aaron, and said to them, 'You have gone too far! For all the community are holy, all of them, and the Eternal is in their midst. Why then do you raise yourselves above the Eternal's congregation?'" (Numbers 16:1–3).

It sounds like a reasonable question, doesn't it? Don't we think of the whole community as holy, or potentially holy? So why is Korach vilified and more—killed by God in a dramatic scene: "The earth opened its mouth and swallowed them up with their households, all of Korach's people and all their possessions. They went down alive . . . the earth closed over them and they vanished from the mist of the congregation" (Numbers 16:32–33).

On a simple level, we understand that one doesn't criticize Moses so strongly in the midst of Moses's book: Moses is the leader, beloved of God. But if we go deeper, we find questions of ego there to make us think. First, Korach questions Moses's and Aaron's self-elevation: "Why do you raise yourselves above the Eternal's congregation?" And yet, we have to wonder where Korach's question comes from. Several commentaries point out that the Torah's phrasing is in singular form; though it is Korach and many others who raise the question, it is written as though it is only Korach, suggesting that, as one commentary has it, "each one sought honor for himself proof that their intent was not for the sake of heaven." So Korach, questioning Moses's self-elevating ego, reveals his own. He is Moses's cousin and now appears jealous of Moses's success and high position. He may want only to tear Moses down, not lift the entire community, as he seems at first read to want to do.

Yet Korach doesn't die when swallowed alive in the earth. His family reappears as psalm singers in the Book of Psalms. And the question he raises still rings true. We know even from the Torah's story that it has validity, because Moses has to engineer an elaborate contest to show who God prefers. We can imagine that if his question carried no weight, it would have been dismissed immediately, not given all the space it has in the Torah, including a portion named for him!

And of course he still lives and his question lives. It continues to worry those of us who are leaders—me and the young rabbi who asked about ego's role in my starting Kolot. What is the role of ego? I have to ask myself. How much do I love being up there in front of the gathered High Holy Day community, for instance, or having my picture taken with Senator Russ Feingold at our recent gala, or hearing reports of praise from one member of Kolot or another? I admit it: I LOVE it. And I, like many rabbis, have to fight that love to remember humility: We are not building "Ellen's congregation," as Kolot was known briefly before it had a name. We are building a community in which "all the community, all of them, are holy," or have that potential, and we are building a community that ultimately intends to serve God in the many ways we understand what that means. You can't just aim for the priest-hood's trappings, another commentary reminds Korach and us; there is also a need for divine service and good deeds.

One year, a besotted participant in our High Holy Day services went up to Kathryn after services and, referring to me, said, "Isn't she wonderful?" Kathryn answered politely, but inside was responding, "You should see her in the morning!"

Everyone needs internal and external reminders of what we are like in the morning when someone is gazing up at us with awe and admiration. The Talmud gives us this good reminder: "No one should be appointed head [*parnas*—provider] of the community unless he trails a box of bugs behind him." (Babylonian Talmud, *Yoma* 22b). It is a creepy image, but a good reminder: We will always have leaders with flaws, mistakes, inadequacies. The need to wrestle with those flaws will maintain humility; the experience will enable the leader to relate to the community's members on equal footing and with the understanding of experience. Ultimately, such a leader can say, "If I, with all my flaws, can be serving God, so can you." Perhaps this is the answer to Korach's question and to that of my young rabbi friend. All the community are holy in our striving to rise beyond our earlier flaws and mistakes, to elevate ourselves—not in an ego-driven way, but in a way of true aspiration.

That is my hope for myself and for Kolot, and so I sign off as I have been doing for these thirteen years:

In hope,

    Rabbi Ellen Lippmann

A Jewish Home
Has an Open Door

Yom Kippur 2007 / 5768

Whenever I come home from traveling anywhere, I do two things. I greet my home by a moment's pause at the mezuzah on the front doorpost. And I go to the ocean, usually at Brighton Beach to remind myself that I am home. Sometimes I swim, sometimes I just stand and gaze for a few moments, taking in the sight of the sea. My home is now, the present, for me, and the sea is eternity, a glimpse of the cosmos fifteen minutes from home.

What does it mean to be home, to make a home? On this Yom Kippur, when our task is to come home to ourselves, what does it mean to come home? Rabbi Alan Lew suggests that we have to leave home to find a home and that it is a profoundly Jewish journey.

We spend a lot of time with words of prayer and pangs of hunger on Yom Kippur. We read and sing confessions and prayers of praise and words of hope. Sometimes these words and songs take us home, in a deep and profound way, and sometimes, frankly, they don't. Sometimes we get so caught up in the words and what good fasters we are that we forget that the words and the fasting and the wearing of white are just tools, intended to help us make that journey home, to the home inside and the home in the endless span of time and space, what some here call God. On this Yom Kippur, how do we find our way home?

When I think of home, of the home I live in and love, I think home means to be safe in a place that you have created, having added furnishings and artwork and human connections to the walls, floors, and roof you have rented or bought. It is, ideally, the place you live: the place you can become who you most deeply are, removing the masks you wear to navigate the world. It is where you express your heart, and let it rest, the place the *Shechinah* dwells with you and gives you peace. How tempting it is to stay home these days, given the hard world in which we live, tempting to stay in bed, in fact, and not get up to face the world. Some days I think "if I pull these covers a little more over my head, maybe the war will go away, people will stop killing each other, we'll have good leaders in Washington. If I can only go back to sleep, the hammering of the new development in the next block will stop, and the one that will block out our morning light won't start to be built. If I stay here, safe inside, maybe Israel and Palestine will make peace while I am not looking, someone will figure out health insurance and reasonable mortgages for all, and education and health care will break out all over Africa." But as Harry Brod of the University of Delaware writes, "a Jewish home has an open door."[19]

I can't hide inside, covering my head and wishing the world away, and neither can you, tempting though it is. At some point, I have to get up and face the world. Someday, what Arthur Waskow calls "global scorching" may make the sea I love roar through Brooklyn looking for me. Someday, and today, young American soldiers will come home, some in coffins, others without limbs or eyes. Yesterday and today, Iraqis lose their homes and their lives and Darfurians lose life after life after life and I have to wonder how I am responsible or what I can do. Yesterday, today, and tomorrow, Israelis are injured and killed by Palestinian rocket fire

19. Harry Brod, "A Jewish Home Has an Open Door," *Sh'ma* 27, no 535 (May 1997) 3–4.

and Palestinians are killed and maimed by Israelis and I always wonder how I am responsible and what I can possibly do.

The truth is that you and I do a fair amount. Every day I hear from Kolot members who do the most extraordinary things, using their power, their music, their art, their organizing skills to try to make this world a better place. Yet the world is manifestly not a better place, and often I at least feel helpless to respond. Harry Brod writes, "I identify the voice impelling me to open the door as the Jewish voice within me. It is what makes my home a Jewish home. The mezuzah beside my door points and beckons inward. Keeping the door locked against others violates the principles it houses."[20] This is the voice of my conscience, reminding me it is time to get up, time to open the door, let in what light is left, and move out into the world again. Yom Kippur gives the voice of conscience time to regroup, refresh itself, before we move on to the real world, the world outside this inward-looking home we create today and carry with us in our hearts.

There are many words in Hebrew for what we call in English "living," as in "Where do you live?" *Leisheiv* is "to dwell or sit," as in dwelling next week in a sukkah or sitting in a yeshiva to study or Abraham dwelling in Beersheva after the Binding of Isaac. *Lagur* is "to live somewhere" and is the word used for the question "Where do you live? *Eifo garah?*" *L'shakein* is the word God uses for divine dwelling, as when God tells Moses to tell the people to build a *mikdash*, a holy central place, and God will dwell among the people. God's indwelling presence is what we call, therefore, the *Shechinah*. Yom Kippur asks us how God will dwell among us. It urges us to ask, "How does my voice of conscience connect to this *mikdash*, this holy place, and how do we invite God in or pray in such a way that we connect truly and not just have a great show of words and fasting? What is written on the mezuzah of the doorway to our hearts?"

20. Ibid., 4.

My first thought in trying to answer this question was of the *Aleinu*. Just as the *Sh'ma* is written in the mezuzot on our actual homes' doorposts, so perhaps our internal doors' opening words are the *Sh'ma's* companion piece, the words we end our prayer with, even as the *Sh'ma* leads us in: *Aleinu l'shabei-ach laadon hakol, lateit g'dulah l'yotzeir b'reishit.* "It is up to us to praise the Lord of all, to give greatness to the Shaper of creation. . . . May *tikkun olam*, repairing the world, make manifest your mighty dominion . . . . *Bayom hahu*—on that day the Eternal will be one and God's name will be Oneness." Dr. Henry Slonimksy once wrote, "On that day, not as yet, alas, but surely on that day God shall be one, as God is not yet One. For how can God be called One, that is, real, if humanity is rent asunder in misery and poverty and hate and war? When humankind has achieved its own reality and unity, it will thereby have achieved God's reality and unity. Til then, God is merely an idea, an ideal. . . . Til now, God merely subsists in the vision of a few great hearts, and exists only in part, and is slowly being translated into reality."

How do we start to translate God into reality? How far do we have to travel to open our doors? The pull to shut them tight is very great, to shut out the fear, the anger, the helplessness we feel in the face of the current war, the aftermath of Katrina, the number of deaths in Darfur, the intractability of Israel and Palestine. Leonard Fein expressed our fears and began our translating when he wrote in a new take on the *Un'taneh Tokef*, "Who will live and who will die? Who by landmine or cluster bomb, who by ethnic cleansing, who by handgun, who by drunken driving, who by negligence and who by malice?" It would be so nice if our homes could be spared, as they are in reality spared most of the world's horrors. How nice if we could just bask in that space: we are not the ones being killed, we are not the ones who have to watch a beloved family member murdered or raped before our eyes, we are not the ones struggling to find any food at all, we are not the ones fearing death at any moment. How nice then just to live our lives and shut out the world. And yet: our mezuzahs and our prayers and our history will not let us bask.

We are reminded: *Aleinu*, it is up to us to repair the world and translate God into reality. So many of us, of you, are immersed in repair of the world. Tonight, we begin to translate God into reality by beginning to open our doors and pour out our hearts. The *Aleinu* is indeed a fine prayer for our hearts' mezuzahs. But it is not the only prayer we need for the journey we make back toward home, the home where we really live. Leonard Fein began to show us how to do that, how to translate a prayer from the eleventh century to the twenty-first and have it hit us where we live. We can sing *Avinu Malkeinu* and the *Un'taneh Tokef* and *HaYom HaYom HaYom* with all our hearts. But without our own prayers, we won't really be opening the doors to our hearts, the home—the *makom*, the place—where it all comes together. I am not sure how many of you say or write or cry or sing or meditate your own prayers.

Tonight, let us write one together, using all we have brought on this journey so far, all we are willing to pour out of our open hearts: [I will begin, you call out a line that tells of your feeling or your thought or your desire or your praise. I'll take notes and create a prayer out of what we pour out.] I'll start: Dear God, I AM ANGRY THAT THE WORLD IS SUCH A MESS AND I AM AFRAID I CAN'T DO ANYTHING ABOUT IT.

Here is the prayer we created together, reconstructed after the fact:

Oh, God, the Source of Life, Your presence fills time and space. We are angry that the world is such a mess and we fear we can't do anything about it. Help us recognize what we can do. Help us find and be the leaders who will repair the world. Help us never to be paralyzed by our fear, rather give us a vision for what the world might be and help us to draw inspiration from the progress we have made so far. Help us remember the power that is in ourselves and let us know that we are not alone. Help us to hear each other better, and share with us the gift of honesty, no matter how many facades

You must break through nor how cynical we may be. Help us to want less so that others may have more. Teach us to start small and close to home, to notice the man lying on the corner cold and alone. We can't even reconcile the members of our own family, so how can we repair the world? But help us to put our passion into action. Let us make the world a better place.

Last week after Rosh HaShanah services, a Kolot member told me he is looking forward to learning about prayer this year, because after all the Rosh HaShanah prayers he wanted to know, "Why do we praise God so much?" Peter, here is one answer: We are translating God into reality. We start by opening our doors. This Yom Kippur is the time and the place to start.

Where Have You Come From, Where Are You Going?

Rosh HaShanah 2004 / 5765

My family and I went shopping for a refrigerator on Sunday, a needed task before the New Year. We all went—Kathryn, our daughter, Emma, and me—searching the crowded aisles of Drimmer's on Coney Island Avenue for the best deal we could find.

We finally settled on our choice and sat to do the paperwork with our salesman. When we talked about delivery dates, he noted that many customers would not want delivery tomorrow, "because of the Jewish holiday." But, he said, looking at us, "I don't see anyone Jewish here." It was stunning to me that this man, who seemed to be Jewish himself, could look at my face and not see anyone Jewish. But we realized later that he wasn't exactly looking at our individual faces. He was looking at the face of our family, and we are not what people think of as a Jewish family.

Stereotypes are what drive a lot of the discussion in the Jewish world about Jews and non-Jews and how we relate or are related. Stereotypes about Jews have so often led to violence against us that we can understand the desire to stick together in tribe or clan, mixing only with our own. Stereotypes about non-Jews have often led to exclusion, denigration, and the disowning of Jewish children as they love and marry non-Jews in our increasingly multicultural society. Yet change is in the air. At Kolot Chayeinu, we wrestle with the implications of change and sameness and try to understand where we have come from and where we are going. The roles and responsibilities of Jews and non-Jews, members all in our congregation, is high on the list of subjects for wrestling. In this wrestling, we are very much a Jewish family, though here too the Drimmer's salesman might not recognize us as such.

Yet look: Seated right here in this room are scores of people who are learning Judaism and teaching their children and celebrating the holidays and putting up mezuzahs and giving their babies Hebrew names and getting married in Jewish weddings. Some of you are Jews who have a non-Jewish parent, some a non-Jewish spouse. And a whole lot of you are not Jews but have become our strong allies. You are each *hager hagar itanu*, "the stranger who dwells with us."

In one of Rosh HaShanah's Torah portions, the God of Abraham speaks to Hagar the Egyptian after Sarah throws her out, asking her, through an angel, "Where have you come from and where are you going?" She had lorded it over Sarah, thrown her superior fertility in her face. Hagar says to God, "You are *El Ro-i*"—"the God who sees me." The well at which they spoke was called Beer-lahai-roi, "the well of the Living One who sees me." How is it that God speaks to this stranger who is brought into Abraham and Sarah's home? Her very name echoes in our ears, reminding us of *hager hagar itanu*, "the stranger who dwells among us," referred to over and over in biblical legislation: "Be kind to the stranger, for you were a stranger in the land of Egypt."

Having been strangers, we knew what it could be like to be a stranger, and we were to treat others in as open and generous a way as we could. But that stranger has morphed into someone we refer to now as a non-Jew, and over centuries we have put more and more emphasis on the word "stranger" and less and less on the possibilities implied in "dwells among us." And yet, here you sit, so many of you, non-Jews who are dwelling among us, strengthening Jewish life, building our community. We should salute you, yet the Jewish community too often denigrates you, castigates your spouse, implies that your presence represents the death of Judaism. You are the no-longer strangers, and in our day it is to the Jewish community that the God who sees us all asks, "Where have you come from and where are you going?"

This sermon is one answer, an answer wrung from the pain and fears and hopes and dreams I see and hear every day as a rabbi and those I know in my own life and deepest heart. It is born of eleven years of Kolot Chayeinu's life trying to carve a new path toward Jewish community and twenty years of my own life as the partner of a non-Jew. Both places in which I stand are places of love and joy and not a little defiance. Both are also lonely places to be sometimes, places of struggle and fear, embarrassment and anger.

So this is a sermon about that struggle, my struggle to reconcile the sometimes surprising components of my life and my struggle to work with you to shape this community's future. These are struggles I know I share with many of you. And, an odd but somehow happy honor, I am just about the only rabbi who can give this sermon. It is the sermon I have been afraid to give. Yet this year, as the New Year approached, I knew that this was the year to speak to you from my heart. At this season, that means confronting my conscience or at least that opposing voice in my head, the one that keeps me from insincerity or too much piety. In my twelfth year on this bimah, I know I can trust you with my innermost fears and joys as you so often entrust me with yours. It also means speaking directly to God, the thing we so often shy away from doing.

Let's start with the year just ended. This past spring, at a retreat in which I participated, the Kolot board was presented with a new set of bylaws, the result of months of labor by a hard-working committee. The draft had been looked at briefly at a congregational meeting, and now the board was asked to examine it more carefully. A few issues were a little thorny, including what to do about choosing a second rabbi (far into the future, I hope). But none evoked anything like the response to the issue of "Who may serve on the board of Kolot Chayeinu?" The drafters left it wide open: any member in good standing of the congregation may serve on the board. Kolot Chayeinu has many members who are non-Jews. Could we agree that board membership was open to Jews and non-Jews alike? We could not.

What we could and did do was talk, argue, raise our voices, retreat into ourselves, and cry—a lot. Some felt very strongly that board members of a Jewish congregation must be Jews. Others felt just as strongly that Kolot was already a different kind of Jewish congregation, one that had created an atmosphere of welcome equality, and must therefore include non-Jews on the board. Added to this was the fact that non-Jews had always been full members of the congregation; how could we deny them participation or representation on the board? Some members and staff were happy, smiling through tears, that this issue had at last been spoken; others wished we could carry on as before and not raise it in all its complexity. Some feared offending those in the room whose spouses are not Jewish, or a new board member who isn't Jewish but is in the process of conversion, which reflects our policy before the new draft bylaws. Some couldn't believe that the person sitting next to them, whom they liked so much, held such a different opinion on what felt like a bottom-line issue. And all the time there were tears, the tears of relief and fear and discomfort and confusion.

Other questions arose, attaching themselves to this discussion: "Well, what do we do in the Children's Learning Program about kids who have only one Jewish parent?" "What do you, the rabbi, do about weddings?" "Who do we consider a Jew here?" All these questions showed legitimate wondering about our decisions and policies. But it was clear they also stemmed from deep emotion, from people's long experience of interfaith marriage or the unwelcoming stance of Jewish communities. The tears were close to the surface. Were some in the room to be exiled like Hagar, while others stayed in the Jewish fold like Sarah? Or were some asserting the right and responsibility of Jews to work for the Jewish future, like Sarah protecting Isaac from Ishmael, while non-Jews who don't hold the same stake are reasonably prevented from board service? The God who sees us almost asked aloud, "Where have you come from and where are you going?"

I am telling you all this because this discussion was the tip of this iceberg, the way we found ourselves engaged in all the questions that come up when a Jewish congregation talks about Jews and non-Jews among us. More than that, it was for those hours our Jewish family, the one where the non-Jewish member can't understand why having a Christmas tree or not having a bris is so damned important while the Jew thinks the spouse with whom he or she has lived for many years is suddenly a stranger. Some may wonder whether this sometimes painful subject is fit for Rosh HaShanah, the beginning of the year, a holy day, this holy eve. Trisha Arlin, editor of *Voices* for Kolot, said a few days ago that one of the things that makes us Kolot is that we can have difficult discussion even on our holiest days and that in fact such dialogue is an expression of the holy. The God who sees, sees us grappling, and calls it good, and asks us, as with Hagar, "Where have you come from and where are you going?" Where have I come from?

My partner of twenty years and I were married in January. (We were married in Brooklyn, there was nothing legal about it, and this is not a sermon about gay marriage, fraught as that issue also is.) As I have said, my partner is not Jewish, and in the year of planning our wedding I came to understand in new ways what many of you have gone through looking for a rabbi, learning which friends support you and which don't, making decisions about the ceremony. The wedding was a mountain-peak, just as our ancestors imagined it. But hovering before, during, and all around it were my questions and fears. What did I hope for from the Jewish world around me, or just from my friends who are rabbis? Absolution? Praise? Simple acceptance would be good.

For most of the twenty years in which I have lived with my soul's beloved, I have also been in the process of rabbinic study and working as a rabbi. So I have heard or read every version of Jewish condemnation of interfaith relationships and marriage, from the biblical Rebekah's fear that Jacob would marry a Hittite woman and Ezra's instruction to the people to separate from the foreign women to my classmates' unrelenting condemnation of intermarriage as the death of the Jewish people. The latest version? At my rabbinic conference in Toronto in June, I joined other rabbis in a study session with a professor of Jewish literature. We were looking at a variety of Jewish views about rabbis as seen in literature of many kinds, from a very early rabbinic contract to *Friday the Rabbi Slept Late*, by Harry Kemelman. As one rabbi read aloud from an early twentieth-century story, he came to the section about a rabbi falling in love with a non-Jewish woman. And every single rabbi in the room except me began to laugh, make fun, question the story, until the voices rose and swirled and I wondered whether I was Isaac as Ishmael played with him or Ishmael excluded from the tent.

Is it so strange for a rabbi in the twenty-first-century to be married to a non-Jew? I am one of two or three, as far as I know, a lonely place indeed, but what a joy to have met a rabbi last year who is also in what she calls an intercultural marriage and to correspond with her. "Intercultural" may be a better term than "interfaith"; Rabbi Harold Schulweis says a lot of couples he sees are actually "interfaithless." And while we are talking terminology, "non-Jew" is such a strange label; Kathryn, for instance, is a permanently lapsed Irish Catholic, student of Buddhist meditation, ally to me in all my Jewish thinking and practice, creator of our Jewish home. But she isn't Jewish. Does that matter to the God who sees me? This is not a rhetorical question, but the very heart of the matter to me. Our rabbi said that our wedding strengthened Judaism. I hope beyond hope that God believes it.

Oh, God, You see me, You know me inside and out. Are You willing to believe in me, believe in my complete devotion to Judaism, which is enhanced by my marriage to my non-Jewish love? Can You believe that she enhances my Judaism, even helped open the door to my being a rabbi? I could stop being a rabbi, but I can never stop being a Jew. Do You know that, You who are the *Chai Ro-i*, "the Living One who sees"?

Once, our ancestors couldn't understand a modern-day gay relationship, yet today we are able to interpret Leviticus 18's condemnation of gay connection in light of all we know of modern open possibilities. Similarly, our ancestors, whether in biblical Canaan or early twentieth-century Brooklyn, could never have understood a modern-day devotion to Judaism by someone who married "out," as they would have said, out to the Hittites or out to the Irish Catholics. So how could they have imagined marrying "in," bringing in new strength and creativity to Judaism? I remember the words of one of my professors who said, "Anyone can say words," referring to the fact that repeating a blessing doesn't make you a Jew. Of course it doesn't. But it can help to create a Jewish home.

I will always remember that the year I lived in Israel to start my rabbinic studies, Kathryn lit Shabbat candles here every week while I was gone. And it was our daughter Emma who started our practice of bringing the *Kiddush* cups of everyone in the family to the Shabbat table even if they aren't present. Kathryn was part and parcel of all the early discussions that began Kolot Chayeinu and has been a regular presence here for eleven years. I ask anyone here to tell me that I am not or we are not contributing to the Jewish future. That's my defiance showing. But this is hard because I have other voices, too, voices that question and worry and wonder.

It is so hard because like many of you I grew up with tribal Jewish notions and loving the Jewish tribe, even if it felt stifling sometimes. It is so hard because underneath my questions I feel my desperation, a desperation made of love for family of origin and

Judaism, often tightly intertwined; love for my partner and child; a desire to please them all; and fear or certainty that I am pleasing none. Sometimes I *know* from reading all those texts and hearing my classmates and a lot of other Jews talk and reading Jewish newspapers regularly and all the years of being a rabbi that I am single-handedly causing the decline, if not the death, of Judaism. I wrestle with that knowing, with that fear.

Yet when we married—when we stood together under a chuppah and yes, said blessings together, that fear receded. So this sermon is also a coming-out: For too many years I walked a fine line of trying to have my cake and eat it too; have my life with Kathryn *and* please all the Jewish classmates and rabbis and teachers and sociologists and guests at the last wedding I performed that I might meet as she and I walked around the city or went to a play. But the cake I was eating wasn't only Rosh HaShanah honey cake, it was also Irish soda bread and for a while in the early days (though no longer) it was Christmas cookies, and at some point I just couldn't please everyone, hard as I tried. Tonight, I officially stop trying.

I stop the years of blanching when meeting someone who may disapprove and trying not to introduce Kathryn or get away as quickly as I can. I stop the apologetic way I sometimes feel or speak to friends about our Jewish practice. I stop trading off honoring my beloved with attempts at an approval that is never coming anyway and which, really, I don't want. *Al cheit shechatati l'fanecha*; for the sin which I have sinned against You by betraying my love. Where have you come from and where are you going?

Planning our wedding made me look seriously also at questions about my own officiation. Early on we realized that if we asked them to, some of our close friends who were rabbis wouldn't officiate at our wedding. They confirmed this and we have had a lot of intense talk with them; we are still figuring out how and if to continue those friendships. We knew who would be our rabbi, and she agreed, so we didn't have to ask others. But it made me think about my own meeting with couples, especially when I turn them down. And it made me know that our wedding could not be different in its way of being a Jewish wedding than any wedding for which I would agree to officiate.

Several years ago, some people here will remember, I refused to officiate at a wedding of a longtime friend who was also a member of this congregation. She was marrying someone who was very involved in his church, and they wanted the wedding to be led by his minister and me. I said no, for reasons I will explain in a moment, and then I referred them to another rabbi who did officiate; they later joined his synagogue. My friend has never forgiven me. I wrote to her every year for four years during the month of Elul, asking that we begin to repair our friendship, if not her connection to this community. Our parents live in the same continuum of care community, so I see her folks and she recently saw my dad. But we never see each other. For the first time, this year, I was able to understand her pain and anger.

I have not changed my mind about the weddings I do and don't do, but I have thought more about it. Let me be clear about what I do as a rabbi about weddings: I officiate on a case-by-case basis for couples where one is a Jew and one not, in a Jewish wedding, and I do not officiate with clergy of another faith. What I do is officiate at a Jewish wedding in which one member of the couple is not Jewish. With clergy of another faith, the wedding becomes a different thing, to me: it is an interfaith wedding or a Christian wedding or something else, but no longer a Jewish wedding.

Once I was asked to do a wedding of a Jew and a Zoroastrian and thought it was so cool that for a moment I forgot that the Zoroastrian priest, too, was not Jewish! I referred them to another rabbi who does co-officiate with other clergy. When I meet a couple, I try to get a sense of how deep and active is the Judaism of the Jewish partner and how involved or not the other partner is in another religious community. I don't ask for promises, such as "Are you going to raise your children as Jews?" because I don't believe in promises and I believe with our tradition that you can't promise what you don't have in hand. Often I say no to weddings, either because of time or location or the reasons I just noted. Sometimes I say yes, and I have had the pleasure of officiating at the weddings of a lot of people sitting here.

I respond to gay and lesbian couples in the same way I do to heterosexual couples: With them (us?) too, I try to gauge the current Jewish connections of the Jewish partner and the lack of other religious involvement of the other partner. While my Jewish decisions may strike some as inconsistent and idiosyncratic, I do make them from my sense of Jewish integrity. Where have you come from and where are you going? My Jewish integrity is offended to learn of the way that non-Jews are sometimes treated in synagogues or other Jewish institutions, including occasionally this one. Remember that my partner is noticeably not Jewish in origin. She's also 6'1" and she's the rabbi's wife. So she may get some comments here that others don't, but I have heard from others too about the ways non-Jews are spoken to, even those who have converted to Judaism but don't look Jewish, whatever that means anymore. I understand that sometimes our old fears and stereotypes are driving those comments—someone told me that to say something like "You're not Jewish so you wouldn't understand" is much like saying "You're white so you wouldn't understand" or "You're heterosexual so you wouldn't understand." And I have said words like those too, from my own fear that my spouse could not possibly comprehend the entire sweep and sorrow of Jewish history as I feel it in my bones. This last in spite of her twenty years of Jewish education with me, everything from reading a 1950s text about what a rebbetzin should do to helping a friend and me understand that a text we couldn't believe really must say that Moses was bowing to God to telling me of the way her amazing high school teacher taught them about the Holocaust. But we can acknowledge our fears without putting the full weight of them on the non-Jews among us who are already our supporters.

That doesn't mean we won't fight antisemitism where it exists, in France or Brooklyn. It does mean watching our words, a good lesson in any case. Let us be kind to the stranger *because* we were strangers in all the lands we lived in before this one, and often in this one too.

I am happy to say that there are other voices. Here at Kolot Chayeinu last spring, we adopted a statement of values that includes this: "Diversity is a hallmark of the Kolot Chayeinu community. We continue and grow as we began, with profound respect for individuality, believing in and striving for broad inclusivity, sharing meals, conversation and camaraderie. Our experience has taught us that a wide range of Jewish background, practice and understanding is necessary to a vibrant community, as is the active presence of non-Jewish members, loved ones, and friends. We are proud to be a community comprising individuals of varying Jewish traditions, sexual orientations, races, and family arrangements." Present at one of the many discussions we had on the way to adopting the Kolot Values Statement were several Jews whose spouses are not Jewish and a couple of non-Jewish members of Kolot. They were adamant that it was this diversity that drew them to Kolot, that made it possible for them to remain in a Jewish community, and that must be stated loud and clear in our statement. At another discussion, Jews with non-Jewish spouses rejected in no uncertain terms the uncertain term "allies" to refer to those non-Jews among us who support our Judaism. They said, "Look. You are referring to the people we love. Why not say so?" And so we did. For the whole issue of Jews and non-Jews in the congregation really turns on that statement: You are talking about us or the people we love. Where have you come from and where are you going?

Where are we going? We are moving into an unknown land, hoping that God is seeing and watching out for us all. I personally hope for as open a tent as possible and as high a Jewish standard as possible. That is why, in spite of or because of the family I choose,

I believe that Jewish children of a Jewish and a non-Jewish parent, either parent, are Jews if they live and practice as Jews. I believe certain Jewish liturgical roles should be limited to Jews. I believe conversion is deeply serious, requiring time, study, and thought, and I am delighted at present to be working with five conversion students.

For the record—and to answer all of you who have asked or are wondering, "Why doesn't she convert?"—Kathryn believes that conversion is the equivalent of a sex-change operation. Post-operation, many people who have had that surgery say that they have come home to who they really are. Kathryn feels she already is who she is. If she could convert to Kolot Chayeinu Judaism, she says, she might do it. But becoming a Jew is becoming a Jew. You can't convert to one small shul. You can convert to Judaism and come to Kolot, and for you and for those who choose not to covert, I hope that here we create a space where the skeptical questions and denigrating comments can be left at the door.

Back in the Kolot board retreat room, we dried our tears. Someone proposed a compromise: that a certain number of non-Jewish members can be on the board. That way, the board will be mostly Jews, but there will be representation of the many allies—I mean, people we love—among us, the no-longer-strangers who are truly dwelling among us. I am all for it, if our lawyers say it can fly. If not, let us find some way to have a Jewish congregation with Jewish leadership that also includes some leaders who are not Jews but who dwell among us.

Some in the Jewish world have called for a new category, a reviving of the ancient term *ger toshav*, to apply to those "strangers" who dwell among us. Those suggesting this recommend that these *geirei toshav* should receive some benefit after all that they do for our community or should at least have some obstacles removed. I am less concerned with terminology and more concerned with new attitudes and new ways of speaking. In place of shut doors and narrowed eyes, we need open tents and the God who sees. In place of denigration, we need celebration. And in place of suspicion, curiosity and welcome. Welcome. Blessed are you who come in the name of *Adonai* the living God who sees us all. And stay tuned. We will be talking about this at Kolot Chayeinu this year. So you might want to start now to think about your answer to the question God posed: *Where have YOU come from and where are YOU going?*

Reform Rabbi Urges Hebrew Union College to Reconsider Decision on Intermarriage

May 17, 2013

An open letter to the board of governors of Hebrew Union College—Jewish Institute of Religion:[21]

I am writing to urge you to reconsider the HUC-JIR requirement that all prospective rabbinical students sign an agreement that "any student engaged, married, or partnered/committed to a person who is not Jewish by birth or conversion will not be admitted or ordained."

It matters to me: I am a HUC-JIR rabbi, ordained in 1991 and partnered with a non-Jew since 1984. In 1993 I founded a now thriving congregation that has engaged hundreds of people in Jewish life. I have worked toward conversion with dozens of candidates. The HUC-JIR requirement might have prevented me from becoming a rabbi, as it will future rabbis whose efforts would be as significant as mine.

My partner is a woman. I was an LGBT student at a time when this status was not recognized at the college and there was no such required agreement to sign. We were married under a chup-

---

21. This article originally appeared on the Forward's website, forward.com, on May 17, 2013, and is reproduced with permission; https://forward.com/opinion/176823/reform-rabbi-urges-hebrew-union-college-to-reconsi/.

pah on our 20th anniversary, in 2004, and were legally married when we could do so in New York State, in 2011. We have a grown daughter who celebrates the Sabbath and holidays. In 1988, my partner began welcoming the Sabbath in our home even when my student pulpit took me away. She attends services in my congregation, reads Jewish texts with interest and annually counts the Omer with me.

And no, she has not converted. She believes strongly that one should feel oneself to be fully a Jew in order to convert, and she defines herself instead as a "permanently lapsed Irish Catholic."

We are like the thousands of Jews across America who commit to strongly Jewish lives with their non-Jewish spouses. Interfaith families tell me that having a rabbi who mirrors their relationships makes an enormous difference to being able to commit to Jewish life.

I believe the board of governors must address this policy from two Jewish standpoints.

First, there is the question of inclusion or exclusion.

In 1864, debating the circumcision of males born to Jewish fathers and non-Jewish mothers, Rabbi Tzvi Hirsch Kalischer stated that it was a "mitzvah to circumcise such children," because, "with children such as these, there is sometimes the possibility that great leaders of Israel will arise from among them."

Rabbi Alexander Schindler and his Reform movement accepted patrilineal descent for membership in the Jewish community 35 years ago. Similarly, we should not push away those who want to become leaders of the Jewish community as rabbis just because they are intermarried. As the governors of HUC-JIR, you must choose between an inclusive vision of Jewish leadership and an exclusive one. Let your bold decisions to ordain women, lesbians, gay men and transgender rabbis show you the way. We are capable of becoming the leaders so desperately needed in the American Jewish community.

Second, there is the question of "What is a rabbi?"

A rabbi is a role model, and there are many kinds of role models. Intermarriage is a fact of American Jewish life. We can do a better job of connecting intermarried Jews to synagogues, rabbis and Jewish life. One way is to knowingly ordain intermarried rabbis.

It is important to remember that a rabbi is a human being. Yeshayahu Leibowitz wrote in commentary on Emor that since there is no more mikdash, the ancient Temple, the function of the service of God is the study and teaching of Torah. Therefore, those leaders who serve as teachers of Torah are otherwise just like any other human being—not intrinsically holy, as some may wish to see themselves or their leaders. The ancient priest removed his special clothing and was just an ordinary human being. Today's rabbis may demonstrate special knowledge, but once the teaching is over, the rabbi is just a human being, not elevated above any other. If a rabbi is a Jew like all others, we should welcome rabbis who are married to non-Jews just as we welcome Jews who are married to non-Jews into our congregations.

I pray that you will use this moment to overturn a policy whose time has gone.

Respectfully yours,
    Rabbi Ellen Lippmann

Part Four

Din

Justice

We Who Believe in Freedom Cannot Rest Until It Comes

Words for Being Honored as a JFREJ Risk-Taker

December 6, 2017 / 19 Kislev 5778

Thank you, [City Council member] Brad [Lander] and [his daughter] Rosa; it is a great joy in my life that our long friendship now extends into the next generation. I am so moved that you two introduced me here. Thank you, JFREJ [Jews For Racial & Economic Justice]—all of you!—for bestowing this great honor on me. Thank you, Kolot Chayeinu! You who worked to enable this night *and* you who are here to support me as you do and have done every day for twenty-five years! Thank you, rabbis from T'ruah and IJS [Institute for Jewish Spirituality] and the JFREJ Rabbinic Council who are here to honor me and all the risk-takers tonight. Thank you, Yehuda Webster and Linda Sarsour and We Dream in Black; it is an honor to stand with you. And thank you, Kathryn Conroy, my wife of thirty-three years; your own risk-taking on behalf of battered women and of children everywhere inspires me, and I could never do what I do without you beside me.

We. Who Believe. In freedom. Cannot rest until it comes.

Dr. Bernice Johnson Reagan wrote it, and it was sung first by Sweet Honey in the Rock. But the words originally came from the great civil rights leader Ella Baker. Thank you, Leah King and the JFREJ band for making them sing so powerfully. Rabbi Alissa Wise once told me that I am an "Ella Baker rabbi." Alissa wrote this week to say, "It's because Ella's hallmark—like yours—was developing the leadership of others + supporting people to be their best most whole selves." Her praise and Baker's words fill my soul, and I want to dig into them tonight as a way to try to capture what I think about my work for justice and freedom.

We. Who's We? "We" is everyone who is working for freedom and justice and who allows me to be myself working in my way as I try to do the same. As my sister risk-taker Linda Sarsour wrote to me last year, "I don't always agree with every thing in every movement space but I sit, I listen, I absorb, and I contend with others' experiences which are not always my own." Thank you, Sis. Me too. I listen, I absorb, I contend, and I try not to draw lines except against those who want to oppress me. I struggle first with my own biases or unfamiliarity or questions. And then I argue and embrace, wonder and love, trying to hold it all. When (in Torah) Moses gave to the people—former slaves—the chance to build a *Mishkan*, they responded with willing hearts and all their skills, including—unusually—the women! Together these women helped to create a center for their journey to freedom. Who imagines they all loved each other? They did not have to. But they did have to respect each offering and each skill if they were to get that *Mishkan* built. We could learn a lot from them.

We who **believe**. What does it mean to believe? Knowledge and smarts are needed. But belief is an act of imagination. It is why last year at the extraordinary protest staged by thousands of Yemeni storekeepers with a lot of organizing by my friend Dr. Debbie Almontaser, I said I was tired of saying no and wanted to say yes. YES. When we say no, we are only reacting. When we say yes, we begin to create a vision of what could be, what might be. Those ancient Hebrew slaves walked through a parted sea saying no: No, we will not stay here; no, you cannot keep us slaves anymore. They feared what they did not yet know. They needed the Torah as a guide, and they needed something they could build: The *Mishkan*! A place for the sacred and imagination to join, a sensual place of deep rich colors and precious metals, barely imaginable skins, and light strong wood. We who believe have to say YES.

*We who believe in **freedom***. What is freedom? Do we say, "I am free, so everyone else be damned"? Or can we say, "We all must be free," with the freedom Toni Morrison wrote better than anyone ever:

> *Laughing children, dancing men, crying women and then it got mixed up. Women stopped crying and danced; men sat down and cried; children danced, women laughed, men cried until, exhausted and riven, all and each lay about the Clearing damp and gasping for breath. In the silence that followed, Baby Suggs, holy, offered up to them her great big heart. She did not tell them to clean up their lives or go and sin no more. . . . She told them that the only grace they could have was the grace they could imagine. That if they could not see it, they would not have it.*[23]

If you have not read Morrison's *Beloved*, read it. I sometimes think she is God.

*We who believe in freedom **cannot rest***. Kolot members here know that I often say instead, "We who believe in freedom *have to* rest so it can come." The ancient former Hebrew slaves got the gift of Shabbat, long before the *Mishkan*: a day for rest and control of their time. If we are lucky, freedom allows us rest; it is why we lean on pillows at our Passover seders, why Shabbat is so important to some of us: our down time lets us sing, march, chant, organize, write, dance, or get arrested for freedom. Lydia Scott, a babysitter and National Domestic Workers Alliance supporter said while marching last January that many black immigrant women like her lack the provisions like time off and sick pay that many working women take for granted. Our sisters need their rest, and we who

---

23. Toni Morrison, *Beloved* (New York: Random House, 1987), 103.

believe in freedom have to rest so we can keep on joining Ms. Scott and all my sister risk-takers here from We Dream in Black and all the women who work without enough rest. From Employers for Justice to the New York Caring Majority, JFREJ reminds me who it is my obligation to hold up.

Tonight we dream, tomorrow we work, and on Friday or Saturday or Sunday, we rest. Someone else will be picking up the work just as your Sabbath begins. And when it ends, you can pick it up again. You have to, because we are not all free to do so. We believe in freedom, so use it, and envision it and make it happen.

We who believe in freedom have to rest so it can come.

Social Justice

Money

Voices, Spring 2010

Dear Friends: It was 1987. I had recently returned from a year of study in Israel and began commuting to rabbinical school in New York via the Broadway-Lafayette F train station. Some of you will remember that in 1987 President Reagan's cuts had taken hold and the Broadway-Lafayette station was a de facto homeless shelter, where people slept, lived, and asked for food or money. I began to think it was impossible to study the basic texts of Jewish ethical behavior without doing something about people in such desperate need three blocks away. So I worked with fellow students, faculty, and administration at Hebrew Union College–Jewish Institute of Religion to start a soup kitchen. It opened its doors in the fall of 1988 and has operated steadily since then, a fact that I find affirming and appalling in equal measure. I will say that one of my proudest moments came when my Talmud professor, teaching us about a *tamhui*, the soup kitchen that was ever present in the shtetls and towns of Jewish Eastern Europe, stopped his lecture to say, "And now we have one here at HUC." Communal assistance to those in need was an obligation in the nineteenth century and still is, in the twenty-first.

That experience led me to become an active member of Interfaith Voices Against Hunger, taking part in monthly protests at City Hall against reductions in food stamps and the shutting of food programs that could not keep their doors open. We learned about Native American corn ceremonies, we engaged in Buddhist walking meditation, we listened to the shofar blast, we gathered in a Christian circle of prayer, and more. We enjoyed each other and those rituals, but in fact they did very little good for the people who still lived in desperate straits in subway stations and homeless shelters and piled up ten in an apartment meant for three.

When I was ordained, I went to work for MAZON: A Jewish Response to Hunger. There, presented the opportunity to give grants to organizations across the country that work to end hunger and feed the hungry, I learned a lot about the relative value of feeding someone a meal and advocating for change in the circumstances that create hunger. Enter the recession of 2008–9. Some of you heard me tell this story during Rosh HaShanah services this year:

I was meeting a Kolot member at a café in a neighborhood near here earlier this year, something I often do as a rabbi without a real office. As I approached the café, I saw a man walking into the street and yelling at a small boy, presumably his son, to come on but the boy was near tears and hung back. The man kept walking and kept yelling. I suspected child abuse—the man was so harsh and the child so small and fearful. As I got closer, I could hear that the boy was saying he did not want to come, because he wanted something in the store behind him. Over and over he cried, "I want, I want." Over and over, the man yelled, "Get over here! Get here right now!" One more time the boy cried, "I want . . ." And finally the man spoke the truth: "I don't have any money."

I thought my heart would break. I thought perhaps the man's heart had broken at that moment of having to yell his shame as everyone around stopped to stare. Later I wept.

Every week this fall I have spoken to or counseled or met with a Kolot member who has lost a job or seen a job diminish due to the recession. The shame that middle-class, formerly comfortable people feel in this circumstance parallels what was felt by that man shouting at his son in the middle of the street.

Recently I have realized that I was seeing more people sleeping on streets and in subway stations than I had in a long time. One word for a poor person, *ani*, is related to the word for oppress or humiliate. It also sounds very much like the word *ani*, "me." Each poor person is an individual, feeling the oppression or shame of poverty in his or her own way. *Ani* is also very like the Hebrew word for answer, *anah*. Rabbi Jill Jacobs, in her book *There Shall Be No Needy*, reminds us that "the psalms regularly describe the *ani* as suffering not only from financial need but also from illness, oppression, loneliness, and depression. This *ani* calls out for divine help, on the assumption that God intervenes to redeem those who are suffering."[22]

So what now, God? We need some strength for *cheshbon hanefesh*, taking stock of our souls. Our task is not only rebuke of others, but also of ourselves. What is each of us doing that keeps the *ani* needy? What in our choices in homes, meals, clothing, and more keeps the poor *ani*—humiliatingly poor? What small measures can I take to help the man on the Brooklyn street who cannot buy his child a sweet or a toy or the Kolot member who needs help paying the rent or food? And what can I do—*rak ani*—just me—to keep those new to poverty from feeling the humiliation that is so often the lot of the poor?

How do we allow the society—country, state, city, neighborhood—in which we live to come to such a moment? I have been working on these questions for more than twenty years. I have wept and raged, written letters and written sermons, made calls and made stew. And yet here we are again, as forces well beyond most of our control wreak havoc they may not intend and do not repair.

Hunger is the tip of the iceberg of poverty, the symptom that makes us all know there is serious illness at hand. When our trusty

22. Jill Jacobs, *There Shall Be No Needy: Pursuing Social Justice through Jewish Law and Tradition* (Woodstock, VT: Jewish Lights, 2009), 50.

editor asked me to write about money, hunger is what came to mind and keyboard. The statistics are grim beyond belief. Children across the country and the world are hungry every day. So are old people. So are many able-bodied adults who want to work. So are some Kolot members who may feel too ashamed to ask for help. The New York City Coalition Against Hunger reminds us that in New York City, 1.3 million New Yorkers (one in six) live in food-insecure households; 417,000 of them are children.

My prayer is that they get help, that the shame diminishes in the face of true community, that the economy picks up, that jobs return, that Kolot's dues return to normal levels, that we get through this bad time as we got through the one of the late 1980s, but without the greed and unbridled risk and use of people as pawns that marked the recovery of the 1990s. My prayer is for more regulation, more compassion, more interest in people than in mortgage rates, more jobs and fewer soup kitchens.

In 1987, I looked around at people in need and began a soup kitchen. Twenty-two years later I look around and ask, "Who is making all those people hungry?" The answer is multifaceted, making it hard to know how to help. I am back to thinking one hot meal can make some difference. It just doesn't solve anything.

Chutzpah! Seeking
Moral Leadership in Torah and Life

Rosh HaShanah 2008 / 5769

It was Yom Kippur and there was a drought in the land.

"Rabbi Eliezer came before the ark and recited the twenty-four blessings (said on fast days), but his prayer was not answered. Rabbi Akiva then came before the ark and exclaimed, 'Our Father, our King, we have no king but you; our Father, our King, have mercy upon us for Your own sake!' whereupon the rain fell" (Babylonian Talmud, *Taanit* 25b).

Akiva—having no patience left—cut through the usual ordered mode of prayer to urge God to respond—and the rain fell. Ever since, the story goes, we have been singing those words: *Avinu Malkeinu, choneinu vaaneinu* . . .

Traditions so often sustain us. Coming into Rosh HaShanah, I could hear the sounds of *Avinu Malkeinu* in my head, as I yearned to hear its haunting melody and words yet again. But not all traditions need to be repeated again and again; some can be altered, some discarded, some replaced. Akiva himself broke through the order of prayer in his time to give his urgent prayer of necessity. Chutzpah! Surely we too are living in a time that requires urgent prayer and an overturning of the usual order— some chutzpah. When I think of Rosh HaShanah in this way, I realize that as much as I love singing *Avinu Malkeinu*, I am

139

sick of the *Akeidah*, the story of the Binding—sacrifice? murder?—of Isaac.

This story is everywhere in the midrash, poetry, art, and yes, our liturgy. And I am sick of it. It contains not a single character I want to identify with, not the God who commands the sacrifice, not Abraham who obeys so submissively, not Isaac who goes along with only one question along the way, and not even the poor ram who loses his life because someone has to. It is our tradition to read this story on Rosh HaShanah and I am sick of it.

Over the cries of "We can't leave it out, it's part of our tradition!" I say, "Let's." Not just because we need change, though that is clear enough in our liturgy, in our nation, in our world. No, I say let's leave it out because what we need now to face the terrifying world is a story of moral courage, of protest, of hope, not one of submission to God, who lays down an impossible command. What we need is an Akiva to overturn the usual in a time of crucial urgency.

Why do we read this story anyway? Dr. Larry Hoffman, our great modern Jewish liturgist, asks, "What kind of story is this to tell the assembled multitude on the High Holy Days?" He then reminds us that the *Akeidah* is the traditional reading for the second day of Rosh HaShanah. The story for the first day was—and often remains—Genesis 21, the story of God's visiting Sarah and promising Isaac's birth, and of Sarah casting Hagar and Ishmael out with Abraham's reluctant assent. But Hoffman notes that at the end of the first day, the Torah would have been rolled to the end of Genesis 21, and the very next chapter, Genesis 22, is none other than the Binding of Isaac. So he thinks it is very possible that the Rabbis chose the *Akeidah* just because it is the next chapter! So by the chance of a roll of the Torah, we have been reading this story for centuries?! I asked Dr. Hoffman about it a couple of weeks ago, hoping he had found more substantial reasoning for its inclusion. But no: it remains the chance—though powerful—result of rolling the Torah. So let's roll it somewhere else.

I do not suggest change just for the sake of change or even just for distaste. I suggest it because I believe that our stories, both personal and collective, shape our lives, and I worry about us continuing to be shaped by the *Akeidah*. While we have wrestled with it for centuries, it is not usually the wrestling that people remember, but rather the story itself and sometimes its terror. God tells Abraham to take his son up on the mountain and offer him as a sacrifice—that *is* what we remember, right?

In talking about change of text and its potential to change us, I am conscious that you may hear echoes of thoughts of change in our world today. That is entirely intentional. I hope that as I speak about change in Torah and liturgy, we can all be thinking about change in our nation. I want to make change in our Torah reading and our nation because of a need for moral leadership that I see far too little of anywhere. Rabbi Donniel Hartman of the Shalom Hartman Institute in Jerusalem wrote recently that, too often, "religious piety is judged by a person's ability to dissociate from their moral and intellectual commitments and make the leap of faith to serve God . . . in Jewish tradition, the most prominent exemplar is the story of the binding of Isaac."[24] Surely Abraham dissociated from his moral understanding when his only response to God's command to offer his son as a sacrifice was *Hineini*— "Here I am."

Rabbi Adin Steinsaltz wrote of that same dissociation last week with regard to our economic crisis:

> *For many people there is a disconnect, a cut between personal life and financial life. One may be a nice, quiet, straightforward person in one's personal life; one may even be genuinely generous and philanthropic. But in financial dealings, the same person may be a cold-blooded shark. . . . In the rare cases when people take note of this discrepancy, the common answer is: this is business—meaning*

24. Donniel Hartman. *Judaism and the Challenges of Modern Life* (New York: Continuum, 2007), 52.

that business has a completely different set of moral assumptions completely detached from other sides of one's personality. . . . The real sense of teshuva is to allow some higher concepts to seep into the kitchen, the bedroom, and the pocket.

Our great prophets preached this same need to bring religious ritual and moral action together. On Yom Kippur we will hear again the crucial words of Isaiah, urging us to use our Yom Kippur fast as a time to commit to the needs of the world. When we act justly, Isaiah tells us, Then, when you call, God will answer; when you cry, God will say, *"Hineini*—Here I am." Isaiah did not mean us not to fast, but rather not to dissociate that religious ritual from our moral commitments. This year, when I read the *Akeidah* and hear Abraham say *Hineini*—Here I am, ready to do Your bidding, even to the point of sacrificing my child—it feels like a dissociation. I want instead to hear God say to us all, *"Hineini*—Here I am," because we have acted justly in our world even as we spend time in religious ritual. Surely, what our world does not need any more of is dissociation from moral and intellectual commitment. Rather, we need more such commitment to face, protest, engage in, and act upon abuses of power and official neglect piling up all around us.

Imagine the idea that God responds, ensures God's presence, when we make that moral commitment. I remember that it was not until the Hebrew slaves of the Book of Exodus grew so oppressed that they cried out to God that God "remembered them" and began to act. In the Torah, God's remembering *is* also taking action, thus God's sending Moses to free the slaves. Larry Hoffman says the central theme of Rosh HaShanah is this kind of remembrance, and hence the story of God remembering Sarah is our central text, the one that comes before the *Akeidah*.

On this Rosh HaShanah, living in our world, we need God's active remembrance and we need a model of moral action and we need to make the changes that will get us there. To get there, we have to make a change in the stories we tell. Philosopher Charles Taylor reminds us that our stories shape not only our identities as individuals, but our moral character as well; he calls Moral Space a place at our very core where the questions of what is right and what is wrong can be answered, and he suggests we need stories that bring us to that space. I don't think the *Akeidah* is that kind of story, giving us as it does a portrait of the passive, accepting Abraham. If we are not to remain in its sway, then we need to change. But how? One way to change a Jewish text is to read it and our own environment very carefully and to bring them together in midrash, a way to seek new truth in an old story. Year after year here at Kolot, for instance, we have heard Arthur Strimling *d'rash* the *Akkeidah* in ways that probe the story's depths and make us think. But in the end, the story itself remains in our minds and hearts.

Another way to change is to leave, toss in the towel, separate from the whole system that gave us this story to begin with. It is amazing how often in Kolot Chayeinu's weekly Torah study sessions this idea of leaving comes up: we have arrived at an edge we cannot justify or interpret to satisfaction, and we are tempted to throw the whole Torah against the wall. Even Moses, arguing strenuously with God to keep God from killing all the people after they built the Golden Calf, says finally to God, "Now, if You will forgive their sin [well and good]; but if not, erase me from Your book that You have written!" (Exodus 32:32). *L'havdil*—in as opposite a scenario as possible, I want to say that if titans of American financial companies get off scot-free, with billions in their pockets, write me out of that story that we see repeated again and again! But if we do not in fact want to write ourselves out or throw away the book, where to now? Following Donniel Hartman, I want to explore a "different religious sensibility within Judaism, which views religious individuals as members of a moral community . . . and as people who are obligated to examine, and if necessary, criticize God's command."

I do not mean we need to leave Judaism or Torah or Rosh HaShanah's rituals behind. Rather, we can dig in deeper and find a new text that will be as rich as the *Akeidah*, but with the moral standing we need now. It is my hunch—and my hope—that in making this significant change, we will also find new vitality, new life in ourselves, our traditions, and our stories. The Torah, Constitution of our people, can find new life and new respect in more eyes. So I ask: "If I were deciding what Torah text to read on Rosh HaShanah instead of the *Akeidah* (Genesis 22, the Binding of Isaac), what would it be, or would I stick with the *Akeidah*, and why?" Here is one of my favorite Torah scholars, Amelia Holcomb, to give us her answer:

> *If I could pick the reading for Rosh haShannah, I would choose to read Genesis 6–9, the story of Noah's Ark. Rosh haShannah is about trying to wash away what we want to change, about trying to act morally, and about learning to adjust, and Noah's Ark depicts these perfectly. G-d realizes that the world has become corrupt and decides to wash it clean. Only Noah, his family, and enough animals to continue every species, are to be left on earth after the flood. I think that God chose Noah because he had strong moral values. Instead of trying to save all people and animals, an impossibility, Noah opted to save every land species from certain extinction, and do the most to protect biodiversity in the history of the world! And, in Noah's Ark, it is G-d who actually gave an oath to do better in the years to come, promising, "I will maintain my covenant with you, never again shall all flesh be cut off by the waters of the flood."*

On Rosh HaShanah, learning that even God can promise to do better reminds us that when we make mistakes, we can work to improve. So let us deliberately roll back just a few chapters in Genesis, to Genesis 18, and anoint another Abraham, this time one who is a fully developed moral being ready to argue with God against God's plan to murder the inhabitants of Sodom and Gomorrah: Abraham came forward and said, "Will You sweep away the innocent along with the guilty? . . . Shall not the Judge of all the earth deal justly?" (vv. 23, 25). Abraham goes on to ask what will happen if there are even fewer innocent people in the city—what if forty-five, what if forty, thirty, twenty, what if only ten? And God answered, "I will not destroy, for the sake of the ten" (v. 32). I am not so naïve as to think that any protest I or we undertake will get such a swift and heartening response. But I do deeply desire that the story that I read every year as the year begins offer me a model of the founder of my people that I can live with and aspire to.

A man willing without hesitation to offer his son as a sacrifice cannot be for me, in our time, that kind of model. This protesting Abraham is the one our ancestors compared with Noah and saw as superior, for just this protest, something they thought Noah had never even attempted.

As we begin the new year, we have a choice of stories, and a choice of two Abrahams: the active protester of injustice and the passive receiver of an impossible command. I can no longer learn about being a Jew from that passive Abraham, and I think you can't either. We need a moral leader, a Jewish leader who does not hesitate to protest even to God when needed, a leader who will elevate us to a moral level we have so lacked, often in Judaism, everywhere in our government.

Will this one relatively small change really make such a big difference? Not for us. But if the children of Kolot Chayeinu grow up hearing a different story every year, if they learn that the original Jew was someone who stood his ground even against God and urged God to act with justice, who knows what may happen? If God is the energy of the universe, then how may that energy shift when we shift? Perhaps even our ideas of God will shift as we imagine not a harsh commander but a partner engaged in conversation and debate. Rabbi Elyse Frishman has written that in so many places in Torah where we read "God commanded," it does not actually say "commanded," but rather *Vayidabeir Adonai*— "God said, God spoke." Frishman suggests that what God always wanted was a conversation, while we humans wanted a command. I think a change of story can remind us that God wants to talk, wants to hear even debate and criticism. That may be why Akiva's prayer gained favor; perhaps even God was bored with the old order of prayer!

On this day of remembrance, let's remember that and make some change. It is a little wild, this urge to change. It's exciting, it's chutzpah-dik: It makes us sit up a little straighter, feel our power stirring, maybe we even laugh out loud at the possibility. But change for change's sake is often empty. On this day of remembrance we need to remember Isaiah, who wanted us to change without abandoning the things that had kept us going for so long, wanted us to link our prayer space and our moral space, letting them interweave in a way that would benefit us and improve the world. Let's not fear change, and let's not change without thought, without care. Quick fixes are no fixes, and we do not have to jump to this idea in a moment, after at least twelve centuries of the *Akeidah* as Rosh HaShanah text. But let's not *not* jump after we have a chance to think about it, either.

Tomorrow, we are going back to the traditional way of reading. We will read tomorrow the story of Sarah and Hagar, so ripe with issues of power and abuse, of hope and abandonment. On Wednesday, we will read the *Akeidah* with musical midrash, letting the music break it up that it may enter our hearts in a new way. On Thursday, I want you to begin to think about your answer to the question "If I were deciding what Torah text to read on Rosh HaShanah instead of the *Akeidah*, what would it be?" Who knows what may happen here next year? I know I want to follow urgent Akiva and the protester Abraham and sometimes Noah and Miriam, and many in our day, including someone like Max from *Where the Wild Things Are*, who made mischief of one kind or another, and who was not afraid of wild things even when they roared their terrible roars and rolled their terrible eyes. Last week I was present at a big celebration of the life and work of Maurice Sendak as he turned eighty. I think of Sendak here because he, like Akiva, had chutzpah! He busted through convention to create something new that has lasted for generations. Here was a gay man who could not be open and who created Max and *Where the Wild Things Are*. It was a new story, unlike anything read to children before, and generations have now been shaped by it.

I'd like to bring a few wild things into Torah and into liturgy and see what happens. This is after all a new year, a year ripe with possibilities, just being born. Right now, let's feel the excitement of change. I am excited and a little fearful just to think about changing twelve centuries of accepted liturgical wisdom. Chutzpah! Let's cultivate a little more chutzpah here. Let's fast *and* free the oppressed, read Torah *and* inhabit moral space, sing *Avinu Malkeinu and* let some jazz into the service. Kolot Chayeinu is, after all, a congregation that refuses to be satisfied with the world as it is. So, in the immortal words of that great Jewish sage Maurice Sendak, "Let the wild rumpus begin!"

Author's note: While Kolot did not stop reading the *Akeidah* on Rosh HaShanah, this sermon did result in many, many private and public conversations and deeper understanding for some of the depths of Torah's reach.

Justice Is the
Ground We Walk On

Rosh HaShanah 2011 / 5772

A well-known story: A potential convert comes to Shammai and Hillel and asks, provocatively, that they teach him the whole Torah while standing on one foot. Shammai is provoked and whacks the man with a rod. Hillel replies, "That which is hateful to you, do not unto another: This is the whole Torah. The rest is commentary—go and study."

I go back to this story often, for its essential message about Torah and its urge to study. I am thinking about it tonight because this Rosh HaShanah is not just another new year here at Kolot Chayeinu. It is the beginning of our next eighteen years. In May, we celebrated Chai Time, eighteen years of our community's life, a life full and rich and accomplished. Nowhere has our accomplishment been seen more clearly these last two weeks than in our overflowing school registration and our community's care for [congregant] Amina Rachman in her tragic illness and death.

I know that Amina would be saying to us all, go and study. She had begun making plans for a new format for our weekly Torah study and other kinds of Jewish learning. Amina was also a lifelong activist and wanted us to start developing a community-wide conversation about race and Judaism and Kolot. It was one of the projects I was looking forward to seeing come to our new Eitz Kehilla Social Justice Facilitation Committee.

This committee is, as its name says, a kind of "gathering tree." It is a committee comprising experienced activists in various realms—education, environment, human rights—who will help you shape an idea you have for a project or a one-shot action.

Do you have an idea for a project you have wanted to create, like Amina did, or a way to get a group to engage in work already being done? This committee will ask you some questions: How many people do you have already? What resources do you have? What is your basic plan? Does it conform with Kolot's expressed values? And then they'll help guide you as you develop it. I think it is exciting! Already recently at Kolot some have been engaged in bank regulation efforts in New York City through Brooklyn Congregations United; some take part in monthly discussions about social justice in this neighborhood through council member Brad Lander's office; some are talking about continuing our work with domestic workers in a new way that links children, the elderly, and people with disabilities who all hire helpers at home; some—thanks to Amina—have had conversations about looking at issues of race in our community; and some, thanks to Barbara Kancelbaum, have cooked or slept at a new neighborhood homeless shelter.

So kudos to all. And kudos to the committee—will you all stand? They have fliers for you and a poster you can check out.

But my dream is not that an amazing organizer like Barbara Kancelbaum organizes another project, though I hope she will. No, my dream is much bigger. My dream is that every single member of Kolot Chayeinu and all of you who are not members do one act of justice this year. By one act, I do not mean putting a quarter in a *tzedakah* box, though I might mean making a *tzedakah* box and collecting all year, then deciding where to give it. I mean taking a monthly slot at the new shelter and cooking a meal or spending the night. I mean writing letters to legislators on an issue that is important to you. I mean organizing others to advocate for a solution you come up with. I mean your Judaism is in your hands.

It is not across the sea or up in heaven, as our Torah portion for Yom Kippur says, so that you need someone else to go get it for you. No, it is in your mouth and in your heart, and you can do it.

This is a big switch for us. We have been used to a model in which our social justice committee decides what it is going to work on and does it, and then tries to get people involved, and others call or write them and say, "I think you should do *this*." The new answer is, "There is no committee that will *do*, and there is no *this*, without you." And if you think it is just you, note that I too have to bring my ideas for projects to this committee. So do members of the committee, as one ruefully said to me not long ago.

You are all created in the image of an active God. You all have the potential for just action toward justice, the ability to right the world's imbalance, the chance to model justice and mercy.

Listen! Rabbi Akiva and Ben Azai are arguing. What *is* the essential teaching of Torah? Akiva says *V'ahavta l'rei-acha kamo-cha*, "Love your neighbor as yourself." Ben Azai disagrees. He says no, it is "on the day when God created Adam he created him in the image of God." Ben Azai argues against love as a basis because loving your neighbor is fine, except when you don't. And when you don't, you still have to *respect* the neighbor because that person was created in the image of God.

The question now is, what are you going to do? The word you may not want to hear is "obligation": we do not give or act or urge because of love or caring; we do so because we are obligated as Jews to do so. But knowing when and what and how—that is when it gets difficult.

As Rev. William Sloane Coffin—not a Jew, but surely a sage—once said, "You can say, with the prophet Amos, let justice roll down like mighty waters, but figuring out the irrigation system is complicated."[25]

25. William Sloane Coffin, *Credo* (Louisville, KY: Westminster John Knox Press, 2004).

So now let's us go and study. For Judaism, justice is literally the ground we walk on. Talk of justice begins at the very beginning of our Jewish enterprise.

At the heart of Judaism's understanding of justice is the idea that all human beings were created *b'tzelem Elohim*, "in God's image." This is foundational; it starts with the first human, whose creation we celebrate on Rosh HaShanah. It is *tzelem Elohim* that makes us see that people are inherently equal *and* deserving of the respect due God's image. That respect came to be called *k'vod hab'riyot*, "honor to those God created."

This respect means that we do not harm this creature of God's, ourselves or others. Rather, we must do all we can to protect and assist human beings because they—we—were created *b'tzelem Elohim*. The biblical Cain who murdered his brother Abel was sent off to wander the earth, but God still provided him with a protective sign. Even people who may have committed acts of terror should not be tortured. Even people who did commit murder should not be put to death. And *kal vachomer*, so much more so those who did not commit crimes.

Essentially, Judaism has two major ways of looking at justice. One is the practical, *tachlis* way of enacting justice: the realm of courts and judges and lawyers and advocates. The other is the ideal, the foundational values that shape what we do and when and how we do it. Tonight, at the beginning of the year, we start with ideals and values. And we begin with Ben Azai and *tzelem Elohim*, for it is the beginning, a way to recognize that we are all one, that we cannot harm one another or ourselves, for we were created in God's image. It is also the beginning of obligation: We don't always love those we come into contact with, so we can't always love our neighbor as ourselves. And what about when we do not love ourselves? But we can act on the obligation of respecting others.

Obligation leads us to the Jewish value of *tzedakah*. Long before it meant putting coins into a nice decorated box and deciding where to give that money, *tzedakah* meant justice, and sometimes righteousness, the way we humans are supposed to act toward others with generosity of spirit and bounty. It is based on an understanding that the world is created in balance and that when it gets out of balance it is our responsibility to set it right.

Tzedakah comes to mean a kind of giving for justice, giving of self and giving of money or goods. Though it is often explained as charity, it is quite different. Charity comes from the Latin *caritas*, the same root that gives us the word "caring." But just as love cannot be the basis for respect of human beings, so caring cannot be the basis of giving. We are asked to give because the world is out of whack and it is our obligation to right it. You can care a lot or not so much, but you have to do it. For that reason, even those who are in need themselves and may receive *tzedakah* are asked to give.

One is supposed to give first, to the poor of one's own close relatives, then those of the extended family, then of the city, and then of other cities and countries. And our sages also said that for the sake of the paths of peace non-Jews as well as Jews should be given *tzedakah*.

And everyone should be given compassion, leeway, the benefit of the doubt. A collection of ethical laws in Talmud is sometimes known as *mishnat chasidim*, "the teaching of the righteous ones." Their theme is action that is morally just, even if the law requires something less. Reaching to do more than is strictly necessary is in fact required.

On Rosh HaShanah, as we sing and read of God as royalty, ensconced on the throne, it is good to remember that our ancestors imagined a scene in which God had two thrones. God would sit on a particular throne when issuing an opinion of strict justice and switch to another when wanting to offer a merciful opinion.

Cantor Segal provided the music last year for the funeral of Rhonda Copelon, a courageous and activist lawyer who took on many groundbreaking cases. By request, Lisa led the enormous gathered crowd in singing Cris Williamson's song "Song of the

Soul," with its lyrics "What do you do for a living, are you forgiving, giving shelter?"

God sits tonight on both thrones and asks us the question Rhonda Copelon wanted those who loved her to remember. What *do* you do for a living? *Are* you forgiving? What is the song of *your* soul? *Tzedek, tzedek tirdof.* Justice, justice we *must* pursue. We must pursue justice using just means. We must pursue justice even if we may never achieve it. We must do and live justice at home and pursue it everywhere else.

This year at Kolot Chayeinu, we are starting anew. We begin tonight a new phase of life, the first of *chai*—eighteen—more years. We begin tonight to take Judaism into our own hands. We begin tonight to learn what Judaism means when it says pursue justice. And we begin tonight, as our ancestors began at the base of Mount Sinai: *Naaseh v'nishma*, we will do first, and as we do we will learn. What is hateful to you, do not do to another. That is the whole Torah; all the rest is deep, rich, compelling, crucial commentary. Go and study. Go and build that irrigation system and let those waters of justice flow!

Social Justice

Accounting for Our Souls

Rosh HaShanah 2015 / 5776

We stand on the cusp of a new year and engage in *cheshbon hane-fesh*—accounting for our souls. For me, the hardest and most nec-essary accounting is the one closest to home, and all year I have been wrestling with what it means to have white privilege. I hope my wrestling will connect with or inspire your own, because this sermon is not just about me. As Abraham Joshua Heschel wrote, "Living is not a private affair of the individual. Living is what humans do with God's time, what humans do with God's world." For me, God's world is right down the street. Listen.

I live in Kensington. Kathryn and I have lived there for twenty-nine years. Back then, we were the newbies among the longtime white working-class folks, the black working-class folks, the immi-grants from Guyana and Pakistan and Ecuador. Now *we* are the old-timers, and every day more white professionals arrive, buying houses they could not afford to buy in Park Slope, joining black pro-fessionals, immigrants from Bangladesh and South America, and a few white working-class folks. So we, who once made the older folks on our block roll their eyes by our arrival, now get to roll ours at how the neighborhood is changing when new people arrive.

I want to tell you about two blocks on Caton Avenue between Ocean Parkway and East Eighth Street.

A couple of years ago a big plot of land was sold along these blocks, and we feared it was yet another giant condominium or high-priced rental building; three of those have been built within three blocks of our home in the last few years. But no. It was a school, a new public school, elementary and middle school as it turned out, and much needed in District 15, which includes our area. I was cheered, though I feared it would block the much-loved morning light in my study. Now that it is built, I still have some light, and I have loved seeing the children in their two play yards, lively, engaged, fun, varied.

The small local market grew and thrived, bringing in organic foods and locally grown items and hard-to-find delicacies. And a food co-op opened a block away.

And then, joy of joys, a café appeared, surely also spurred by the school and its teachers and parents, and too by the increased number of white professionals, the folks who work from home or have flexible schedules, the people who like to sit in a café to do work or hang out or join friends there.

I think I went there every day after it opened. I am a little embarrassed to tell you how much I am in love with this café.

But sometime in the midst of my second week I had to start owning up to my over-the-top love for this café and had to face up to the way it embodies my privilege. Because, you know, I *am* one of those white professionals who works from home and likes to sit in a café for meetings or out-of-the-house work or seeing friends.

The café and the expanded grocery store and the food co-op and the new school have everything to do with the new people moving in for whom such necessities or amenities appear in a way they do not in other kinds of neighborhoods. Prices of houses are five times what we paid when we moved in, and the diversity on our street, a block over from Caton and Ocean, has declined. The children in the three schools in the area are more often white, less black, less Asian, though more Latino than they were five years ago. And since Nicole Hannah-Jones wrote that extraordinary article in the *New York Times* in June, called "Finding a School for My Daughter in a Segregated City," Kathryn and I have been keeping an eye on our schools. We just got statistics last month but have been noticing for some time that there are parents lingering at school arrival and dismissal time, clearly parents, mostly white, who have time to do so, as other sorts of working parents do not. It is clear some balance has shifted and may be shifting further, and we lament that reality while we also know we can get an unbelievable price for our house if we sell it.

And then there is my café. Many local people get their sandwiches and coffee at the market next door instead for a fraction of the café's cost. But the café is crowded most of the time. And I sit drinking cappuccino and knowing that while I am paying through the nose for the coffee, it is still a privilege, and I did nothing to earn it. I can't hide from the fact that this privilege is bought by gentrification and decreasing diversity of race and class. I have to recognize that what drives the schools toward a tipping point, what led to all those apartment buildings being built, also fuels my beloved café.

I have two pockets. In one, a note appears saying, "For you, the world was created." In the other, a note says, "Hypocrite! What are you going to do about your privilege?!"

For me the world was created: I am white, an Ashkenazi Jew, raised in a middle-class family, some of whose branches have been in this country since the 1850s. I grew up in northern Virginia, land of *Loving v. Virginia*, the American Nazi Party, segregated schools, and a fair amount of overt antisemitism. *And* I went to decent schools, got to go to college, have two master's degrees and rabbinic ordination. Kathryn and I, richly blessed, have been able to pay the rent and then the mortgage for many, many years.

There is no doubt that I am privileged. Many of you are too. The privilege is about having enough money and it is about being white, and seeing how the two interweave.

Every time I sit in the café, loving its good coffee, I know I am a hypocrite. How can I bemoan the local schools' tipping point when I benefit so much from it?

Rosh HaShanah is the birthday of the world or maybe, as some teach, the anniversary of the sixth day of Creation, when God created human beings in the divine image. The angels said, "Don't do it. They'll wreak havoc." But God said, I'll create one, one alone so that no one can say to another, 'My ancestor is greater than yours.'"

God had a very nice idea. But what havoc have we wrought?!

Every kind of harm. Police shootings of black men and women. Again, again, again. Again. Increasingly segregated schools here in the capital of the world. Displacement of people from their homes. Whole neighborhoods—stores, churches, clubs—virtually wiped away. And through it all we who have enormous privilege can sit in cafés and bemoan the state of the world without having to give up anything.

Have I made you uncomfortable yet? I am uncomfortable and can use the company.

Listen, we white people at Kolot are not bad people. Perhaps more than many white people and even many white Jews, a lot of us recognize that we live in a racist society, with racist institutions and systems. Many of us have worked for wage increases and better working conditions for the people of color who wash cars and serve fast food and box up computers. We have protested police killings of black men and women and have worked for a change in the way New York City oversees the police. We have declared our intent that Kolot itself become an anti-racist congregation, a rarity in the American way of religion, which is almost always segregated. We are blessed to do this work with Jews of color and non-Jews of color who help keep us honest and on track.

But what many of us who are white have not done is look at ourselves as white and at the way that whiteness plays in to the racist systems we deplore. I don't want New York City to keep having the third most segregated schools in the country. I don't want to lose the amazing diversity of my neighborhood. I don't want to think of myself as blind to our society's realities or to the very real suffering of people I ought to see as my neighbors, the people Torah commands me to love as I love myself. I do not want to keep living as though nothing is wrong with where I stand in what is so clearly a racist society.

The closer to home this reality hits, the more urgent our need to face it. So when that racist system we all know so well—gentrification—began to roll down the slope to Kensington, I started to have to pay attention in a new way. I frankly do not know what to do about forces like development's greed and gentrification's spread, though I have dabbled on the edges of protests for affordable housing and been glad the city is attending to it.

But what I can do and what you can do is to look at our own privilege. How do we begin to counter or sacrifice some of the small and large ways we white people benefit?

The first thing we have to do is open our eyes. This is not as easy as it sounds. It means reading and talking and confronting hard truths and thinking about what we might have to give up. Long ago my friend Bobbie Samet gave me a simple tool that awakened me to small-scale racism like nothing else had. She said, spend a week describing all your encounters in terms of their white participants, since most of us who are white also have white friends and colleagues and do not usually name people's race unless it is different from our own. So: *Last week I went to dinner with some white friends and we went to see a movie about white people and then I went to work and had a meeting with my white co-workers and after work I had a drink with my white neighbor.* That opens the eyes, or will after a week.

We can also stand up for racial justice in small intimate ways. Injustice happens that way, one to one, so why not justice? You know the term "micro-aggressions"? One definition I found said they are the everyday verbal, nonverbal, and environmental slights, snubs, or insults, whether intentional or unintentional, that communicate hostile, derogatory, or negative messages to target persons based solely upon their marginalized group membership.

Many of us here probably do them unintentionally, but opening our eyes means we have to try to stop.

I suggest we counter them with what I want to call "micro-supports." My white wife Kathryn told me one small story: She was driving when she saw that a black person had been pulled over by the police. Knowing the way these encounters often go, she pulled over in front of the car that had been stopped. The officer came over to ask what she was doing, and she said she had stopped to send a text because of course she would never drive and text. But what she was really doing was supportive witnessing, which may have kept the encounter of this one black person and this one police officer from going bad. That is micro-support. We could all do it.

Maybe you are a subway rider. My black neighbor Camille Dentler told me that her daughter, a wonderful, talented teenager, often tells her mother that she is shunned by commuters getting off the subway at the Fort Hamilton Parkway station. White men have even clutched their shoulder bags when she is nearby. Maybe white people in the neighborhood can offer micro-support by greeting people of color and walking with them. It does mean you have to know them. As Camille says, "When we speak and engage people, it's a different experience."

We can also:

- Make sure that people of color in restaurants are served as quickly as we are.
- Make sure our children speak with respect to their caregivers of color.
- Make sure we try to develop friendships and collegial relationships with people of color.
- Make sure we do not assume everyone in a group has the money for a trip or a meal out.

I was reminded this summer by white Jewish anti-racism trainer Martin Friedman that we Jews need to focus more on being Jews, on our own history of being oppressed and our own immigration stories and our own traditions of justice. Some of us Jews are white, he noted, because we have had the opportunity to say so and to claim it. Martin wrote, "One of the costs of our [white Jewish] comfort and our privilege is Black and Brown lives. As long as we align ourselves with whiteness we contribute to the deaths of Black and Brown people at the hands of institutions. Their deaths are part of the cost of our comfort, safety and privilege.

"The other loss," he wrote, "is the loss of what it really means to be Jewish. That it means to not stand idly by when our neighbor bleeds. That it means true *Tikkun Olam*. . . . Let's choose our Jewishness over Whiteness. . . . Let's choose life."[26]

I have two pockets. In one, there is a note that says, "You can keep sitting in that café. Just close your eyes and enjoy." In the other, a note says, "Stop wallowing, guilt does not help, be a stand-up Jew, you might save some lives."

On the corner of Caton Avenue and East Eighth Street, there is a traffic light! It was installed this past spring thanks in large part to my friend and our City Council member Brad Lander, and because of Brad I got to say a blessing for that light. It was installed because of the new school and tragically because a fourteen-year-old Bangladeshi boy named Mohammed "Naiem" Uddin had been killed at the next corner by a hit-and-run driver. The light is a *mechaya*, a giver and protector of life.

My black friend and Kolot board member Ernst Mohamed taught me about CPR, lifesaving! It is what I am really talking about here, the ultimate saving of lives, literally and in every way that matters to life. CPR is a method of imagining and moving toward the future we want to see. Context. Purpose. Results. C-P-R. It works backward:

26. Martin Friedman, https://rabbibrant.com/2016/08/14/guest-post-observations-on-the-jewish-response-to-the-movement-for-black-lives-platform-from-a-self-loving-anti-racist-white-jew/.

We start with the "R"—the *results* we can imagine: I want Bangladeshi children and Latino children and black children and Asian children and white children to be safe on Caton Avenue, and I want them to have safe good schools, and a good fair justice system, and have futures filled with opportunity and open doors and the chance to relax, give up the vigilance that is otherwise their harsh inheritance.

Then we think about the "P"—the *purpose*: A rebalancing of our society is needed, so we put the needs of poor people and people of color first even when it is uncomfortable for some of us.

The "C"—*context* is the basic, most crucial foundation for what we envision, the *achat shaalti*—the one thing that drives us. For me, the context is I am a Jew and Judaism demands this.

For all this to be true, for the large saving of lives I pray for, we have to understand that we may have to give something up. It may be just the comfort of our closed eyes, or it may be the extra time it takes to offer micro-supports when micro-aggressions come so easily to mind and mouth. It may be the stretching of the unused muscle of imagination. Or it may mean the active engagement needed to really hear and do, to insist on justice as well as one-to-one equality.

V'chayah im shamoa tishm'u, begins the middle paragraph of the *Sh'ma*. If you listen, really listen . . . what will happen? God gave us two ears and just one mouth, so we can listen twice as much as we speak. Let's listen.

Black attorney Bryan Stevenson, author of *Just Mercy*, says, "When we get close, we hear things that can't be heard from afar. We see things that can't be seen. And sometimes, that makes the difference between acting justly and unjustly. . . . If you are not proximate, you can't change the world."

I have two pockets. In one, there is a note: The world was created for me. In the other, its necessary twin: I was created to change the world.

What about the Woman?

Erev Shabbat before the March for Women's Lives, April 23, 2004

Two men are fighting. One pushes a pregnant woman. She miscarries, without other misfortune. The one responsible is then fined according to what the woman's husband decides (adapted, Exodus 21:22). This odd scenario is the biblical basis for all of later Jewish legal understanding about abortion.

On Sunday, Kathryn and I and maybe a million other women will be marching in Washington to express our deep concern about the many issues affecting women's health and lives, but especially to say that the right to an abortion in the United States must not be taken away. It seems an apt time to say some things about Judaism and abortion. So, this scene from the Book of Exodus.

Later Jewish understanding develops along two lines, and essentially all commentators follow one of those two lines. First, based on the scene I read and a Mishnaic text, there develops an understanding of what a human is and when one becomes a human, called *nefesh* in Hebrew, one of the words for soul. As Rachel Biale, author of *Women and Jewish Law*, notes, "The woman is a living person, a *nefesh*, and anyone who harms her body or kills her must pay in kind. The fetus is not a person in this sense. Destroying it through causing an abortion is not a capital crime and carries no capital punishment."[27]

27. Rachel Biale, *Women and Jewish Law* (New York: Schocken Books, 1984), 220.

In *Mishnah Ohalot*, we find a description of what we know as late-term abortion or, called by its opponents, partial birth abortion. But here we learn that until the head or majority of its body emerges from the womb, it is not considered a person, and its life is considered inferior to the mother's life. There are some Talmudic authorities that consider a fetus a potential person and see killing it as similar to murder. But in general, the mother's life takes precedence, and some later authorities permit abortion even in non-life-threatening circumstances. Then the Rambam, Maimonides, weighed in. He looked back at the Mishnah text about late-term abortion and said it was justified, *not* because the fetus was not yet a *nefesh*, a person, *but* because when it endangered the woman's life the fetus might be seen as a pursuer, and a pursuer who threatens one's life may be killed in self-defense. The only problem is that a pursuer is also fully a person. And much of the commentary that comes after Maimonides focuses on the fetus as pursuer, rather than on the fetus as non-*nefesh*. Thankfully, some authorities still see the fetus as a non-person and therefore are able to justify abortion for many ways in which a woman's life may be in danger.

This is probably enough for tonight on the legal aspects of the question. So let me return to the scenario with which we began, because I want to think about that pregnant woman. I want to think about her because I think that in all our attention to legal details, American or Jewish, we too often forget that we are talking about real women with real pregnancies that cause them distress for many reasons. If we look at the original scene in this light, I have a lot of questions: Who are these three people? Why are the men fighting? Did one of them get the woman pregnant? Is one her lover and the other her husband? Is one her brother and the other his friend? Is one her father and the other her brother? Does she have children? How did she get pregnant? Is she happy about it, or nervous, or angry? Why is she standing near the men fighting? Does she get into the middle of the fight deliberately, in an effort to abort, or is she just a bystander and the fight gets rowdy? How do the men push her? On purpose? By accident? What in the world is going on?

The Hebrew word for pushing is unusual. Since it is unusual, Rashi feels the need to explain that it means both "pushing" and "hitting," and he shows us several other places in the Bible where it is used, all having something to do with striking or stumbling on a rock. But when we look closer at those texts, we also see their contexts, and perhaps Rashi's underlying message. All his examples of the use of this word have to do with God's protection. Psalm 91, for example, tells us "Because you took the Eternal as your haven, no harm will befall you. . . . God will order angels to guard you wherever you go. They will carry you in their hands lest you hurt your foot on a stone" (vv. 9–11). The word in question here is "hurt,'" as in "hurt your foot." That is what connects to the woman who is pushed—same word. Maybe he meant to say that her being pushed was only as injurious as hurting your foot on a stone. But see the world of protection and security that opens up through that word.

We have to be God's angels here and provide some of that protection and security for a woman today who chooses abortion. We still have to work to ensure that she is able to choose it. But I think we also want to bring her choice out of the shadows, the place outside the camp. We need to develop some set of recognizable stages, perhaps, or status changes, for the woman who decides on and then has an abortion. When someone dies, we Jews have a clear set of stages that are not exact for each mourner, but come pretty close. But when someone has an abortion, we may not want to know her sadness, her anger, her fear. Do we ask if someone wants to announce her abortion during our time of sharing joys and sorrows in services? Do we create a ritual for this important life passage? Do we talk to her months or years later about her thoughts, her grief for what might have been, her joy at having made the right decision, her feeling of being alone?

Kathryn went to Japan last year and while there she visited one of many temples that has a statue of Jizo, a bodhisattva, patron of women, children, and travelers between this life and whatever comes next. Women bring a flat stone, on which they may or may not draw a face; on it they place a bib and put it next to the statue, commemorating abortions, miscarriages, and deaths of children. This would not be the Jewish way—statues, etc. But to have a way to remember and be comforted, well, that should be our way. Just because we are part of a tradition that doesn't necessarily see a fetus as a person doesn't mean we can't recognize that a woman who has an abortion suffers a loss. She may be delighted, or hopeful, or relieved, but for many that feeling of loss is also clear and long-lasting.

As a woman says in a ritual created by Rabbi Leila Gal Berner, "It is the blessing and the curse of being human that we have the capacity to make choices. Sometimes the choices can make our lives rich and beautiful. Sometimes the choices are filled with pain, or it feels as though we have no choice at all. Nothing can make the ending of a pregnancy easy. We affirm you in your painful and difficult choice." In this ritual, those who gather share the woman's pain, allow her to affirm her self, help her acknowledge surviving and being thankful, and support her in seeking healing. As God's angels, we might do all of these things and more.

For us as Jews, it is the woman's life that takes precedence, and we must help to support and heal that life. Let us be angels who serve and support, bless and comfort. We do it for joy, we do it for illness, we do it for death. Why, then, do we relegate abortion to that place outside the camp where it may fester? Our task, as we march or support the marchers from here, is to remember the choosing women as we remember the freedom to choose.

Hagar Spoke to God

Rosh HaShanah 2005 / 5766

Last year at this time I told you about buying a refrigerator at Drimmer's. This year, it's the vacuum cleaner. We had a good vacuum cleaner for years, but it finally started to wear out, and Carol, the woman who cleans our house, said, "You have to buy me a new vacuum cleaner." So I went to Lowe's, talked to the vacuum cleaner guy, and picked one that seemed really good and likely to last for years. It is sort of an upright and with a hose—a great combination. Carol hates it. She never says so; I can just tell. So why did I buy a vacuum cleaner whose main user hates it? Why didn't I ask her what kind of vacuum cleaner she prefers? Or ask her to come shopping with me? I have to admit, in this season of admissions, that I just didn't think. I needed a new vacuum cleaner, I shopped when it was convenient for me, I picked by price and the word of the in-store expert, and I never thought, "How will this be for Carol to use?"

I want to talk tonight about thinking and about the people who work in our homes: the maids, nannies, and health-care aides who make so many of our lives possible and thus hold our homes together. Thinking about them and about us and our homes raises all the large issues of race and class that we have focused on since the recent hurricanes, but through the small intimate lens of home. We have to think about feminism and what is still called women's work and the price of housing and fair wages and immigration. And most important, we have to think about our homes and how our values—our passion for justice, our work for fairness in many large realms—work in our homes. All this because of buying a vacuum cleaner.

Now I am aware as I speak that not everyone here hires some-one to work in your home. You may not see it as priority, or you'd love to but can't afford it, or you do it only rarely—cleaning for a special occasion, say. Or maybe you tried it and didn't like it—you want to stay home with your kids, if you're lucky enough to choose to do so, or you think you do a better job of cleaning, or you don't want to live with the questioning and guilt that often accompany this kind of hiring, or you object, on principle, to the idea of some-one cleaning up after you or acting as a servant. So I recognize that this is not a situation in every one of your homes. But it is a major story in many, many homes in this city and across the coun-try, and as such, we all need to be interested.

For me, it is a fascination as well as a lived reality: What does it mean to bring another woman—almost always a woman—into your home? What does it say about race and class in America that most domestic workers are not white and most of us employers are or that we who think of ourselves as middle class are able to afford to pay others to do work in our homes? What would we do without these workers? What can we do with them?

I confess that I have been ambivalent about how to speak about this with you. Part of me remembers a line reportedly spoken by Reinhold Niebuhr: "The purpose of religion is to comfort the afflicted and afflict the comfortable." Surely most of us sitting here tonight are the comfortable, and we may need to confront some uncomfortable truths. But part of me also knows that the people of Kolot Chayeinu are good, honorable people who hire domestic workers the way you do so much else—with clarity of purpose and respect. Maybe you are already doing the things I will sug-gest here. So which is it? I have wondered. Do I speak to you as if afflicting the comfortable, or do I ask you to help me from your place of greater wisdom and experience? Both are probably true, and you may hear some of both in what follows. I ask you to try to listen with open ears and open hearts, taking in what makes you uncomfortable and nodding in recognition at what you already know.

Let me start with a story: It begins with a couple, a man and a woman in this case, who realize they just can't do everything they want to do and also take care of everything at home. So they do what so many of us do—they bring in another woman who, they hope, will do what they are unable to do. But what they don't do is think. They hire a woman from a different culture than theirs, with different language and different expectations, and they don't think about what it will mean to bring her into their home, their lives. They forget that she will have desires of her own, her own expectations and pride and worries. And so what happens is not what they expected: The woman they hire is haughty with them, not easy-going and compliant as they had imagined. And to their surprise, they each respond to her differently, the man finding her delightful, the woman jealous, unsure, sorry she ever thought to bring in someone—another woman!—into her home. Finally, things get really bad and the woman fires the other, sends her packing in fact, though the man surreptitiously gives her some provisions for the road and some help for her future. They don't hire anyone to replace her, but the suspicions and fears that were raised in their minds while she was there stay with them, and nothing is ever the same.

The woman is Sarah, the man is Abraham, and the woman they hire is Hagar, almost always referred to as Hagar the Egyptian, a stranger who comes to dwell with them, a *shifchah*, a maidservant. And the work they need her to do is, of course, to produce a child when Sarah is unable to do so. Sarah is *akarah*, not able to have children (Genesis 11:30), but *akarah* can also mean "rootless, detached, removed." Or maybe there is something wrong with her *ikar*—her essence. And Abraham cries out to God, "What can you possibly give me, seeing that I shall die childless?" (Genesis 15:2). He is *ariri*, childless, but also *ariri*, stirred up, protesting. They are not happy, and into this time of unhappiness comes Hagar the Egyptian, the *mitzrit*—the one from that narrow place. Sarah says, "Maybe I will be built up through her," or maybe she says, "I will have a child through her" (Genesis 16:2), and Rashi tells us that she is bringing her *tzarah* into the house—*tzarah* being an associate wife, but *tzarah* also meaning "trouble"—*tzuris*. And *tzuris* is what she gets.

Bible translator and commentator Robert Alter calls this the first domestic squabble, though squabble is a small word for the large emotions that can get stirred up. You know what happens. Hagar lords it over Sarah when she is able to conceive quickly, as Sarah never could, and Sarah reacts by treating her so harshly that Hagar runs away. The Ramban—Nachmanides—says Sarah sinned when she did this, and so did Abraham by letting it happen. Abraham had said to Sarah, "Look, your maid is in your hands; do with her as you think right." *Hinei, shifchateich b'yadeich; asi lah hatov b'einayich* (Genesis 16:6). We could atone for their sin by reading this instead as a prescription for all domestic hiring to come: Look, your maid is in your hands; do the good that is in your eyes. In other words, do what you know to be the good, the right, rather than reacting on the basis of conflicted emotion alone.

Doing what is good and right takes a lot of work, psychologically, financially, intentionally. Doing what is good and right means, first, seeing that you are hiring a human being, a person with all the complexities of any human being. For us Jews, that means remembering that every human being is created in the image of God, with God's breath within them. In the context of our story, it means remembering that Hagar spoke to God. When she ran away and again when she was thrown out, God spoke to Hagar in a way she could hear, and she spoke back, understanding God as *El Ro-i*—"the God who sees me." When we get ready to hire someone to work in our homes, we must see that person as fully human, seen by God. And let's do the same for ourselves.

Nachman of Bratslav tells us that when thinking about *t'shuvah*, we should give everyone the benefit of the doubt, including especially ourselves. So let us remember that we work hard, all of us sitting here tonight. We work long hours and it is hard if not impossible to work, spend time with our children if we have them, or our pets or our friends or relatives, do the extra voluntary things we all try to do—including Kolot's activities—and still be able to clean our houses and care for our children or our aging parents without hiring someone to do some of it for us. So this is not about beating ourselves up; it is about trying to do the hiring thoughtfully, in both senses of the word.

First, being thoughtful about hiring means taking a look at Jewish tradition, which presents us with a clear need for fairness in hiring, fair though not extravagant wages, reasonable hours, provision of food, and honoring a contract. This requires us to remember that when we hire someone, even—or especially?—to work in our homes, we are becoming employers. We are not taking in a new member of the family, though sometimes it can come to seem like that to us and sometimes it seems like it to the other person as well.

My mother went back to work when I was about twelve, and she hired a woman to clean our house. When I was about fifteen, something happened between my mother and that woman. I don't remember what, but the woman disappeared from our lives completely. My mother tried for weeks to reach her by phone and then by mail, to no avail. How bereft my mother was, weeping at the sorrow of this loss. She had thought there was love between them, when in fact the other woman saw this as a job, no more. Last week I heard an opposite story, about a woman who left her longtime position after some kind of problem arose and waited for weeks for the employer to call her, to no avail. I worked as a maid for a family in a wealthy suburb right after I graduated from college. They had both a three-year-old and a white kitchen floor, and they had *tzuris* in the house long before I got there, some of which was inflicted on me in the form of harsh treatment and little praise, even for washing that white floor twice daily. But I knew I was not in it for the long haul, that I had gotten a degree and could venture into the wider world of work after doing this as transition. It was a job, no more.

But when I worked as a chambermaid in a motel, the other maids were in it for the long haul. I tried to think about that, making those beds and cleaning those kitchenettes day after day, week after week, year after year, I tried to imagine that. As lovely as it was to sit with them all in one of the rooms at 1:00 p.m. and watch the then-new *All My Children* on that room's TV—I could not. This job thing also gets complicated because the work involved is what we have long called "women's work"—cleaning, cooking, laundry, taking care of children or parents. And we are hiring another woman to do what we women aren't able to. We feel guilty as though we should be able to do it all, and we worry that our children will love her more, and occasionally we fear that our mate will find her more attractive, and here she is living or spending many hours in our house. I wondered if men worry about all this until Brad Lander bravely told us at Open Tent that he feels guilty that the person who works for them and whom they try to pay well still, should she want to, cannot afford to be a tenant in their home.

How about the person—almost always a woman—being hired? She may be worried about her immigration status, as so many of those who do domestic work are recent immigrants. She may be thinking about her own children, as often women leave their children in less-than-perfect child care to come to tend ours or to clean our houses. She may be resentful of having to do this work or envious of our comparatively luxurious homes. If she cares for our elderly parent, she may hate doing the bodily cleaning that is necessary, or complain that she is not a nurse yet is expected to know what she does not know, or tire of our parent's complaints. Most often, she is just trying to make enough money to live and pay her bills, and perhaps have some left over to send to relatives in the old country. Isn't it amazing, therefore, to find so many domestic workers who show great affection for our aged parent or our children; they are able to see into the heart of the matter and accept the rest for what it is.

Yet while we are probably pretty careful about what we pay and the work we expect, domestic workers elsewhere are often badly mistreated, paid slave wages, kept long hours, never given a break. Let me say a word here about race. Usually the woman we hire is a different race than ours: African American, African Caribbean, Asian. How often when we who are white see a black or Hispanic woman wheeling a white child in a stroller do we think, "That's the nanny," whereas when we see a white woman wheeling a black or Hispanic or Asian child, we think, "That's the adoptive mother"? Either of those statements may be incorrect, but the fact that they arise so quickly highlights our assumptions about race. Somehow, in spite of our best intentions, I fear we are teaching many of our children that black and Hispanic women are our servants. Why is an "au pair" often a young white person, whereas a "nanny" is so often black or Hispanic or Asian? And while we don't use the same overtly racist language our parents may have when they spoke about the "schvartzes," we are sometimes helping to create a dichotomy of race and class that we probably thought we would help to bridge.

I am not always sure how to build the bridges, but it is clear that we have to fight our assumptions as we fight for people of any race to be treated fairly when doing domestic work. Fortunately, some domestic workers have begun to organize, in New York City forming Domestic Workers United in 2000 to fight for better pay and conditions. In 2003, they had a victory: the mayor signed Intro #96 and Resolution #135, compelling agencies to take crucial measures to ensure the protection of workers' rights. It only covers workers who work through an agency, however, and we are often hiring workers on their own. But other help has arisen as well. Domestic Workers United and others are suggesting a contract that we can show you copies of and urging employer and worker to enter into a fair contractual relationship. DWU estimates that there are more than six hundred thousand women working as nannies, companions to the elderly, and housekeepers in the greater New York metropolitan area, many of them immigrants from various countries in Asia, Africa, the Caribbean, Latin America.

In last Thursday's *New York Times*, Rick Marin wrote a review of a book called *Laundry*, by Cheryl Mendelson, a former Columbia professor of academic philosophy. In the review, Marin wrote, "For New York's laundry liberals, a variation on the limousine liberal, Latin America exists to lament right-wing regimes and to supply housekeepers. They haven't ironed a shirt since Iran-contra. And they can't imagine why anyone of their class would want to." When I read "laundry liberal" and know that Rick Marin is talking about the Upper West Side, where Professor Mendelson lives, I fear that he is talking about Jews, though the issue of hiring help in one's home applies to all who can afford to do this and should, I am urging, do it right.

Since we are Jews sitting here together on a night designated for thinking about doing right, it seems crucial that we Jews be thoughtful about and to the people who work in our homes. Being thoughtful means more than thinking, more than remembering we are employers and must act accordingly. I know that so many of you sitting here do act thoughtfully, do try to do what is right. Yet so many people don't that it is possible some of us don't either, not out of malice but out of busyness and lack of thought. I was the one who bought the hated vacuum cleaner, remember?

So let's remind ourselves that thoughtfulness also means being a kind employer, one who treats our employee with thoughtfulness. It means sticking to the hours we have set, even when we could use just one more hour to finish that project at work or get to the gym. It means allowing for sick days or family leave; our domestic workers too have children and parents and need to be able to spend time with them when necessary. It means being sure there is Shabbat built into the contract: From biblical days forward, everyone in a household, including servants, is supposed to rest on Shabbat, so let's be sure our full-time workers have a day or two of rest. If those workers live in our homes, let's be sure they have a nice, private space in which to live, free from our children's or our own prying eyes. And let's try to be thoughtful about our employee's benefits, including health insurance. Thoughtfulness may also mean creating a good, respectful way to end the working relationship. How do we fire someone respectfully, as we would if doing it at our jobs? Do we give severance pay of any kind? And what of the worker who has been with us for many years? We have all seen on the Kolot member announcements the pleas for someone to hire the most wonderful nanny. I hope people are finding jobs that way. And how do we mark the end? With a party and a small gift, as from a regular job? With a good reference letter? With any kind of retirement benefits, if the worker has reached retirement age? "Don't cast me aside when I am old," says our Yom Kippur liturgy. Let's pay it heed.

We don't have to figure all this out ourselves. As I said, there are resources available to help, and we have provided some in your *machzors* tonight. I have been helped a great deal in my thinking by the combined understanding of JFREJ [Jews For Racial & Economic Justice] and Domestic Workers United and give special thanks to Temim Fruchter, Kolot member and JFREJ organizer. I urge you to contact them to get help. We will be having a discussion about all this during Sukkot, on October 23—during Sukkot because it reminds us of how fragile our homes can be. I hope many of you will come to keep talking. And later in the winter we at Kolot will be engaging in a series of one-on-one conversations, *sichot* in Hebrew, about the things that concern and engage us most. I hope we will talk about homes as well as the larger world, domestic workers as well as other issues of justice.

We need help. That is why we may hire someone to work in our home in the first place, not to help them, though it often can, but to help ourselves. To keep our homes working, standing, we bring in another woman to do what we cannot do. A *shifchah*—a maidservant. *Shifchah* was also the ancient word for female slave, and for some the line between slavery and employment is pretty thin. Appalling as we find it, there are employers who essentially enslave their workers, giving no rest, no time away, no living wage. The Rambam, Maimonides, taught that one who holds back the wages of a worker is as though taking that worker's soul. We need help. I want to suggest some ways we can think differently about these questions and perhaps come to some better solutions. For it is not just our individual homes that need another adult to help with the work.

Our collective house—our society—is also faltering on the altar of the individual family. Somehow one nuclear family or one person is supposed to be able to do what an entire extended family or community used to do. We are supposed to take care of our children and our parents ourselves, we are supposed to earn a living ourselves, we are supposed to cook and clean and do the laundry and make the school cupcakes all ourselves. Why? When I was a small child, my parents belonged to a babysitting cooperative. Do they still exist? They should. Why hasn't co-housing spread as a way to share common relaxing and dining and laundry space while still maintaining private living quarters? Why aren't we learning lessons from the kibbutzim, like some variation on the children's houses, even while the kibbutz communal life shrinks? In our house, we talk about joining with friends to create our own assisted living facility down the road, sharing costs for a health aide who could live with us as well, each in our own apartments, but with some shared space and many shared costs. That is what co-op living might mean, beyond fighting over the costs of a new roof, which are of course also important.

When Abraham complained to God that he would die childless, *Genesis Rabbah* suggests that Sarah rebuked him for thinking only of himself. We don't want to be guilty of the same thing. We somehow have to begin to think of ways to see beyond ourselves and our own narrow needs, to change our society a bit as we help ourselves. I am amazed that in a neighborhood like Park Slope, where there is a major food co-op to which so many Kolot members belong, and some co-op nursery schools, that there hasn't been more of a move toward cooperative child care in general, cooperative hiring of house cleaners, and even more cooperative living. Wouldn't it be amazing if we could help organize a cooperative of house cleaners or nannies? Kolot member Mary Ann Wilner used to work for just such a cooperative, Cooperative Home Care Associates, a home health care agency in the South Bronx, begun in 1985. Mary Ann tells me that the premise was that workers would do better for themselves and the company if they were invested in the company and that salary and benefits could be better than normal in their industry. There are now close to one thousand workers in the company in the South Bronx, many of them new immigrants—many from Central America, but some from Africa too, as well as African Americans. In an industry that suffers from extreme turnover rates, CHCA has very high retention. It also offers benefits and training that are very unusual in an industry where workers are often seen as expendable. Basically the mission has been: by valuing workers and giving them a good job, workers will in turn take pride in their work and deliver high-quality care to frail and disabled consumers.

My friend Rabbi Sarah Reines reminds me that we have to think about domestic work as honorable work. Let's begin to turn things around, to take a new view that may totally change our perspective. Rabbi Valerie Lieber suggests that we see domestic workers the way we see our lawyer or our accountant, as someone we hire to do necessary tasks for us that we can't do ourselves and that require special skills. We would then be not employers but clients, the ones contracting with the specialist for the work to be done. We do it with painters and builders, who literally help our houses hold up, so why not with the people who metaphorically hold them up day in and day out? As a beginning here, I know some of you who hire the same nanny or house cleaner have decided to share the cost for her health insurance or other benefits. To take that step, we have to be willing to talk about our money, one of the hardest things for us to do. Are we willing to do that?

The Hebrew word *k'saf* or *k'sif* means "to be frightened or ashamed." The word *kesef*—same root—means "money." Let's not let money make us frightened or ashamed; let's have it work for us, instead of the other way around. I made a little discovery while studying about this issue in Jewish sources. As I said, *shifchah* is the word for female servant, or maidservant, or handmaid. If you place a *mem* at the beginning of the word, you get the word *mishpachah*, "family." Hebrew linguist Dr. Joel Hoffman says he doesn't know of any other words with that root. Just *shifchah* and *mishpachah*, the maid and the family. Without that *shifchah* in our midst, our families would be much diminished. And without the *mem*—the *mamon* (money) and the *midot* (qualities) of thoughtfulness, intention, and care—the *shifchah* in our midst would be much worse off. It is our task to continue to remember that *mem* every time we encounter a *shifchah*, so that our *mishpachot*—our households, our families—will stay strong and vital and just.

In conclusion, I want to tell you about a sign I saw years ago in Israel at a bus stop. It gave thanks to the bus driver for doing this important and necessary work. We ought to have such a sign in front of each of our houses where a nanny or house cleaner or elderly companion is working. Thank you, dear domestic worker, for doing this important and necessary work.

Women

Rights for Domestic Workers

June 2, 2007 / 16 Sivan 5767

I want to talk about second chances and about domestic workers, the hardworking, low-paid people—usually women—who clean our houses or care for our children or accompany our elderly parents. I have talked about them before at Kolot, but I speak now because this week we can try to give them a second chance at the benefits granted to other workers.

I'll start, though, with Pesach Sheini, the amazing offer of a second Pesach given by God to those in the wilderness who for ritual or logistical reasons were unable to celebrate Pesach Rishon, Pesach in its original time. Interestingly enough, that Pesach Rishon is also Sheini—it is the first time the people are to celebrate Pesach *after* actually going through the Exodus from Egypt. So second chances all around: a second chance to go back and reflect on the experience of the Exodus via ritual reenactment, a second chance a month later to have that experience if one couldn't do it in the month of Nisan.

Jocelyn reminded me of this passage when we spoke the other day about this service with the wonderful participation by these *b'nei mitzvah* students. She pointed out this surprising passage: God instructs Moses to instruct the people to make the Passover sacrifices, and, says the Torah, "they offered the Passover sacrifice in the first month, on the fourteenth day of the month, at twilight, in the wilderness of Sinai." But there's a problem: there were some people who were ritually impure at the time—they'd had contact with a corpse—and could not offer the Passover sacrifice on that day. They asked Moses, "Why must we be barred from presenting *Adonai's* sacrifice at its set time along with the rest of the Israelites?" And Moses said, "Stand by, and let me hear what instructions God gives about you" (Numbers 9:4–8).

God's answer might have been to tell them to be part of a group offering the sacrifices, but not to do it themselves. But doing it oneself is important, and so God's answer is to offer the people Pesach Sheini—a second time to offer the Passover sacrifice, in the *second* month, on the fourteenth day of the month, at twilight. Not Nisan, but Iyar. *Next* month go do it—if you were kept from doing it for two reasons: you were defiled by a corpse or were on a long journey: *tamei lanefesh o v'derech r'chokah* (Numbers 9:10–11).

And thus we come to the domestic workers. Why here? Because they are in effect asking for a second chance because of being *v'derech r'chokah*: they were far away in time or place when our state and nation enacted laws to protect workers. If this were a Torah story, they might now say, "Why must we be barred from attaining our rights along with the rest of American workers?" And someone—a Moses of their group—might say, "Stand by and let me hear what instructions God gives about you."

One instruction God gives is right here in this *parashah*: "There shall be one law for you, whether stranger or citizen of the country" (Numbers 9:14). I would extrapolate: if other workers—longer time in this country—have rights and benefits that protect them as workers, then these strangers—the new immigrants who do so much of the work that keeps so many homes and families going—these strangers must have those rights and benefits too.

They are asking for them. And it turns out this is not the first time they are asking. This is not Pesach Rishon or perhaps even Sheini. As Albor Ruiz, a columnist in the *Daily News*, reminded us on Thursday, "This is the third time the Domestic Workers Bill of Rights is being introduced in the state assembly and the second time in the state senate."

When labor laws were passed, these workers were *r'chokah*—far from here, or not yet born, not part of the original fighters for justice. But God gave our ancestors who were *v'dereh r'chokah* a Pesach Sheini, a second chance at the table. And if we can pull together, we may be able to offer these workers their well-deserved second chance too.

This coming Thursday evening there is a town hall meeting at which domestic workers will have a chance to speak to legislators and other political leaders, supported by people like us, people who employ domestic workers or who once worked as maids or nannies. I am going to it—to lend support, to add to the numbers, and most importantly, to say that I as a Jew understand my tradition to be saying these rights are overdue. It is time for a second chance for people who make my life run as smoothly as it does. I hope you will join me.

Two Voices

Rosh HaShanah 2003 / 5764

My sermon for Erev Rosh HaShanah 5764 was in two voices—mine and that of **Dr. Debbie Almontaser***, a local and national Muslim educator and peace activist. This is an edited version of the very long sermon we spoke together.*

INTRODUCTION, by Rabbi Lippmann: I went last Sunday to hear the Dalai Lama speak in Central Park. As we waited in a long line on the park road, we listened to a couple of small boys who were waiting with their father. They saw several monks who were dressed similarly to the Dalai Lama, in red and gold robes. They pointed them out to their father, saying, "Look, there are some Muslims." Their father explained that in fact they were Tibetan Buddhist monks. But their misunderstanding stands with us. Since September 11, 2001, we have been interested in, perplexed by, worried about, and misunderstanding Muslims here and around the world. For Jews, this concern is heightened by ongoing Arab anti-semitism and by the horrific violence in Israel and Palestine. We watch with cautious interest as Jewish and Muslim neighborhoods in Brooklyn thrive side by side. Dialogue groups have sprung up around the country, and some of you are participants. Interfaith efforts aimed at greater connection and understanding abound. Here in Brooklyn many of you have protested the detention or deportation without cause of Muslim, Arab, and South Asian men. We have all learned a lot, myself included. Yet children in New York City can still easily confuse Buddhist monks with Muslims in religious garb. We are all as curious and impolitic as children. For all these and more reasons, I invited Debbie Almontaser to speak with me here as we enter this new year, Rosh HaShanah or Ras a Sannah. The issues that have grabbed me for some time, that tear at my heart and my kishkes, all seem to involve Arabs and Muslims. And I felt that I could not speak alone again without also speaking to and with someone who could teach me, argue with me, and give me hope, the gift sorely lacking for so many of us. . . . Maybe there is nothing more we can do than to stand here together as a new Jewish year begins, to say, "It is a new year, and we must find new ways. To do that, we have to start talking."

DEBBIE: I am honored and humbled to be invited here on this Holy Day, and very happy to be able to speak with you all.

ELLEN: I met Debbie on September 15, 2001, which was Shabbat Shuvah, the Sabbath of Return that year. We had invited the Dialogue Project, begun by Marcia Kannry, to join us for discussion following September 11. Debbie and her husband Naji were among those who came, and Debbie woke us up to what it felt like to be a Muslim American in the wake of 9/11, by telling us how afraid she was of being attacked in those hard days, as she is a Muslim woman who wears the hijab and is thus identifiable. Several members of our groups offered to help, by driving her or escorting her. That was the good part, the part that made us feel connected and hopeful, able to help a neighbor in distress. But we also heard that day and for weeks that followed an opinion voiced there by a Muslim man that Israel and the Mossad were in fact the ones behind the terror of September 11. It was the kind of thinking that made us Jews feel alienated and afraid, disconnected and unhopeful. Those feelings—the connected and the alienated—have persisted for us and for Muslims here. So when Debbie and I first spoke about talking together here, I said we could only do it if we spoke of the hard questions as well as the easy ones, the ones about terrorism and occupation as well as the ones about how similar our language and cultures are or about our American immigrant experiences. Just so you know, as I wanted to, Debbie was born in Yemen and came to this country at three, after her father had been able to send enough money back to get his wife and daughter. She grew up in Buffalo. I was born here, into a family of longtime American Jews who came from Germany in the 1850s and from Russia and Poland in the 1880s. Since we met, I have been in Debbie's home, and she in mine. We are not yet friends but are becoming so. Debbie has become a major activist on behalf of her people here, and we have seen each other somewhat often at protests and gatherings of one sort or another. And *she* went to a special dinner with the Dalai Lama after his Central Park talk! So let us begin. We start with text, for both of us are informed and inspired by our sacred texts. And we begin with the same story, told two ways, reminding us that our traditions spring from the same source. We start with the story of Sarah and Hagar, two women trapped in place, coming from different places. Their story is foundational for Judaism and Islam.

FROM TORAH: *Sarai, Abram's wife, had borne him no children. She had an Egyptian maidservant whose name was Hagar. And Sarai said to Abram, "Look, Adonai has kept me from bearing. Consort with my maid; perhaps I too shall have a son through her." And Abram heeded Sarai's request. So Sarai, Abram's wife, took her maid, Hagar the Egyptian . . . and gave her to her husband Abram as concubine. He cohabited with Hagar and she conceived; and when she saw that she had conceived, her mistress was lowered in her esteem. And Sarai said to Abram, "The wrong done me is your fault! I myself put my maid in your bosom; now that she sees that she is pregnant, I am lowered in her esteem. Adonai decide between you and me!" Abram said to Sarai, "Your maid is in your hands. Deal with her as you think right." Then Sarai treated her harshly and she ran away from her* [Genesis 16:1–6].

ELLEN: I have such trouble with this story. I try to find myself in Sarah and can't find a way in. I keep wishing for Sarah and Hagar to be friends, instead of mistress and maid.

DEBBIE: Sarah figures very little in the Quran's version of our story.

FROM THE QURAN: *For many years, Abraham and Sarah lived as exiles, and during all that time they had no children. Sarah, having passed the age of childbirth, suggested to Abraham that he marry her maid and companion Hagar. Abraham and Hagar married, and Hagar bore him a son who was called Ishmael. Many years later, God rewarded Sarah for her patience and faith by giving her a son of her own named Isaac, and tidings of a grandson named Jacob.*

DEBBIE: Our situations in the world today are also very different. Jews are comfortable in America now, after three or four or more generations and easily fit into society. Muslims, especially observant Muslims, show our identity wherever we go. Many Muslims in New York City are immigrants who come from all over the world and find it difficult as Muslims and immigrants. The "War on Terror" has produced new terrors for us. . . . The proposed Patriot Act 2 will be a disaster for us all *because* it will not leave anyone untouched. Since September 11, essential rights and freedoms that were once guaranteed to all Americans have been substantially degraded, especially for Arab, Muslim, and South Asian men. Many Americans still don't realize the significance of what we have lost.

ELLEN: I have been surprised that there haven't been more Jews protesting the detentions and deportations that have already taken place. We have short memories if we forget the times and places in which we were the suspected ones, the different ones who could not fit in, the ones ordered to special registrations. The violence and fear in our world make it complicated for us.

DEBBIE: I want to say clearly that Islam is not a religion of terror or violence. The root word of Islam is *salaam,* which means "peace." The word *Muslim* means "submissive to God, the creator, the bearer of peace" and refers to a follower of Islam. Its root word is also "peace." Many verses in the Quran denounce the taking the lives of others. To the question "Why so many Arab and Muslim terrorists?" I would rather ask our world leaders, "Why is there so much poverty in this day and age? Why are there so many people who are disfranchised and stripped of their human rights as individuals?" These are the things that lead people to terror, not religion. Religion is misused, to frame terrorist acts. Terrorism is a problem that exists in all religions and ethnic backgrounds. I think a terrorist has no identity, no religion, and no nationality in the human race if his motives are to take the lives of people. The 9/11 terrorists who acted in the so-called name of Islam do not know anything about Islam, if that is how they misused it. Muslims do not acknowledge them as Muslims but as creators of havoc.

FROM THE QURAN: *Abraham, Hagar, and baby Ishmael set off on a journey. For days and nights they traveled, until they finally arrived at a barren valley in the desert of the Arabian peninsula. It was a desolate place with no vegetation and no water. There they stopped, and Abraham gave Hagar their remaining provisions of food and water. Surprised, Hagar asked, "Will you leave us here then?" Abraham made no reply. Once again, Hagar asked him if he would leave them in this place, and again Abraham made no response. She then realized that Abraham must be following a divine command and she asked him, "Did God command you to leave us here alone?" Abraham replied that such was the case, and Hagar declared, "We have God with us, no harm will come to us." And so, Hagar and Ishmael were left alone in this barren valley.*

FROM THE TORAH: *Early next morning Abraham took some bread and a skin of water and gave them to Hagar. He placed them over her shoulder, together with the child, and sent her away. And she wandered about in the wilderness of Beer-Sheva. When the water was gone from the skin, she left the child under one of the bushes, and went and sat down at a distance, a bowshot away; for she thought, "Let me not look on as the child dies." And sitting thus afar, she burst into tears* [Genesis 21:14–16].

ELLEN: So Abraham leaves them alone with their fear and sorrow. Who is Abraham now? This year we are the ones left alone with our fear and sorrow. And nowhere is that fear and sorrow focused more than in Israel and Palestine. This may be the toughest thing we have to face together. We are both connected to the place, the land—*haaretz*, Jews say. I lived there for nearly a year when I began rabbinical school, in 1986 and '87. I was back early in 2000. It was peaceful when I was there, and I have had to learn what was going on with Palestinians at those times, when it wasn't peaceful for them.

DEBBIE: I have never been there. For me, Israel is the place of the holy sites of Islam, and the source of Judaism, Christianity, and Islam. That is sacred ground—God's place.

ELLEN: And what of it as a Jewish state? Do you think of it like that? How?

DEBBIE: Israel and Palestine are wounds we as Jews and Arabs share. Israel today is a state that I feel does not encompass the moral values taught in Judaism. I pray that one day it will exemplify what I respect and admire about Judaism. . . . Last year, I helped create a series of workshops for Muslim youth, with a few Jews and Christians participating. At the end, they created a mural about their hopes for the future. On the mural was the Star of David. One of the young men who helped with the project said that a few of the children felt very comfortable acknowledging Judaism through the Star of David, but not the Israeli flag. One of the boys said he sees the flag as an oppressive symbol, but sees the Star of David as a religious symbol that in Islam must be respected and honored, because the Jews are the people of the Book. It's amazing that children can distinguish between the religion, the people, and the political situation, while adults have a hard seeing the difference. Gandhi talked about it; Mandela and Martin Luther King also: there can only be real forgiveness when we can separate the people from the political structures that we live within.

ELLEN: Sometimes it is hard to make such distinctions, and we may not always want to. Judaism is not just a religion, any more than Islam is just a religion. We Jews are also a people, struggling with our political situation and our connections as people. When I work with people toward conversion to Judaism, we always have at least one conversation about their relationship with Jews they don't feel related to. Often that means very Orthodox people they see on the subway or fundamentalist Israeli settlers they read about in the paper. And I say, "It may be that they feel like distant cousins whom you'd never want in your house. But they are cousins, and you must remember that." *Pirkei Avot*, the *Ethics of the Fathers*, says it this way: *Kol Yisrael areivim zeh lazeh*—"Every Jew is mixed up with, responsible for every other." So I must acknowledge that Ariel Sharon and Israeli settlers are my cousins, even when I think that at best they make one wrong decision after another. I abhor targeted assassinations. The wall Israel is building is walling people in, creating ghettos, another abhorrence for Jews, for whom the ghetto was created. The bulldozing of houses is terrible, punishing an entire extended family for what one son or daughter has done. Checkpoints, incursions, the list goes on. And I write letters and send money to peace groups and am thinking about how to get over there this year—maybe we'll go together, Debbie. And I grieve as well as rage: Because I remember riding buses in Jerusalem and sitting in cafés in Tel Aviv, I can only feel that a part of me is murdered when a murderer explodes in a bus or café or university. Those killed are my people too. Do you feel that way? Are they your people, the suicide bombers? And the ones killed by Israel, are they?

DEBBIE: For me, any child killed is a child killed regardless of their faith or ethnic background. The killing of innocents of all ages on both sides tears my inner soul to pieces. And the poor soldiers who are forced into the violence pay the price by losing their lives. The tactics of suicide bombings go against every teaching in Islam that I love and cherish because it is forbidden to take the lives of others as well as your own life. Your life and the lives of others are sacred in God's eyes. Many people in the Arab and Muslim communities look at me like I'm crazy. They feel that I am not sympathetic to "the cause" because I denounce suicide bombings. But what is their end? Is there peace? Will there be a Palestinian state? I work to change people's minds, especially among young people. Sometimes I think adults' minds can't be changed. But I am a teacher of children and youth, so that is often where I put my energy. Like Hagar, I try to save a child.

FROM THE TORAH: *God heard the cry of the boy, and an angel of God called to Hagar from heaven and said to her, "What troubles you, Hagar? Fear not, for God has heeded the cry of the boy where he is. Come, lift up the boy and hold him by the hand, for I will make a great nation of him." Then God opened her eyes and she saw a well of water. She went and filled the skin with water, and let the boy drink. God was with the boy and he grew up* [Genesis 21:17–21].

FROM THE QURAN: *The heat was fierce and there was no shelter under which they could take refuge. Before long their provisions began to run low, and in desperation Hagar started looking for some water. Leaving Ishmael sitting on the ground, she ran to the top of a small hill called al-Safa, hoping to see some sign of travelers who might be passing by and who would help them. There were none to be seen. Hagar went down to comfort Ishmael and then climbed up another hill, al-Marwa, in the hope of finding some help. Again she was disappointed. From al-Marwa she ran to al-Safa, and then back to al-Marwa again. Seven times she climbed these hills and each time she saw nothing. Finally, when she returned to Ishmael, he was too weak to even cry. With great sorrow, Hagar bent down to pick him up, when lo and behold a spring gushed forth from under his feet! Hagar thanked God for saving them and gave her son some water to drink. It was not long before passing caravans noticed that birds had begun to gather in the barren valley where a spring of water now gushed. Soon travelers took to halting there and gradually people began to settle in this place. They called their little town Bakka, or Mecca. It was in this very town that, many years later, the prophet Muhammed was born from the descendants of Ishmael and where he began preaching the message of Islam.*

ELLEN: Rabbi Ben Hollander reminds us that there was no miracle in this story. God did not *provide* Hagar a well or spring of water. Rather, she opened her eyes in a new way. She lifts her son up, first, and then sees the water. What do we have to lift up, care for, or move out of the way before we can see new ways of life and hope? Maybe we need to forget history, start a new religion. In our new religion, Sarah and Hagar would be friends, or lovers, planning to have a child together, or two children, each loved, cared for. There would be laughter and listening, Yitzchak, Yishma-el. For now, maybe what we can start to do is teach our children. Here at Kolot Chayeinu, we have a chart of the Arabic alphabet, and someone came to teach the kids the letters. We have talked about what goes on in Israel and Palestine. Last spring, in a retreat about Israel, they participated in a mock checkpoint and also had to decide if they would serve in the Israeli army and what they would do about scarcity of water there. This year they started school by singing "Od Yavo Shalom Aleinu"—"Peace will yet come to us and to everyone, shalom, salaam." They also learn about the joys of Israel, joys I hope they will one day be able to see and experience.

DEBBIE: For the Muslim youth, I will continue as I have in the past to expose them to events and conferences that exemplify coexistence. I will never forget the look one of the girls had on her face when I took her with me to a Women in Black vigil. She was shocked to see Jewish men and women who cared about the Palestinian cause. Or the time two boys and my daughter heard Jeff Halperin, a Jew, speak at Columbia University against the demolition of homes in Palestine. And the time they went to B'nai Jeshurun to hear the bereaved Palestinian and Israeli parents share their pain. Events such as these have helped the kids see New York and even Israeli Jews from another light. They now know there are many who are acknowledging their pain, and thus they too have developed empathy for civilians killed in Israel.

ELLEN: In the mural project, you asked the kids at the Muslim Youth Center to express their hope for the future. My hope for the future is that the Israeli flag will not be stained with the blood of Jews or Palestinians and will not be seen by us or by Muslim youth in Brooklyn as a sign of oppression. My hope for the future is that children in Israeli and Palestinian schools will learn each other's history as clearly as it can be told and will not be taught to demonize the other. My hope for the future is that all New York children will one day know enough about the Jews and the Buddhists and the Muslims that they won't mix us up. And my hope for the future is that one day we will be mixed up—*areivim zeh bazeh*—we will live as neighbors, colleagues, learners, and friends, sharing our common culture and learning of our differences, responsible for each other: *Yad b'yad, yed b'yed*, hand in hand.

DEBBIE: My hope for the future is that Jews and Arabs/Muslims can reunite to bury the hurtful past we've shared, as did Isaac and Ishmael when they came together to bury their father Abraham. I hope for this in my lifetime. My hope for the future is that we continue efforts such as this to educate our communities about one another's culture and traditions.

On the Death of
Osama Bin Laden

May 2011

I have been grappling with many thoughts since I learned early
this morning the news that Osama bin Laden had been killed. At
one moment, I was stunned, happy, worried, puzzled, and horrified. How about you?

Some of you will remember that I spoke at Union Square in
October 2001 as we went to war precipitously in Afghanistan. I
felt that vengeance was not enough of a reason for it and fearful
of what kind of war we might wage if driven by pure vengeance.
In my Yom Kippur sermon a week or so earlier, I quoted from
Deuteronomy 20:19, in which God instructed against destroying
trees as part of the wartime siege of a city. I said: "When you make
war you have to take care . . . emotion-driven vengeance is not
an option." The trees teach us about how, in war, to take care of
human beings, God's most precious creation.

My great fear then, almost ten years ago, was that we—the
U.S.—would kill thousands of non-combatants. I frankly hoped
we might quickly capture Osama bin Laden and bring him to justice. And I have hoped that, in a back of the mind kind of way,
every year since.

And now he is dead. Am I sorry? Not at all. Do I wish we could
hear him in a court of law instead? Absolutely. Rabbi Brad Artson

wrote in 2001, "Justice is the result of a process designed to produce fairness and accuracy in pinpointing proper culprits; revenge
follows no such process and often is indiscriminate in its targets."
Surely Bin Laden was a proper culprit, and bringing him to trial
would have served justice well. It would have taken enormous
capacity for compassion and for justice, a hard thing to imagine in
the tenth anniversary year of 9/11.

So now he is dead. And while I am not sorry, I am very sorry
that so many people's response was to gather in what appeared
to be vengeful groups, drinking, shouting, waving flags, laughing,
and singing.

Two weeks ago, we all sat around seder tables and took drops
of wine from our cups as we recited the names of the plagues God
inflicted on Pharaoh and the Egyptians. We took out those drops to
show we intentionally diminished our joy at that human suffering.
Some of us may have told the midrashic story of how, when the
just-freed Hebrew slaves danced and sang at the other side of the
sea as Egyptian soldiers and horses drowned, God rebuked them
(or rebuked dancing, singing angels) by saying, "They too are my
creatures, and you would dance and sing at their demise? (BT
M'gillah 10b)"

It is understandably human to be at least somewhat happy that
the man who masterminded the killing of nearly three thousand
Americans is dead. But it is unnecessarily vengeful to sing and
dance and drink and party to celebrate.

Two other things occur to me today. One is that this killing
must not somehow set off a new round of anti-Muslim, anti-
Islam speech and violence. President Obama was careful to say,
"We must—and we will—remain vigilant at home and abroad.
As we do, we must also reaffirm that the United States is not—
and never will be—at war with Islam. . . . Bin Laden was not
a Muslim leader; he was a mass murderer of Muslims. Indeed,
al Qaeda has slaughtered scores of Muslims in many countries,
including our own."

Second is the uncomfortable understanding that this killing will be good for President Obama politically. I am saddened to realize that what so many of us want in a leader is a "tough guy." I have wanted our president to be tough in many ways: in stronger bank regulation, in broad programs of job creation, in pushing for health care reform. I was not really thinking about him being the one who would find and kill Osama bin Laden. But he is. And it will play well in many parts of the country, perhaps too with those who danced and sang at Times Square or Ground Zero last night. I pray he keeps the sober tone he spoke with last night and does not get drawn into triumphalism of a sort we do not need.

Osama Bin Laden is dead. I hope his movement shrinks, though I fear the opposite. I fear our own tendency to vengeance and triumph. I fear my own forgetting that every human being was created in the image of God. I am not sorry he is dead. But I refuse to dance and sing.

On Being Honored by the Lambda Independent Democrats

April 10, 2005

Thank you all. Many thanks to Debra Silber for her lovely presentation; it is my honor, Deb, to receive this from you, and to join the long line of outstanding activists who have received it before me, including so many (I am happy to say) who are members of or connected to Kolot Chayeinu. I am so happy that so many Kolot members are here as well, because I could never do what I do without their support and friendship. That goes double for my beloved partner of twenty-one years, Kathryn Conroy. We were married under a chuppah last year at twenty years and know that we are truly married and are only waiting for the state of New York to recognize it.

Mostly, I am incredibly honored to receive the Peter Vogel Award. I didn't know him, but my friends and Kolot members Phil Saperia and Skipper Edwards did, and they told me about this warm and gentle man who worked tirelessly for equal rights for us LGBT people while forming a deep, loving ongoing partnership with Don. *Zichronam livracha*, may their memories be for a blessing. Alan Fleishman reminded me that Peter was one of the early heroes in the work against HIV and for LGBT rights, so we all stand on his shoulders. I feel like I stand taller for it.

I am standing here because last spring I took a very public stand for gay marriage rights in New York. I've never seen so much press!

But what was really moving that day on the steps of City Hall was the wedding itself: two wonderful women, Ruth Finkelstein and BC Craig, with their four-year-old son Sam really getting married as their friends and family and Kolot members and a zillion rabbis looked on and wept, really getting married even though as I said then, "By the power vested in me by the state of New York to do any wedding but this one."

It was an amazing day, and it added to the amazing days in San Francisco and Massachusetts and New Paltz, and for a little while in spring we thought we were going to have legal gay marriage all over the place. Now it's spring again, and we are wiser, perhaps, but we are going to have it. It's just going to take a little longer than we hoped. We Jews spent forty years in the desert after the parted sea, forming strategy teams and contacting elected officials to get to true liberation. So another spring looks like a drop in the bucket. And I want you to know that on May 24 busloads of clergy people are traveling to Albany to try for another amazing spring day in our long exodus.

"Exodus" means "coming out" and so we are in this fight. I know there are a lot of people who think this marriage stuff is a distraction from working on the really important issues. I understand what they say, but it looks to me like the fight for marriage equality carries with it the fight against so many kinds of discrimination at once that it is really an efficient way of moving forward. And while "exodus" means "coming out," the Hebrew name for that book of the Bible is *Sh'mot*, "names." In Hebrew, the emphasis was on who came out, and the "big Who" that made it happen. *HaShem*, we say, "The Name," referring to God. And I do think it is with God's help that Ruth and BC, Phil and Jim, Skipper and David, Emily and Patty, and yes, Kathryn and I have gotten married and will some day be married legally. May it come *bimheirah v'yameinu*, speedily in our time.

I invoke God deliberately, in part because we have a pretty good relationship and in part because God is invoked so often by those who oppose us. So it is crucial to say that there are hundreds and thousands of people who connect to God and who believe that gay marriage is right and good. I have gotten so sick of hearing phrases like "It's Adam and Eve, not Adam and Steve." So I want to end here with a little story I wrote, a corrective of sorts in response to those hate-filled voices. Some of this story was written long ago, and some just the other day [and some after the event].

A Bible story for us all: On the day that God made earth and heaven, no shrub of the field being yet on the earth and no plant of the field yet sprouted, God had not caused rain to fall on the earth and there was no human to till the soil, and wetness would well from the earth to water all the surface of the soil, then God fashioned the human, humus from the soil, and blew into his nostrils the breath of life, and the human became a living creature. And God planted a garden in Eden, to the east, and placed there the human. And God took the human and set him down in the garden of Eden to till it and watch it. And God said, "It is not good for the human to be alone, I shall make him a fitting partner to be beside him." And God took more of the humus from the soil, and fashioned another human, and blew into this one's nostrils the breath of life, and this human too became a living creature. And the first human said, "This one at last, is bone of my bones and flesh of my flesh." And the two of them were naked, these first humans, and they were not ashamed. And the human, who was named Adam after the *adamah*, the soil from which he came, called his partner's name Ezra, for the help he had brought to his life and soul.

In another corner of the garden lived Eve and Lilith, those first women, also born of the breath of life and the earth beneath their feet; they too tilled the soil and grew their food and flowering plants, and they were beginning to raise another generation. Their children would grow to play with the children of other pairs, this time of men and women together, play peacefully and without the angry calling of names. And so they all lived, tilling the garden and enjoying its fruits, until a snake came into their lives bringing shame and uncertainty, and their bliss was destroyed.

Ever since, the descendants of Eve and Lilith, Adam and Ezra, later mockingly called Steve, have yearned to return to that garden, to the life of partner with partner, matching helpers both. So to you, their descendants, I say, it is now our job to redeem their dream and make real that return. As we make our exodus from the narrow place of shame and uncertainty, we remember all the names and pledge to carry them to the broad expanse of freedom.

Pesach Sheini

May 29, 2010 / 16 Sivan 5770

How many people here have ever heard of Pesach Sheini, the second Passover?

Jonathan Mark, reporter for the *Jewish Week* newspaper, calls it "a club-fighter of a holiday so obscure and cauliflowered of ear that it doesn't even have an English name."

Pesach Sheini is an innovation described in this week's *parashah, B'haalot'cha*:

> *And* Adonai *spoke to Moses, saying, "Speak to the Israelite people, saying: When any of you or of your posterity who are defiled by a corpse or are on a long journey would offer a Passover sacrifice to* Adonai—*they shall offer it in the second month, on the fourteenth day of the month, at twilight. . . . But if a householder who is pure and not on a journey refrains from offering the Passover sacrifice, that person shall be cut off from kin." (Numbers 9:9–13)*

This decision comes after an appeal to Moses by some householders who were, the Torah says, impure by reason of a corpse and appealed to Moses to appeal to God. Their appeal was "Impure though we are by reason of a corpse, why must we be debarred from presenting *Adonai*'s offering at its set time with the rest of the Israelites?" (Numbers 9:7).

This is a problem. Why should they be debarred? Moses does not know, so consults God directly. This happens four other times in Torah, when a question leads to a new law. In this case, the new law is to establish Pesach Sheini, the second Pesach for those who are ritually impure or too far away to be able to do the Pesach sacrifice at Pesach Rishon—the first Passover. Later commentators question the sincerity of those who need a Pesach Sheini: Are they really too far away, asks Rashi, or just far from their Jewish commitment?

Pesach Sheini becomes the holiday of second chances. Reporter Jonathan Mark says it evokes Passover, but it's just one day, not eight, you can eat bread, there are no restrictions, and there is no seder. Some today eat leftover matzah that day (talk about second chances!), but this day is less about matzah and more about leftovers. Mark notes beautifully, "There is really nothing to do on Pesach Sheni but 'give those who ache from old errors back all their mistakes.'" But a modern commentator named Yonathan Sredni writes, "One might think that today we are too far removed from those Biblical days. Even if I take initiative and have the strongest desires and purest motives and am sure I am in the right and that I really deserve what I am asking for, what guarantee do I have that God will follow through?"[28]

So today I want to give Bill Clinton back a mistake and celebrate the House of Representatives' decision to repeal "Don't Act, Don't Tell." Repeal is not done yet; the Senate has to weigh in, but it probably will come to pass. Way overdue: It was a mixed blessing of a law from the beginning, better than what had come before, sort of, but damaging in all kinds of ways to good soldiers who were gay or lesbian. Repeal is a kind of Pesach Sheini—a way to give back the mistake, to address the yearning of gay and lesbian soldiers and would-be soldiers to be counted and not debarred.

I have two problems with it, though. One, I can't help thinking that the Israelites who offered a sacrifice on Pesach Shieni were

28. Jonathan Mark, "Pesach Sheni—There Are No Sins, Only Second Chances," in The New York Jewish Week, April 28, 2010, http://jewishweek.timesofisrael.com/pesach-sheni-there-are-no-sins-only-second-chances/.

seen as second-class citizens and so of course have been the gay soldiers known to everyone as gay but unable to say so, to stand tall, to serve proudly. I am not convinced that repeal will change that. And two, I am not all that happy that the biggest victory in some time for gay rights is one that allows gay soldiers the same rights as anyone else to be blown up by a roadside bomb. I wonder why any young men and woman want to serve in the wars we are engaged in now. But they do, so I guess we are supposed be glad young gay men and women can too. It is like being glad that someone who had to deal with a death and could not attend to Pesach can complete his obligation a month later, alone, no ceremony, no family table, no communal connection.

War is still hell, as it was when Memorial Day was established in 1868. So it is a mixed victory at best to have Don't Ask, Don't Tell repealed. Let's give President Clinton back his mistake, let's be glad for those who want to serve as open, proud gay men and women, and let's work hard for peace.

And Pesach Sheini? I love it when Moses has to ask God what to do and God tells him. I love it that God can innovate and that Moses can innovate, and I only hope that we as a society can think of better ways to innovate now, for Jews and for LGBT Americans.

Kicking Off
Pride Week in Brooklyn

June 4, 2012

[Cantor Lisa B. Segal sings *L'maan Achai V'Rei-ai*.] Thank you, Rev. Charles L. A. Watterson for inviting us, and thank you, Rev. Carmen Mason-Browne for hosting and leading us. And thank you to all of you for being here tonight as we begin LGBT Pride Week in Brooklyn! Special thanks from me to Kolot Chayeinu members Shelly Weiss and Mackenzie Reynolds for sending thoughts that show up in my talk tonight.

Last August, my partner and I went to Borough Hall with a handful of close family and friends and got married. We caused a bit of a ruckus by singing as we stood in line—"Going to the chapel and we're gonna get married"—and laughing and taking pictures. Next to us in line were a young Orthodox Jewish couple, a young white couple from Russia, an African American couple with five children, and another couple with one child, all three dressed to the nines in red satin. It was a picture of Brooklyn and no one batted an eye at any of it. Marriage brought us together.

When we walked out on the street on our way to more celebration, we both realized that something had shifted. We had thought this marriage, unlike our more formal wedding seven years before, would be sort of like getting a driver's license. It wasn't, unless you count my first driver's license, the one that set me free and let me go out into the world with more authority than I had ever had. For us, being married by the state in a shabby little chapel in a government building turned out to mean a lot. But what it meant was not pride; what it meant was being recognized. Being seen.

Everyone wants to be seen. That is truly what brings us together. What a community does more than anything else is create a frame in which each member can be seen. Seen and not judged, seen and offered opportunity, seen and embraced.

That is what LGBT community does, ideally. Even as we all recognize that the L, G, B, and T parts of the community are different and have different needs, and even as we recognize that even within those subcategories everyone is an individual with different needs and desires, being part of this community has long helped us be seen in a way we could not always be in the larger world, especially, sometimes, in our churches, temples, mosques, and synagogues. What a step, to stand here in a church and speak these words tonight!

In the Jewish community, we read mostly consecutive portions from the Torah each week through the year. In last week's portion, in the Book of Numbers, we read a section called *Naso*, which means "to lift or raise." It begins with a census of the people of Israel as they are traveling through the wilderness. But while we talk about "counting heads," the Torah speaks of "lifting the head"—*naso et rosh*—as a way of counting people. I am always amazed by this lifting. Picture what it means: Lift your own head. What happens? Usually more of you lifts. And your face can be seen. Imagine then the experience of moving along row after row of people—millions, it must have been in that wilderness—and lifting their heads so they stood taller and their faces were clearly seen. Instead of just counting people, they were making people count. Every single one of those millions counted. And every single one of the millions of LGBT people in this country needs to count.

That is where we who already feel the lift come in. We have to lift the head of every one. And we have to shine light on the dark places, the places where people are bowed down in fear and isolation and bigotry.

This week's Torah portion is called *B'haalot'cha*: "When you raise the lamps." It is an instruction to the ancient priest serving in the ancient Temple. Today, we are reminded to shed light in ways that illuminate—that light up, and maybe lighten up. The Lubavitcher Rebbe, of all unlikely people for me to quote, said that "the spiritual significance of the lighting . . . is that one should be a 'lamplighter' who ignites latent potential within [the human soul]." He said that "the endeavor must be to kindle the lamp 'so that a flame arises of its own accord.' In teaching and influencing one's fellow, the objective should be to establish him or her as a self-sufficient luminary: to assist in developing the talents and abilities so that the human lamp independently glows and, in turn, kindles the potential in others."

This is how we shine a light to enable each one to know "this little light of mine, I'm gonna let it shine." But we need to shine an ever stronger light too into the most hidden corners. In the Jewish community, we have an often repeated phrase: "Never again." It refers to the Holocaust and means both never again mass killing of Jews and never again genocide anywhere if we can help it. So tonight we too need to say, "Never again."

Never again to be cast away by those who use the Bible to dismiss us; never again a college student jumping off a bridge to his death because his roommate mocked his sexual connection; never again a parent unable to be with a child because of misguided lawyers and enacted prejudice against LGBT folks; never again a trans person attacked on the street just for being transgender; never again LGBT deaths due to neglect and abandonment; never again state-approved killing of LGBT people anywhere in the world. Never again!

And the antidote?

To me, it is to say, Thank God. Thank God for the wisdom, clarity, heart that God places in human beings and thank God for the times those gifts are used for the good; thank God for the "It Gets Better" videos; thank God for LGBT centers in cities across the country and all kinds of other LGBT organizations; thank God for gay churches and synagogues who paved the way; thank God for churches like this one and synagogues like ours and the amazing efforts of gay Muslims that will one day create a gay mosque and then an all-inclusive one, and those of every religious group who open rather than closing the doors; thank God for the activists and advocates of every generation who pushed hard and keep pushing; thank God for whoever helped change Barack Obama's mind; thank God for fighting back, for resistance; thank God for the glory of so so so so many more people than ever having the courage to come out as queer, as trans, as gender variant, even in the face of this crazy world we live in.

Thank God. Thank God. Thank God. Amen.

Part Five

Emet

Truth

Truth

Forgiving God

Yom Kippur 1998 / 5759

Rabbi Elimelech of Lizhensk used to tell this story to his *chasidim* every year before Yom Kippur:

Once there was an ordinary Jew named Chaim who ran a country tavern, and it was his custom to write down, between one Yom Kippur and the next, all the wrongs that he had committed against the people he served: Sometimes he did not give them the full measure of vodka, occasionally he did not give them the right change—whatever his sins, he wrote them down. And he wrote down in another book every wrong done him by the landlord from whom he rented the tavern or by the peasants of that place.

One year, things went badly for Chaim. That year he got up early on the day before Yom Kippur and sat down to speak to God. "Ribono shel olam, *God in heaven,*" *he began,* "*I know that I am a plain Jew. But in no way does this permit me to be a thief. Yes, You and I both know that I am a thief. Take a look in this book—I will read it to You word for word.*" *And Chaim read each of his small thefts out loud, finally toting it all up to twenty-three rubles and change. He banged his head, and cried out to God,* "*Master of the universe, I am horrified. I cannot go the synagogue. Of course I know that today everyone will be present for* Kol Nidrei, *but I cannot do it. I am not ashamed before people, since they know nothing of me, but before You.*

"Truth to tell," Chaim continued, "I don't know why my family or even other Jews should go to the synagogue. I at least know the great secret. I know that not only I, but also You, God of the universe, will not be in synagogue. It stands to reason, for I have another little book. Let me read to You from that book, too. Look! Here, some peasants forced their way into my bar and wrecked it. Well, these are not my peasants, they are Your peasants. Therefore, God, You owe me 50 rubles. And take another look. A few days later, a couple of soldiers blew in. Everyone began in a good mood, but when they got drunk, they started in. They beat me up, they took the whiskey, and they ran off. The damages, with no exaggeration, came to 70 rubles. These were not my soldiers," Chaim shouted. "They were Your soldiers, so I wrote the damages to Your account. Do You want to know what You owe me for the whole year? You, God in heaven, owe me, Chaim, the thief, 226 rubles!

"I've been thinking," Chaim went on. "If I, a simple human being, am ashamed before You because I stole twenty-three rubles, and I am therefore not going to the synagogue, how dare You, who owe so much more, come to such a holy place? But that raises a serious question: What will it look like if Your Jews are in the synagogue and You, dear God, are not there? So, Ribono shel olam, I have a deal to offer You, a good deal. Do You know that I, Chaim the inn-keeper, am ready to forgive You for all the evil that Your servants have done to me? I am willing to forgive and forget. And what do I want from You? Just one small thing. Just as I am saying to You, 'I forgive You,' say the same precious words to me. . . .

"No, no, on second thought, that's not such a good deal. If I am already doing business with You, I want it to be a big deal. I don't think only of myself, ordinary man that I am. I want You to ask for forgiveness, and I want You to say, 'I forgive you,' to all the sinners standing in the synagogue tonight. Yes, the entire people."

Chaim remained standing there, frightened by his own brazenness. He stood with his head bowed and, suddenly, as if he had heard an

answer, he called to his family, "Hurry, hurry, it's Yom Kippur; we
must go to the synagogue. With the help of God, we will have a good
year."

Rabbi Elimelech, telling this story each year, rubbed his hands
and said with great joy, "Now, that's the way to talk. Our God in
heaven loves the kind of language Chaim used. This is the way—
yes, this is the way in which we can effect a good year."

I have become a chasid of Rabbi Elimelech. Or maybe I am
Chaim's student. I stand here tonight to reckon with God.

I come by it naturally. Last week, as my mother prepared to
end our weekly conversation, she said, "When I go to shul on Yom
Kippur, God had better ask for my forgiveness." It has been an
extraordinarily hard year. My mother suffers from clinical depression, and this year a depression gripped her and would not let go
for six months. It had lifted for a few days when she began falling
down unexpectedly. In testing for the falls, the doctors discovered cancer in her lung. They removed the cancer and part of her
lung, and since then she has had kidney trouble and neuropathy
and possibly diabetes. My mother has gone to synagogue all her
life; she lives by Jewish rhythms and teaches others what she has
learned. She became a bat mitzvah as an adult and served as the
president of the synagogue in a painful year. All her extra time
and money go to support the congregation she has helped to build
from its days in a church basement. As she sits in shul this day,
God, I say to You, You had better ask her for forgiveness.

But don't stop there, God. Look around here tonight, too—take
a good hard look. The people You see here are not perfect. They
are ordinary people, hard-working, trying hard. They keep their
records, admit their shortcomings. They, we, lie sometimes to keep
peace or to take the easy way out. We turn our backs on people
when their needs are inconvenient, and we ignore the human cost
of the clothing we wear and the price we pay for housing. We are
impatient, we snipe at those we love, we make fun of those we

don't. Our lists are long, and we are ashamed. Should we even be sitting here tonight, of all nights?

Should You? We have a book for You, too, God. Let me read to You from that book. Look! See the entries pile up: Here a mother battles cancer, here another's mother loses to mental illness, here a baby dies, a mother, a father die too soon, a sister cannot live on her own. You owe us, God, You owe us. Here a baby born in our circle didn't breathe, breathed with machines only, lives now a narrow life that leaves her parents' hope in tatters. Here someone tests positive for HIV, here for breast cancer: medication, surgery, radiation—and tears—are daily fare. You owe us, God, You owe us.

My teacher Rabbi Michael Chernick prays in a shul in New Jersey. A few years ago he started to notice someone new there, a man who sat quietly every Shabbat in the midst of the congregation. The congregation would rise for prayer—but not this newcomer. The congregation would sing, and join in communal prayer, and in silent meditation—but not this newcomer. Rabbi Chernick watched him for some weeks, puzzled by this behavior. Finally, he could take it no longer. He went to the man and asked him, "Why? Why do you come each week, but not participate in any of the prayers or the songs? Why?" The man replied, "I survived the Holocaust. The rest of my family was killed by the Nazis. I cannot pray. But I come each week to the synagogue and don't participate, so that I can show God how angry I am with Him."

There is evil enough in this world to break our hearts, to break Your heart, God. But You created evil, placed it in equal possibility with good in every human heart. When we look into the face of evil, then, where should we turn for compensation but to You? When a young man, barely more than a child, can watch his friend rape and murder a little girl, to Whom shall we turn? When children take guns from parents' closets and murder those parents, or their classmates, to Whom shall we turn? When people the world over make enemies of neighbors, or turn again to hating old enemies, using banishment and torture and rape and brutal killing to "cleanse" their world, to Whom shall we turn? You owe us, God, You owe us.

We owe You, too. We, too, turn our backs on crimes in progress, on spiraling rents, on second-class schools, on invasions of privacy. We do not always teach our own children well, so who are we to question children without conscience? We like to live among our own kind, so who are we to look down on those who hate their neighbors? Our lists are long, and we sit here ashamed of our failings. We will confess tonight, and tomorrow, and into the year: we are good people here and want to do right.

All right, all right, we know that we owe You for joy, too: Two babies have been born in this congregation in the last two weeks, and people have met here and fallen in love, and others have learned new Torah and stepped gingerly into prayer and repeated a new song over and over in their hearts. We have seen art and heard music and raised voices of protest—our records show these lines of profit, too. But our name is our mirror: One among us reminded us all long ago that our name could not show only feasting and joy. Life is not all joy and celebration, he said, it includes sorrow, too, and anger—all the voices of our lives.

So we know we owe You, God, we owe You. But we have to make a deal, a good deal. I don't know if by the end of Yom Kippur, of a day of fasting and prayer and the beginnings of atonement, I will be ready to forgive You for all the evil Your servants have done, for all the injustice we have suffered at Your hands. We will remember this day the sorrows and the joys, and I may stand ready to forgive You. I cannot speak for anyone else here. But ready to forgive or not, I want You to say those precious words, to ask for that forgiveness, to look into our faces and see the anger and the loss, the disappointment and the tears, and to ask for our forgiveness.

And I want You to give us Your forgiveness: look into our hearts and see there the cowardice and the smallmindedness and the greed to which we have confessed. I know that You can see even into the corners of our hearts that we are afraid to search. Look into those corners, God, and still give us Your forgiveness. I do not ask only for myself, simple human being that I am. And I do not ask only for my family, for those I love. No. On this Yom Kippur, I want You to say, "I forgive you," to all the people gathered in this synagogue tonight. And I want you, looking into our faces, to ask: Forgive Me, forgive Me.

"For transgressions between people and God, Yom Kippur—the day of atonement—atones."

Leaning Back into God

Yom Kippur 2006 / 5767

"Remember, you can always lean back into God," my spiritual director told me. This was at a time when I needed to lean into something. Spiritual direction is relatively new for Jews, borrowed from a long-established practice in Catholicism but also hearkening back to the teacher's role in early Chasidic Judaism. "Lean back into God," I thought to myself. "What the hell does that mean?" And then I leaned back in a chair perfectly tailored to this suggestion, with a high surrounding back, and felt the chair and God's presence and was comforted. My spiritual director did not make this up, I have discovered, but rather was passing on wisdom she had learned. I too now pass this on, and so often when I have said, "Lean back into God," I can see people's shoulders relax, their breathing calm.

Last week I spoke about Israel, overcoming a certain amount of fear to speak to you honestly about that thorny, complicated, deeply felt place. The traditional pillars of Judaism are God, Torah, and Israel. Speaking about Israel feels like a piece of cake compared to talking about God in this place, where long before we wrote a mission statement we understood that at Kolot Chayeinu—in Kathryn's memorable phrase—doubt was an act of faith. I always understood it to mean that being able to move from complete disbelief to doubt was itself a leap of faith! Yet here I stand to speak of faith and of God.

A few weeks ago a Kolot member told me she really appreciated my piece in the *Voices* issue about the *Sh'ma*. As I was thanking her, she said that her neighbors, who belong to a more traditional shul in the area, had told her that they understood that I don't believe in God. This seems to be because I quoted "doubt is an act of faith" in an article in the local paper and spoke about Kolot's wide-open doors to people of faith, doubt, uncertainty, or disbelief—such a reasonable mix in an uncertain world. Somehow this translated into "the rabbi doesn't believe in God." So this sermon is in part a response, or at least a hand held up to say, "Wait a minute." It is also a response to all of you, the seekers and doubters, the skeptics and yearners I have met with over the years who wanted to have some way to think about God that wasn't what you had learned in Hebrew school and didn't require leaving mind or heart behind. For the record, I do believe in God, though I don't think belief is the issue. Believing in God is really a way of saying, "I am willing to swallow this or that depiction of God that fits with what I believe already."

So for me, for instance, Kolot member Sheila Bock's wonderful description of God as an electrical field fit perfectly into my sense of God as enticing, powerful, and dangerous. "Our Father, our King" doesn't fit so well, though last year when I had huge important arguments with my own father *and* met a real king, those names fit more easily. Behind the names then, as we sang that glorious music, I could sense a presence with whom to argue fiercely and before whom to feel real humility. "Our Mother, our Queen" opens a whole different image for me of nurturing and yearning, beneficence, and distance. Judaism doesn't ask for belief so much as recognition and acceptance. *Sh'ma, Yisrael, Adonai Eloheinu, Adonai Echad.* Listen, Israel, the God whose name we cannot pronounce is our God, and only that One.

What is the proper response to that phrase that we say over and over in worship, at bedtime, before death? Certainly not a philosophic discourse, though that is perfectly appropriate in some conversations about God. My answer is "yes." Yes, I am listening. Yes, I am a Jew. Yes, the Unpronounceable is my God. Yes, only. One. A famous wag once said, "Jews are the people who believe in at most one God." With a God you can't see who has a name you can't say, there is a great possibility for doubt and disconnection. For me, this means I have to stay awake more, pay more attention to the small moments and places in which I can sense God's presence: the lake in Prospect Park when it sparkles in early-morning light; Kolot's K–1 class singing *Mah Tovu* for the first time; saying the deathbed confession with someone in the last moments of life; contented silence with my beloved.

My list can go on and on, and so can yours. For me to access that list, or take note in the moment, I have come to need silence. Last year I turned off the radio I used to listen to as soon as I woke up and every time I got in my car. I miss some news these days, but I bought myself silence and space in which I am sometimes lucky enough to experience God. For me, experiencing God is the question, not whether I believe. In the silence, I find myself singing: sometimes whatever we sang here most recently, but sometimes a perfect prayer for the moment.

A couple of weeks ago, I was really annoyed at someone who was just pushing my buttons. When I got in the car, into my enclosed silence, I began without thinking to sing "*Hareini, m'kabelet alai . . .*"—the prayer with which we begin Shabbat morning services that urges us each week to love our neighbor as ourselves. When I realized what I was singing, and how I had been feeling about that annoying person, I said to God, "OK, I get it—I get the message to love my neighbor as myself, even this one who is at present the most annoying neighbor around." I didn't even have to lean back.

But what do I lean back into, when I lean back into God, which I do somewhat often now that I have been given the possibility? I lean into a sense of presence, a support made tangible by whatever chair I am in at the moment, a response without voice. Does this make sense? I have learned how to meditate a little, and I am very bad at it, partly because of what the Buddhists call "monkey mind" and partly because I need the chair back and can't sit up straight for long without it. I admire those who can sit for hours with straight spine. I wonder at those who can live in this world without any sense of support beyond family and friends. I can't do that either.

I have always leaned on God, starting with a child's human image—that old man in the sky—but moving to a larger, less tangible sense of presence, force, light, darkness—life. When I lean back into God, I lean into life, into the force that gives and takes life, the force that makes me, me. *Elohai n'shamah shenatata bi t'horah hi—atah v'ratah, atah y'tzartah, atah n'fachtah bi, v'atah m'shamrah b'kirbi*, "My God, the soul You gave me is pure—You created it, You shaped it, You breathed it into me, and You guard it within me." A disgruntled young Jew once called Judaism "an old man saying no." It isn't that anymore, not only old men anymore and no longer Old Man God, though Old Man River has a certain appeal. God is the flow of life, the cleansing, dangerous water in which we try to swim day after day after painful joyful day. Into that water, I lean back and feel its solidity, its fluidity, its force. It pushes back, and my back is supported. God has my back, and so I can lean.

Now let's begin at the beginning: *B'reishit bara Elohim eit hashamayim v'eit haaretz*, "In the beginning, God created heaven and earth." Isn't that how we have always heard the line that begins the Torah? Yet centuries and reams of commentary tell us that *b'reishit*—the very beginning—is an oddity, a strange formulation of the word that means "at the beginning" or "at first." So some read it as "When God began to create." And others see it midrashically, as "with wisdom God created." But then the "God created" part gets interesting. It should say *Elohim bara*, "God created," but it says *bara Elohim*. This oddity made the writer of the *Zohar* look deeper, until he saw that there was a space between *b'reishit* and *bara*. Into this space he suggested we put the life force of the universe, the vast energy we cannot name. Then, with all of this new understanding, we can read, "With wisdom, the life force created *Elohim*"—so that we mere mortals could have a God we could grasp and try to comprehend. When we pray to *Elohim*, who is now truly *Eloheinu*—our *Elohim*—we can know that we are praying to a mere shadow of God, yet still attempt to connect to what lies beyond the shadow. *Baruch atah Adonai Eloheinu Melech haolam*: We stand in humility before the breathing heart of the universe, who allows us to see our needed shadow God and who encompasses time and space. We address that shadow God as *atah*, a masculine pronoun, because our ancestors could only conceive of a masculine God. More recently, feminists have used the formula *b'rucha at*—"blessed are You," feminine form.

This debate reminds me of a story a rabbi I know told, of being a child in a classroom taught by Rabbi Arnold Jacob Wolf, one of the great fierce Reform social justice rabbis. The rabbi, who was then a child, declared loudly, as our Kolot children always do, "I don't believe in God!" Wolf looked at him for a long minute and asked, "What makes you think that matters to God?" What makes us think it matters to God whether we say *baruch atah* or *b'rucha at*? It matters deeply to us, and therefore is important to think about and struggle with. But God is beyond gender, beyond body, beyond being made in the human image. God is. And is everywhere, through all time and in all space. So what are we doing here on Yom Kippur? To whom are we confessing, to whom pouring out our hearts? Spiritual direction has taught me that it is crucial to take note of our deepest experiences, to articulate them and thus to remember them during the long dry spells when we feel no connection to the life force within and surrounding us.

I began spiritual direction in just such a long dry spell, dry and angry, and was eased by the memory of earlier Jews who had prayed angry prayers to God and the possibility that I could too. I did—and then was able to feel God's comforting presence too, the need I'd had beneath the anger. Yom Kippur is a long session of spiritual direction, time, and space for us to connect to time and space, a place and a way to take note and articulate and remember our deepest experiences. We strip away color and taste and smell and move inward, finding a space parallel to the space we create around us on this holiest of holy days. And there we take note and say silently and out loud: This is what I loved, and this is what I hated, and this is what I want to change and saying it makes it more likely that I will. Singing it makes it even more likely that I will remember these words but can sometimes shield us from the depth of our examination. It is from that depth that we act, bringing our connection to God into tangible, needed action. Our ancestors understood this as God's desire: God wants us to feed the hungry? Pay the worker? Free the captive? We connect to our ancestors and to God when we feed the hungry or free the captive—this is how Jews for centuries have heard God's voice. We hear what they heard through their words.

But only when we can spend time in Yom Kippur's deep examination and honest assessment can we even begin to imagine moving outward. Seen in this way, it is hard to blame God for the things humans do, hard even to blame God for what we call "acts of God." God is more verb than noun, more process than fixed, more moving river than king on throne or steam bath attendant. Each of us has the chance if we want to take it of jumping in that river and swimming with it. As Noah Chasek MacFoy reminded us at his bar mitzvah, there will always be boulders in that river, but they are either insurmountable obstacles or an opportunity to take a new way and see where it gets us. That decision is often up to us. "This commandment which I command you this day is not too wondrous for you, nor too far away. It is not in heaven, that you should say, 'Who will go up for us to heaven and bring it down to us, that we may do it?' Nor is it beyond the sea, that you should say, 'Who will cross the sea for us and bring it over to us, that we may do it?' *Ki karov eilecha hadavar m'od b'ficha uvilvav'cha laa-soto*—No, it is *karov*—very near to you, in your mouth and in your heart, and you can do it . . . holding fast to the One who is your life and the length of your days" (Deuteronomy 30:11–14, 30:20). We will read those words tomorrow morning.

Tonight, I ask only that you hear them, and try to take them in. "This commandment which I command you this day is not too wondrous for you, nor too far away. . . . You can do it . . . holding fast to the One who is your life and the length of your days."

Doubt and Faith

Rosh Hashanah 2017 / 5778

ELLEN: Fourteen years ago my wife, Kathryn Conroy, noted casually to me that Kolot is a place where doubt is an act of faith. I laughed out loud. And remembered it. Sometime during Rosh HaShanah services that year, I mentioned it. And members began referring to it over and over. It touched something true. It became part of our mission statement, placed prominently on our website, our Facebook page, our T-shirts. Something about those words made people, many of you probably, think you could come as you are—be fully yourselves, for if you can bring your doubts to shul, you can bring a lot else besides.

As I prepare to retire, it has been clear to everyone working on the transition that the Kolot mission and values are the linchpin of Kolot's future, the things that will carry current members forward and new members into a new era grounded in the abiding values of this community. What better to talk about as we begin this new year, then, than the most-quoted phrase of Kolot's mission. How and why do doubt and faith remain crucial?

One thing I can tell you is that a few weeks ago, during one of our first August services in the park under the Tallis Trees, I asked the gathered community to think about God. Not to offer thoughts then, but to take some questions with them to mull over during the week ahead. As I asked the questions, I became aware that there was in that green and shady space a deep hush as people listened. This was important! Was it more important this year than last, as we all have lived through this year of horrifying changes in this country and elsewhere? Or was it that we at Kolot have become so used to speaking about doubt that it is stunning when we speak about God without conditions? Whatever caused it, the hushed attentive reaction made me think again that speaking about faith, and about doubt, was needed as this year begins.

This year! Shock wave after shock wave, protest after protest, vigilance, urgency. And then the hurricane season: Biblical, terrifying, deathly. Doubt and faith.

So for my last Rosh HaShanah at Kolot, I asked Kathryn if she would join me to talk about faith and doubt and what she saw in Kolot members back then. We have never spoken together anywhere except at our wedding, but as Yehuda Amichai wrote, "Doubts and loves / Dig up the world / Like a mole, a plow." I wanted us to dig into our hearts and dig up this world a little. We hope our personal reflections will spark yours.

[Kathryn Conroy joins Rabbi Lippmann on the bimah.]

ELLEN: Let's start right here on Erev Rosh HaShanah:

A Chasidic teaching tells us that people and God connect intimately during the month of Elul when "the king is in the field" before returning to the palace to ascend the throne, a chief image of Rosh HaShanah. The month of Elul ended tonight as the month of Tishrei began. The king now reenters the palace and mounts the stairs to sit on the *kisei ram v'nisa*—the elevated throne on which Rosh HaShanah's great King now sits.
KATHRYN: Really?

ELLEN: Of course not. But I have thought about this imagery a lot this year, especially in the past few weeks, not just because I love this sort of anthropomorphic image-making, but more because I have yearned so deeply for some great power somewhere to *do* something . . . I have thought a lot about the old English biblical word "smiting," frankly wishing there were some smiting going on, *if* I got to decide when and where. Years ago the poet Susan Griffin wrote, "I like to think of Harriet Tubman . . . who was never caught, and who had no use for the law / when the law was wrong, / who defied the law . . . / I like to think of her especially / when

I think of the problem of feeding children. / The legal answer / to the problem of feeding children / is ten free lunches every month, / being equal, in the child's real life, / to eating lunch every other day. / Monday, but not Tuesday. / I like to think of the President eating lunch Monday, but not Tuesday."

KATHRYN: I like to think *now* of the president being spit on by a neo-Nazi or grabbed by an ICE agent on a street somewhere or suffering the effects of a leaking oil pipeline or losing his health insurance right when he needs major surgery.

ELLEN: I don't really think about God like this. Except when I really do.

KATHRYN: I don't. But you are the one who once wept at the graves of the biblical Abraham and Sarah, though you don't really believe they existed.

ELLEN: Well, it *is* Rosh HaShanah when Abraham and Sarah seem very real. So let's just posit that the king has left the field and is ascending to the heavenly throne. What better time to confront and embrace or reject or wonder about the ancient, royal, male, decreeing, or inspiring or comforting God of our tradition? What better time, as this new year begins, to face the despair of the year that is ending, trying to locate some new faith and recognize our very real doubts?

KATHRYN: When I first said that Kolot Chayeinu is a place where doubt is an act of faith, I think what I meant was that I was seeing adults doing adult Judaism. I believe that mature faith has to incorporate doubt, otherwise it is mindless belief. Mindful (such a hackneyed word right now), mindful belief has to incorporate doubt. Otherwise it *is* mindless; it is not adult faith. Ambiguity and ambivalence mark adulthood. I am ambivalent; I can hold two diametrically opposed feelings at the same time and not be crazy. Like Ellen weeping at the graves of people she does not think ever lived. Or me really wanting to write and speak this sermon with her *and* ready to pull out every day since I said yes.

Often life is ambiguous: unknown, uncertain. But we too often act as if that wasn't true. I try to ask myself, *What do I really, truly KNOW?* All of experience exists on a continuum. The continuum of belief might run from Absolutely Yes to Absolutely No. From "Absolute Belief and Faith" to "Absolute No Belief or Faith."

ELLEN: Completely certain atheists and completely certain people of faith hold up the poles. Between those two clear poles stand the rest of us, where we two stand. Between the certain poles is the realm of doubt.

KATHRYN: We are both doubters, but our doubt has taken us in different directions. I have moved from an early Catholic childhood steeped in dogma and certainty to a place of comfort as an agnostic. *What do I really truly KNOW?*

What I *know* is that I am truly most comfortable knowing that I do *not* know. I embrace uncertainty, surprise, and mystery. Years ago I fell in love with a bumper sticker that said "Militant Agnostic: I don't know and you don't either."

ELLEN: I have moved from regular Jewish practice and prayer in my childhood to—well, an adult life of regular Jewish practice and prayer. But the adult version is different, deeper, more often tested, and with the strengthening of doubt. *What do I really, truly KNOW?*

I know that people can be heartbreakingly cruel, and breathtakingly kind. I know that birth is a miracle of immense proportions. And I know firsthand that people die. This is partly why we have these High Holy Days, to try to come to terms with life and death, as well as with our hopes and prayers for a good year ahead.

Death is a fact of life, and a fact of war, random, planned, created, accidental. I have learned with the deepest sorrow of my life that children die. When children I know have died, at twelve or twenty-four, I have yelled—really yelled—at God in anger and fear and confusion. *And* I have asked God for comfort for the parents, praying to *El Malei Rachamim*, the God who is full of compassion, wondering where that compassion is and how I can possibly say so and knowing that I can't do anything else. I am not the bereaved parents. Some of you are, and I do not know how you get out of bed. Your willingness to do so, your determination to continue living, takes my breath away, and I bow before you. One of you said recently, "I'm angry at a god I'm not even sure I believe in." I get that. And yet I do not stop yelling or beseeching God or decide there is no God. I am certain enough that something is there to yell at.

KATHRYN: I don't know that a god exists though I lean toward thinking probably there is something (even the physicist Stephen Hawking has come to that). But a personal god? A god to yell at or beseech? A god to turn to in distress? Never.

I grew up Catholic. When I was a child we went to church and the Jewish neighbors went to temple. They had their prayers, we had ours. Maybe everyone had prayers? I said mine faithfully, if a little thoughtlessly, for many years. We had prayers and a saint for everything: choosing a mate, passing a test, finding lost objects, we even had one for lost and impossible causes. Sometimes I miss that certainty; mostly I don't. My childhood assumptions about prayer did not last into adulthood.

ELLEN: On a main road near where we vacation upstate, some people put out a series of four separate signs in a row that read: "Did" "You" "Pray" "Today?"

We drove past it frequently this summer and often I would read it aloud: "Did - you - pray - today?" And almost every time at almost the same moment, Kathryn would say "yes" and I would say "no."

KATHRYN: I said yes because I *do* pray! Prayer for me now is not rote though I do recite some daily intentions. Now prayer for me is spontaneous and "gut felt" much more than "heart felt." It comes from the belly, not the chest. I consider myself praying when I spontaneously feel and acknowledge gratitude, which I do very often; when I contemplate death, which I do daily; when I am deeply concerned about someone or something so much that the rest of the world fades away for a moment; when I see someone perform a small act of kindness when they don't think anyone is watching. Those moments are me praying.

ELLEN: I said "no" because the question makes me think of formal prayer and I was asking myself, "Did you sit or stand with a siddur or other words of prayer in your head or hands and read or chant them today?" Most days other than Shabbat I do not do that. *But* almost every day something happens or I see something that makes me think one of Jewish prayer's big four: "Please, thank you, oops, and wow." And when I think one of those, I try to spend a moment of intentional focus:

"*Please* bring healing to my friend even though the predictions aren't good." "*Thank you* for the strength that keeps so many people resisting truly awful government decisions." "*Oops*, I forgot to call that person and I know my call might have helped them a lot." "*Wow*, the lake in the park looks so beautiful this morning, sparkling in the sun." Sometimes I even add a blessing: a traditionally Jewish way of marking the moment, joining me, the event, and God in a prayer that insists on deep attention. I have already told you that I also sometimes yell and beseech God.
So did I pray today? Yes.

Every evening Kathryn and I read a poem aloud, which is to me a form of prayer, if by prayer we can also mean a touching of our heart or soul or kishkes, what Kathryn calls "guts," by evoking something deeper than ordinary life.

KATHRYN: The poet Mary Oliver writes, "Understand, I am always trying to figure out / what the soul is, / and where hidden / and what shape— . . . I believe I will never quite know. / Though I play at the edges of knowing, / truly I know / our part is not knowing, / but looking, and touching, and loving."[29]

ELLEN: "Looking, and touching, and loving." Did you pray today?

KATHRYN: "Our part is not knowing." Did you pray today?

ELLEN: Kolot Chayeinu is a place where doubt can be an act of faith, because you cannot be confident and faithful at the same time.

29. Mary Oliver, "Bone," in *Why I Wake Early* (Boston: Beacon Press, 2004) 4–6.

KATHRYN: I describe myself as a permanently lapsed Irish Catholic with some practice in Zen and Judaism. I regularly practice kyudo, Japanese Zen archery, which is a form of moving meditation, and zazen, which is meditation sitting on the cushion. I regularly begin Shabbat on Friday nights with Ellen with candles and *Kiddush*, and I do those things without her if she is away. We celebrate all the Jewish home rituals; there is a mezuzah on our doorpost. We say a blessing in Hebrew before every meal. I come to some services here at Kolot and occasionally elsewhere, really appreciate Rosh HaShanah and Yom Kippur (which I actually use as a personal retreat), and love that we count the Omer starting the second night of Passover.

I am a product of Catholic education, kindergarten through college. In elementary and high school I had nuns from two different orders, and not one horror story. When I was in eighth grade we studied the Holocaust. During high school the nuns were involved in the civil rights movement; two of them marched with Dr. King from Selma to Montgomery. When I was at the end of high school and into college the nuns and Jesuits I knew, and knew of, were involved in anti-war work. I learned from their example that part of a life of faith was attending to the world around us and working to make it a better world. They described it as "faith in action." However, study of religion in school was more of an intellectual exercise than anything else. We memorized the catechism and took courses in theology. We were never taught to pray, only taught prayers. Complete faith was assumed and doubt was tightly regulated.

Growing up I especially loved the stories about an individual saint's moment of doubt followed by their anticipation and acceptance of martyrdom for the faith they had just questioned. But our own doubts? Never discussed. It was assumed that everyone had doubts but that everyone came to grips with them and then was more committed for having struggled. But for me, doubt became more important than faith; doubt became my faith.

ELLEN: I was never asked if I believed, because it didn't matter. At five I knew God existed and was sure Abraham and Sarah had lived. At nine I was less sure. But as the late great Rabbi Arnold Jacob Wolf said, when confronting a nine-year-old who proudly exclaimed, "I don't believe in God"—"What makes you think it matters to God?"

What mattered to Wolf and to centuries of Jews before him was action. Rabbi Wolf once greeted me as we boarded a bus for a demonstration in Washington by asking, "What are you reading?" What are you reading, what are you doing, how are you living? Those are the ways Jews have always acted, the way we show relationship with God. God wants me to put up a mezuzah? So I'll put up a mezuzah. And in the doing of the act and its blessing somehow there is a small subtle shift in my home because a little bit of wood and parchment are stuck to the door. It says to the world, "A Jew lives here." It says to me I need to be careful about how I act in my home and out in the world. Holy. Sacred. God's in there somewhere.

KATHRYN: So this agnostic and that person of faith (pointing to Ellen) live in that house with a mezuzah on the door. And we both have a sense that we must commit to what is important in life, that relationship and obligation and discipline matter. For me, discipline is doing something you believe you are obligated to do even when you doubt its efficacy. Doubt is not disbelief.

ELLEN: Judaism urges me to enter into a covenant, a relationship with God predicated on mutual care and obligation. I have learned about a relationship with God by being in relationship with people, especially Kathryn. We argue and solve, admire and criticize, trust and lean on one another in a regular ebb and flow—*ratzo v'shov*—of connection. I have committed to one person to stick with it for as long as we possibly can. So I know that I can also stick with God for as long as I possibly can, arguing and solving, trusting and leaning on. Sometimes, God, you make good things happen. Sometimes you inflict the unbearable. But really, why can't you just do a little smiting when I want you to?

I can almost hear God asking me the same thing.

KATHRYN: Things are very bad right now. I don't have to enumerate; you all know the list as well as I do. I still have faith in our form of government, if not in those doing the governing right now. I do harbor some fear, a few doubts, but I think democracy will bear out in future. It is our job to make that so.

ELLEN: *Aleinu.* It's up to us. Or as my e-mail signature says, borrowing from the poet Charles Wright, "God is the fire my feet are held to."

KATHRYN: I don't protest because of god. No personal god, remember? So why do I believe in and engage in social action? I don't know. Maybe it's the DNA that goes back to my grandfather in Strokestown, Ireland, and the rebels there. Maybe I got some of it from my aunt who fought for a woman's place in publishing in the '40s. Maybe the kernel of it was from the nuns and their "faith in action." I don't know. But as an adult, I can live ethically and compassionately without requiring of myself absolute, blind belief in something. Doubt is my act of faith that it is possible.

ELLEN: I don't require of myself absolute, blind belief. I don't have it and wouldn't want it. But I think I live as ethically or compassionately as I do because the God I have learned to live with requires it. I probably more often think "Judaism demands it" than "God demands it," but in my head there is the faint sound of the prophet Micah (6:8), telling me what the unnameable God requires of me: "Only to do justice, love mercy, and walk humbly with my God." Justice, mercy, humility. Brief words. Tall order. I could try to get there without God, but I don't think I'd be as successful. I'm not all that successful *with* God!

KATHRYN: Ellen and I have an annual pre–Rosh HaShanah ritual that feels important here. Each year we go to the Rose Planetarium at the Museum of Natural History, buy tickets, ride the elevator up, and watch the space show. They only change the space show every couple of years so sometimes we see the same show two years in a row. It doesn't matter. Whether we hear the voice of Tom Hanks or Whoopie Goldberg or Neil deGrasse Tyson, what we see is the vastness of the universe, and the reality that we—who like to think of ourselves as fairly accomplished and important—are just specks of skin and water, mere flecks in a cosmos of multiple universes and countless stars.

ELLEN: Last Friday, Neil deGrasse Tyson taught us that there is no center of the universe, but that wherever you are you think that is the center. The prophet Hosea asked (14:3), "What lets you see there is more than you?" A midrash teaches that the heavenly throne that God ascends tonight is *the* thing that distinguishes human achievement from the divine. We humans can do a lot, it notes, but *we* do not have the *kisei ram v'nisa*, the elevated throne that is God's alone. We do not have the view from on high, from space or from the throne. Kathryn doesn't know if there is a God or not. I kinda think there is. *What do we KNOW?* That we are obligated to work on our home and on our world, and that we must do it with the humility due the universe, which is way bigger than we are. If there is a God, we are not it. And neither are you.

KATHRYN: This year I have doubted more than ever. I have doubted the strength of our democratic systems, even while having faith in those systems. I have doubted my place in a country too many of whose citizens clearly do not want me here, do not want so many of us here.

ELLEN: "Doubts and loves / Dig up the world / Like a mole, a plow." What did you dig up this year? What did you lean on to find meaning or solace or haven or the push to resist? Kolot Chayeinu is a place where doubt is an act of faith. It has to be, because certainty would kill us all *and* the community we've built where we can come as we are.

KATHRYN: Why would I suggest "Doubt is an act of faith" for Kolot? Because Kolot is a community built on diversity including diversity of opinions and beliefs . . . Kolot is made up of people who believe in God; who don't believe in God; who believe that God personally intervenes in their lives; who assume God completely ignores them; and everything in between. And no one is threatened by the others' dis/belief . . . They attend the same services and sing the same songs, together. Maybe, just maybe, each has something to learn from the other.

Doubt is an act of faith at Kolot because the community is adult enough to embrace a diversity of opinion about even the most heartrending topics . . . The only rule that I have experienced at Kolot is that one person cannot oppress another.

ELLEN: Do justice, love mercy, and walk humbly with your God.

KATHRYN: Do justice, love mercy, and walk humbly.

ELLEN: Doubt away. What makes you think it matters to God?

Part Six

Shalom

Peace, Wholeness

Are Trees of the Field Human?

Yom Kippur 2001 / 5762

When my mother died, many people, including I think some of you, planted a tree in Israel in her memory. One friend brought us a rose bush to plant. It is a thing Jews do when someone has died; we plant something living to help us remember a person who has died. One reason we don't have cut flowers at funerals is because we are not supposed to kill something living to commemorate death.

I like to think of the trees that were planted in my mother's name, though of course we all know that when you go they bring you to just the tree that is yours, all of us winking and understanding that they plant a bunch of trees and bring whoever comes to see one of them. So I guess what I like is to think of trees growing, bringing shade, anchoring a piece of land. I like looking at that rose bush, too, seeing the new flowers bloom in the spring. My mother was never a gardener; born and bred in Manhattan, she liked other aspects of suburban living. But even so, those roses and those trees somehow symbolize her life, the vitality of it, the growth, the fruits of her labors.

When Adonai Elohim, *the God of compassion and justice, made earth and heaven . . . God planted a garden in Eden . . . and placed there the Adam, the human creature, whom God had formed. And from the ground God caused to grow every tree that was pleasing to the sight and good for food, with the tree of life in the middle of*

233

the garden, and the tree of knowledge of good and bad. (Genesis 2:4, 2:8–9)

You're thinking that this is a sermon about trees or ecology or even death. It isn't. It's a sermon about war, and about how trees teach us knowledge of good and bad in war. It's a sermon about war because we are staring into war's ugly face and wondering what will come to pass. It's a sermon about trees and what they can teach us:

When in your war against a city you have to besiege a long time in order to capture it, you must not destroy its trees, wielding the ax against them. You may eat of them, but you must not cut them down. Are trees of the field human to withdraw before you under siege? (Deuteronomy 20:19)

That's from Deuteronomy. When you make war you have to take care. Wholesale destruction is not an option, therefore emotion-driven vengeance is not an option. Just wars, first and foremost, require thought. Philo, the first-century Jewish philosopher from Egypt, extends the Torah's reach, writing, "So great a love for justice does the law instill . . . that it does not even permit the fertile soil of a hostile city to be outraged by devastation or by cutting down trees to destroy the fruits."[30]

Josephus, the first-century historian, says further that one cannot incinerate the enemy's country or kill work animals; despoiling the countryside without direct military advantage comes under the ban on profligate destruction. By the twelfth-century, Maimonides excludes all wanton destruction in war, including smashing household goods, tearing clothing, demolishing buildings, stopping up springs of water, and destroying articles of food.

The control Maimonides urges not only prevents wanton destruction, it also builds other kinds of control. The prohibition

---

30. Cited in Reuven Kimelman, "Warfare and Its Restrictions in Judaism," https://www.bc.edu/content/dam/files/research_sites/cjl/texts/current/forums/Isr-Hez/kimleman_war.htm.

on cutting down fruit trees, he wrote, was "to teach us to love the good and the purposeful and to cleave to it so that the good will cleave to us and we will distance ourselves from anything evil and destructive." As Dr. Reuven Kimelman of Brandeis University has written, "If the destructive urges provoked by war against nonhuman objects can be controlled, there is a chance of controlling the destructive urge against humans."[31]

Are trees of the field human to withdraw before you under siege? If a tree, could it flee, should not be cut down, how much more so should we understand that a person fleeing—a non-combatant—should not be cut down. The sixteenth-century commentator Moses Alshikh notes that just as God has mercy on the trees, "all the more so it is fitting that God have mercy on God's children." And from the first century CE, Philo calls, "Does a tree, I ask you, show ill will to the human enemy that it should be pulled up roots and all?"[32]

My greatest fear, as our country prepares to go to war, is that we will kill thousands of non-combatants, people in the targeted countries who have no say and no part in this war. We don't even have a clear target, so how can we not harm innocent people? We have just lost more than six thousand people from our city, a veritable village wiped out. And I want to ask with Christine Gomes, a teenager quoted in today's paper, "How many people do we have to kill to make Americans feel better?"

In the midst of the Vietnam War, Rabbi Abraham Joshua Heschel wrote, "We stand at the crossroads of our history. The atrocities we have committed are part of our record, of our consciousness. Either we accept and vindicate it and establish techniques of atrocities as a legitimate mode of national policy or repent earnestly, confessing our sins, making amends, and adopting measures that would prevent similar crimes from happening in

31. Ibid.
32. Ibid.

the future. . . . The issue we should all ponder is moral, not legal; responsibility, rather than guilt; prevention, rather than punishment. What steps must be taken by our leaders to prevent the possibility of our people committing war crimes in the future?"[33]

Heschel suggested then that the president "appoint a guardian of moral discipline whose responsibility it would be to see to it that military operations be carried out in accordance with international rules of warfare as accepted by the American government.[34] It's still a good idea, better than the new position of Home Security director, and when our day of introspection ends I am going to write to the president et al. to suggest it now. We need it more than ever, as troops of a new generation of eighteen-year-olds cry on their families' shoulders and assemble in military preparedness. Their tears are for fear and separation, but I hope they also clear their eyes so that they can see the forest from the trees.

Are trees of the field human? Our ancestors had a field day with this, likening trees to humans in all the ways they hoped humans would pay attention to. Trees have knowledge, they said; after all, the prophet Ezekiel told us that God once said, "Every tree of the field will know that I am *Adonai*" (Ezekiel 17:24, deliberately misread). A midrash on Ecclesiastes noted that just as humans do, trees must make an accounting for themselves on the day of judgment; they have consciences, it seems. Another midrash posits trees as witnesses; if a man goes to a prostitute in supposed secret, the trees will know, and somehow that knowing is enough to suggest the errant John should turn away from such pursuits.

The trees' witness ought to be enough. Cut down innocent trees and you have already breached the limits of just war. Cut down civilians and you are beyond the pale—the Pale from

---

33. Abraham Joshua Heschel, "Required: A Moral Ombudsman," in *Moral Grandeur and Spiritual Audacity*, ed. Susannah Heschel (New York: Farrar, Straus and Giroux, 1996), 220–21.
34. Ibid., 221.

which so many of our more recent ancestors fled lest they be cut down. We Jews know something of unjust attack and war. There is no question that the attack we have all just suffered was unjust in the extreme. By the trees' standard, it is beyond any imagining. And we are right to want some response, some answer, some bringing to justice. But we will be wrong if what we bring is vengeance instead. We American Jews may have something to teach the Israelis in this regard, now that we have experience of being the victims of terror. When Israel cuts down olive trees and groves, it is a sign of vengeance overtaking justice; a line is already crossed. Israel didn't cause the attacks on us, of course, nor did the vast majority of American Muslims nor did American Jews, though all have been blamed for them in these weeks, another sign of crossing a line into vengeance. The desire for vengeance is very strong, and we can probably all understand it if we look hard enough inside. That's why we are taught not to cut down trees. The trees are a fence around our vengeance, keeping it from breaking out.

Rabbi Brad Artson recently noted that in the old Silverman *machzor*, the High Holy Day prayer book many of you probably grew up with, there is a line that says literally, "*Avinu Malkeinu*, avenge the spilled blood of Your servants." But Silverman, in translating, gives the line as "*Avinu Malkeinu*, bring to judgment those who have shed the blood of Thy people." And Rabbi Artson asks, "What is the difference between justice and revenge? Both share some of the same emotions, including the desire to get even. One critical difference, though, occurs in the realm of action: justice is the result of a process designed to produce fairness and accuracy in pinpointing proper culprits; revenge follows no such process and often is indiscriminate in its targets." He reminds us that the Torah insists, "Do not take vengeance and do not bear a grudge" (Leviticus 19:18).[35]

35. Rabbi Brad Artson, e-mail commentary, Ziegler School at University of Judaism.

As I have often noted in our Torah service, not all of the Torah's ways are pleasantness and only some of its paths lead to peace. But on the question of war it is quite clear: negotiate first, offer peace first, treat captives kindly, don't cut down trees. The Torah itself is called the tree of life to those who hold it dear: *eitz chayim hi la-machazikim bah*. If we forget our bearings in the midst of war's heat and cut down trees that offer no harm, then we are in a real sense cutting down the Torah and its offer of justice in war. You may eat of it, but you must not cut it down. Today is a fast day, yet even today, especially today, the Torah's fruit is here for the eating, the chewing over, the digesting, the ingesting that make it a tree of life. But after today, if we cut it down, destroy its teachings of justice, we will be in grave trouble.

Are trees of the field human? Some of our commentators asked the question differently: How are humans like trees? The *Mishnah B'rurah* says we should treat a young child exactly as we would a young tree, tending it carefully, teaching it as age and development suggest, protecting its fruit until it is old enough to stand on its own and give fruit freely. And Rabbi Judah Loew of Prague, the golem-maker I spoke of at Rosh HaShanah, suggests that a person is an upside-down tree: The tree has roots planted in the earth, and branches and leaves that extend from the mainstay trunk. The person has roots stemming from heaven, and hands and feet that extend from the body and the soul, taking the needed action. The human has a godly soul, he taught, and an earthly body; the tree has only earthly nature. If you cut down a tree, therefore, you cut something God created. If you cut down a person, you cut a part of God.

When I think of my country bombing a woman in Afghanistan who has already been living a miserable, constricted life there, I think of cutting God. When I think of demolishing the scanty, poor fields of crops that may still try to grow there, thus moving people from hunger to starvation, I think of cutting God. When I think of children being raised there like undernourished young trees and imagine their horrible deaths at our hands, I think of cutting God. And when I think of the ways in which my country has already trained and fostered terrorists, added to poverty and misery around the world in a greedy, perverted path to world trade, and pulled away from needed cooperative ventures—think land mines, say—then I think of cutting God, and I am ashamed.

Our friend Tony Kushner wrote yesterday:

Striking the correct balance between justice and compassion is a very tough thing to do, a struggle. Perhaps it is the soul's principle struggle as it addresses the world without and the world within. Perhaps, if you believe God made us, we were made for this purpose, to demand mercy from the Law. Fallible as we are, we are always in need of mercy and well-suited to this task. . . . I believe that justice must be large. A narrow small-minded vengeful justice rapidly decays, becomes injustice. Injustice breeds terrorism, injustice is terrorism's first and richest food. To arrive at real justice, compassion is needed.

When in your war against a city . . . you must not destroy its trees.

This is where we get our compassion, from the trees and from our upside-down roots and our godly souls. Last week I wanted a golem to let loose on terrorists and terrorism everywhere, those out-of-control golems. Ten days later, I know that the earth is better suited to growing trees than to shaping golems. Part of me would still like an easy, harsh revenge: Hunt 'em down and kill 'em. Hunting them down is of course a major enigma, and killing them is almost certain to entail killing other people; it always does. For that reason, we all have to step back, take a collective breath, try to see the forest and the trees. Judaism is not a pacifist tradition, though we have always had our pacifists. Just war is rather a Jewish hope, just and without wanton destruction, without the cutting down of trees that are better off feeding us, without the indiscriminate killing of innocent people. When our target is unknown, and our troops are gathering, indiscriminate killing doesn't seem far behind. But a golem—a hard-to-control weapon of our making—is not the answer, tempting though it seemed at first. Let's rather look to the trees, remembering their humanity and their ability to remind us of ours.

Are trees of the field human? Human enough to have knowledge and conscience and to serve as witnesses to the full range of human evil. I wish at our moment in time that every soldier, sailor, pilot, marine could repeat the well-known prayer of Reb Nachman of Bratslav, or some version of it appropriate to their own place and faith:

> Master of the universe, grant me the ability to be alone.
> May it be my custom to go outdoors each day among the
>   trees and grasses, among all growing things, there to be
>   alone and enter into prayer.
> There may I express all that is in my heart, talking with
>   You, to whom I belong.
> And may all grasses, trees, and plants awake at my coming.
> Send the power of their life into my prayer, making whole
>   my heart and my speech through the life and spirit of
>   growing things.

And then let them remember, if they remember little else, that one simple verse from the Book of Deuteronomy:

> *When in your war against a city you have to besiege a long time in order to capture it, you must not destroy its trees, wielding the ax against them. You may eat of them, but you must not cut them down. Are trees of the field human to withdraw before you under siege? (Deuteronomy 20:19)*

The Story of September 11, 2001

Erev Rosh HaShanah 2001 / 5762

September 11, 2001, was a beautiful day. The sun shone, the clouds and mugginess of the day before disappeared, the air was clear, a little cool. Someone took the baby for a walk on the Promenade, someone slept late, someone got up early to work at the Primary Day polls, someone headed for a 9:00 class. I had an 8:30 meeting at Dizzy's. And you were . . .

This is how our story will begin, once it is told and retold and edited and shaped and given as a gift to the people whose lives it tells. Telling our story is how we move forward, how Jews have always moved forward after times of destruction and despair. The despair doesn't disappear from the old stories. It is woven in, somber threads along the bright threads of hope, the sparkle of an envisioned future.

After the Temple was destroyed—Solomon's Temple, the first—the poetry of tears flowed in *Eichah* / Lamentations (1:1, 4:1):

> Alas!
> Lonely sits the city
> Once great with people!
> She that was great among nations
> Is become like a widow;
> The princess among states

Is become a thrall. . . .
Alas!
The gold is dulled,
Debased the finest gold!
The sacred gems are spilled
At every street corner.

September 11, 2001, was also the twenty-third of Elul in the year 5761, and it was a beautiful day. The horror arrived early, on wings of destruction, and the mother on the Promenade watched in terror, the late sleeper listened in shock, the poll watcher ran to safety, and everywhere we gathered around televisions and radios to try to learn what had befallen us.

After the destruction of Herod's Temple, the second, Rabbi Yochanan ben Zakkai called his brother-in-law, part of a local fighting group, to come to him. He said, "Devise a scheme for me to leave the city. Perhaps the saving of a few lives may still be possible." His brother-in-law, Abba Sicara, said, "We have agreed that no one may leave the city except as a corpse." Yohanan replied, "Then have me taken out as a corpse." This is what they did and carried him out in a coffin until they arrived at the place where the king, Vespasian, stood. Then Yochanan rose and argued with the king, ultimately negotiating with him so that the no-count town of Yavneh and its sages was given to him in safety. The midrash in which this conversation is recorded says, "He should have said, 'Let Jerusalem off this time; don't destroy it.' But Yochanan thought Vespasian would deny such a request, and then there would not even be the saving of a few." So he went to Yavneh and there he created the beginning of a new kind of Judaism, rising from the ashes of the destroyed Temple and city. His form of Judaism—the Rabbinic Judaism of study and prayer in place of animal sacrifice—is still ours, though it is greatly changed. Stories after destruction can change the world.

September 11, 2001, was a beautiful day. As we watched in horror, the great towers that marked our city collapsed, and people fled from the fall, the smoke, the fire, many running into Brooklyn to safety across the bridges. And there, they were greeted with cups of water, the small solace that those in safety could quickly provide. The generosity that would swell in days to come was evident everywhere, in hours-long lines at blood donation centers and hospitals, in dozens of volunteer chaplains and counselors offering their services, in the help and support given our firefighters and police and rescue workers in the midst of their losses, in the money and goods that overflowed the capacity of the recipients. Somehow remembering Yochanan, people tried to save even a few if they could.

A midrash on Lamentations, clearly borrowing or influencing other traditions, tells us:

> *The day the Temple was destroyed, a redeemer was born. It happened that while a certain man was plowing, his heifer lowed. An Arab passed by, heard the lowing, and asked, "Who are you?" He answered, "I am a Jew." The Arab said, "Jew, O Jew, unharness your heifer and unhitch your plow [and go into mourning]." "Why?" "Because the Temple of the Jews is destroyed." "How do you know this?" "I know it from the lowing of your heifer." While they were conversing, the heifer lowed again. The Arab said, "Jew, O Jew, harness your heifer and hitch up your plow, because the Messiah, deliverer of Israel, has been born." "What is his name?" "His name is Menachem, 'Comforter.'"*

September 11, 2001, was a beautiful day that broke our hearts. We sought comfort everywhere, in conversation with neighbors and strangers, in hugs from loved ones, in retrieving our children from school partly just so we could see their faces, and in gatherings of prayer and song. Ancient words and melodies soothed us, the chance for silence renewed our strength. Everywhere across the city, churches, synagogues, mosques, and temples opened their doors, and people hitched up their backpacks and laced up their sneakers and headed out to find comfort.

For our Arab and Muslim neighbors, comfort was hard to find. Immediately following on the heels of the attacks, the slander began: "It's those damn Arabs," someone told me when I went to vote, not realizing what had befallen us. I reminded her of Oklahoma City's bombing and how wrong we who blamed the Arabs had been. "Mark my words," she said. "It's going to turn out to be the Arabs." And how many of our thoughts differed. But when it began to seem that it had indeed been Arabs, Muslims, who killed without regard for life or status, Americans, New Yorkers, Brooklynites began to seek revenge by turning on Arabs, Muslims, who had nothing to do with the destruction. Children in school, women wearing headscarves were harassed and attacked, men were beaten and even killed. "I just want to be able to mourn for my friends who were killed there," a Muslim man said to me at our discussion on Shabbat. When it begins to turn out that the enemy is the person next door, then we must be very careful not to turn the person next door into the enemy.

It is told that after the Second Temple was destroyed, God in heaven wanted to mourn. But not knowing how, God called the ministering angels and asked them how humans mourned. "They hang sackcloth over their doors," the angels replied. God said, "I will do likewise." "They extinguish their lanterns," continued the angels. "I will do likewise," God said. "What else do they do?" "They walk barefoot," and God said, "I will do likewise." "They rend their robes." "I will do likewise." "What else do people of flesh and blood do to mourn their dear ones?" "They sit in silence." And God said, "I will do likewise."

When the biblical Aaron's sons Nadav and Avihu were killed by a strange and unexpected fire, we are told that Aaron was silent. A medieval commentary says their death and their father's silence were as though the sun went dark. And when the sons of Yochanan ben Zakkai, now the leader of the great academy of Yavneh, died, his students' attempts at wordy comfort all failed, serving only to multiply his grief. Aaron's silence became his touchstone. In the very heart of sorrow, silence may be the only response.

September 11, 2001, was a beautiful day. The sun shone, light sparkled on the pond in Prospect Park, our neighborhoods were oddly peaceful. And at home and at work, we watched, stunned into silence. Ash filled our throats, smells invaded our noses. Wordless embraces were for many the best comfort. Silent, we pondered small twists of fate: Why had someone slept late that day? Why had someone taken a September vacation for the first time? Why had someone arranged to take Tuesday morning classes instead of Monday, instead of sitting at a desk a block away from destruction? Why had someone driven by the towers twenty minutes before they were hit? And in reverse: Why had someone decided to stop to shop and have breakfast in the mall under the towers? Why had someone gone to deliver coffee to a new customer on a high floor that morning? Why? Why? Why? Our silent questions reverberate, haunting us. Is it *bashert*, fated? Did God have a hand in, on Tuesday? And if so, what hand? Can we believe in a God with hands, anyway? Or a God who determines this fate for these people? Or a God who watches, silent, as the humans that God created live out their full capacities for good and evil?

After the Holocaust, two main theories about God emerged: Either God was all-powerful and therefore somehow encompassed even Nazi evil, *or* God was less than all-powerful, but solely good, and therefore evil lived outside of God's self. This week, we are confused, wanting God's comfort, raging against God's hand in horror. "I'm really angry at this God of yours," someone writes in an e-mail. "Do you think I'm not?" I write back. I don't know what role God played here, but I cannot live in a world that is not God's place, knowing God as *HaMakom*, the place of the world. I sense mystery in those small changes that led to being safe or being in danger, because so often, for me, God is in the gaps we can't understand. I agree with the man on the street who said on the radio this morning, "A bunch of wonderful people died for nuthin'!" Perhaps the issue then is how we die—not the circumstances, but the life we leave and its legacy, not the "died for nuthin'" part but the "wonderful people" part.

My classmate Rabbi Danny Wiener wrote a sermon for Rosh HaShanah just after the 1998 airplane crash off Nova Scotia. In it, he tried to come to terms with the words we will read tomorrow and next week that speak of a book in which it is written on Rosh HaShanah and sealed on Yom Kippur "who will live and who will die." He wrote that at first, he "could not believe in a God who would choose to down this plane, while allowing Osama bin Laden to live in relative security, plotting his next destruction of innocents." After much searching, Danny came to see that the words of that prayer that we know as the *Un'taneh Tokef* are less a divine proclamation and acceptance of our fate and more a "poignant and heartfelt expression of the fragility of life . . . that counsels us to focus on what is most important, to put our petty grievances aside, to amplify our joys and to endure our tragedies, to cherish life's opportunities and to appreciate its limitations, to pray that we are with loved ones again in a year's time, but if this is not to be, then to pray that we have left worthy and rich legacies for others as much as we have lived contented and fulfilled lives for ourselves."

Rabbi Shneur Zalman of Liadi, an eighteenth-century Chasidic rabbi, asked a disciple, "Mosheh, what do we mean when we say 'God'?" The disciple, taken aback, was silent. He asked a second and a third time. Finally, he asked, "Why are you silent?" "Because," came the reply, "*I* do not know." Shneur Zalman rejoined, "Do you think *I* know? And yet I must say it, *I* must say, God is . . ."

September 11, 2001, was a beautiful day. Some may have uttered prayers of thanksgiving on seeing such beauty, other simply reveled in it, wanting to be out and about in the sunshine. And then disaster hit, out of nowhere, unexpectedly, and the beautiful day took on an unreal cast, the super-brilliance of a movie, the way the day looks as you ride in a funeral procession and wonder how the world goes on. Its unreality mirrored the unreal horror, which would also come to look like a movie, a bad one, a B horror film of people fleeing a monster made of smoke. And all any of us wanted was a monster to hit back, to be as strong as the evil, to keep us safe.

In seventeenth-century Prague, it's said that Rabbi Judah Loew, the great rabbi known as the Maharal, sought to protect his community from an enemy attack, and so fashioned a golem, one of the many forms of magic created in the European ghettos of the time. There were devils of all kinds living in legend, and dybbuks, and *k'silim*.

> *A golem was an artificial man [until Cynthia Ozick saw fit a couple of years ago to create a female golem in her novel* The Puttermesser Papers*] in which a ba-al shem, Master of the Name, could breathe life by pronouncing one of the secret divine names according to a special formula, and using earth to shape the creature. The idea comes from the biblical story of God creating Adam from the earth. Jeremiah was said to have made one, and so was the writer of wisdom Ben Sira. A golem came to life when the name, in its special order, was put into its mouth and was "de-activated" by reversing the name. But sometimes they got out of hand and created their own terror.*[36]

I've been wishing for a golem this week, wishing like a child for something that could counteract the terror of the week. Our ancestors who were used to living with low-level terror understood this and created for themselves a host of supernatural beings. And maybe we have created golems, beings who started as benign who've gotten out of hand. We will learn in time what role we—our country—had in creating and training those who have wrought such havoc against us. For now, maybe a golem isn't the thing to wish for, unpredictability not the best road to comfort.

36. Paul Johnson, *History of the Jews* (New York: Harper Perennial, 1987), 265.

Our story already has enough unpredictability built in. We don't know the ending, for instance. What happens from here? Do we go to war? Against whom? How? Do thousands of innocent people get killed because thousands of innocent people got killed? Will there be retribution? Against New York? When? How?

Shall we say, "September 11, 2001, was a beautiful day, and it was just the beginning"?

We will have time aplenty for speculation and new fear. For now, we have fear enough. Let's leave the speculation for another week. Instead, as children have for centuries, let's lull ourselves to sleep with images of comfort and security, the angels that surround us in reassurance:

> *B'shem Adonai Elohei Yisrael: Mimini Micha-el, umis'moli Gavri-el, umil'fanai Uri-el, umei-achorai R'fa-el, v'al roshi Sh'chinat El.*

> In the name of *Adonai* the God of Israel: On my right hand, Michael / Who is like God. On my left, Gavriel, God's strength. Before me, Uriel, God's light. Behind me, Rafael, God's healing. And above my head, *Sh'chinat El*, God's indwelling presence.

Incomparable presence, strength, light, healing, and spirit within. We need you all. We need presence to feel comforted and not alone, to feel arms around us, hands to hold, whispered words in our ears. We need strength to go on, to face challenges now and yet to come, the true strength of careful response and not just revenge. We need light to see clearly by, light instead of irrational heat, to see our neighbors as neighbors and not enemies, to see a true enemy before we go to war. We need healing of our wounds, our hearts, our city's heart, healing before moving on. And we need to remember the *Shechinah*, mothering presence, dwelling within us, our own inner core, God's still small voice.

September 11, 2001, was a beautiful day that stopped time. We learned what other nations have learned—that we are vulnerable and must own up to it. We remembered that we have shown a superpower's least appealing characteristics and must examine them. We suffered great losses of life, of vitality, of character. Some among us suffered personal losses, a cousin, a friend, a colleague. It is a minor miracle that all members of our congregation are safe, and it teaches us something about strata of society that we will look at later. We felt unsafe, and in some profound way, we may never feel safe again. But surrounded by strength, light, healing, and God's presence, we will go on, if for no other reason than that time stopped only briefly, and we have to go with it. We will mourn for some time, weep at unexpected moments, forget why we went out or who we were calling, bump into things, and keep going. Be kind to yourselves. Don't expect too much. Find pleasure in small things and shrug off annoyances. Remember to tell your friends what a friend of mine called to tell me today: "I love you."

September 11, 2001 / the twenty-third of Elul 5761, was a beautiful day. It was someone's birthday, someone's anniversary, someone's funeral, someone's first day of school. It was a day like any other, only prettier. And then it changed our lives.

Israel/Palestine

Ellen Faces Her Fears
and Talks about Israel

Rosh HaShanah 2006 / 5767

On the day the ceasefire began, Kolot Chayeinu had a discussion about the fighting between Israel and Gaza and Lebanon. We spoke in small groups about how the fighting had affected each of us and what we hoped would happen there next. When the groups reported back, one spokesperson noted that many in his group had talked of their confusion, not knowing quite what to think. This surprised someone from another group who asked, "What are they confused about?!" I sat quietly then, but inwardly was shocked at the surprise. How could they not be confused? I sure was! And I know many of you were confused then too, finding your long-held positions shaken, your certainty a little less certain.

One Kolot person, for example, a longtime far-leftist, found herself defending Israel to a group of Muslim friends. You never know. Some people who came to that evening's discussions were afraid, especially if they held opinions usually seen as further to the right, because they felt that Kolot is generally more left-leaning and their opinions might be dismissed or shouted down. It wasn't that way that night—even with our range of opinions we had really respectful conversations. But I understand their fear as I prepare to talk to you about Israel after this summer's fighting. I too am a little afraid to speak to this gathered Kolot community, so much so that the first drafts of this sermon were shaped as a letter to a third party, allowing me to escape from speaking to you directly. But of course there is no escape, for me as your rabbi and for any of us from confronting the situation and our responses.

Before I say more, I want to take note of this community tonight. Among you here are those who supported Israel in its fighting this summer and wish it had been able to continue. Here are people who saw Israel as the aggressor from the get-go and still do. Here too are people who supported Israel initially and then became convinced that the way Israel was fighting was a wrong, unwinnable strategy. Here are those who became convinced that Israel's killing of so many civilians was immoral, whether Hezbollah helped engineer it or not. Here are those who have friends in Lebanon and who worried about them, as many others here worried about Israelis in danger. And here are Israelis with family who had to move to stay safe and others with family in the Israeli army. Here sit American Jews who have lived in Israel, others who travel there often, many who have never been.

In our community are artists and writers who connect to writers and artists in Israel; activists who spend precious time working with Palestinians in the West Bank; activists who work and teach in Israel; Jews who fear the results for them of Israel's tarnished reputation in the world; and here are some who rarely think about any of this at all. There are people in this community who have lost a child and whose hearts reach out to those in Israel, Gaza, and Lebanon who lost theirs this summer. Here are some who wonder if they could watch their children go into army service and others who wish all the Israeli soldiers would refuse to fight—or at least refuse to serve in the occupied territories. Even the staff of Kolot spans the poles, with an Israeli Jew now on staff who leans more to the right and an American Jew who used to live in Lebanon and spent a lot of the summer worrying about friends there. I stand tonight in the center of this span of experience and opinion. To the leftists here, I am a frequent disappointment: Why didn't I condemn Israel in no uncertain terms when I returned from vacation in early August!? How can I say I love Israel when it behaves so abominably? How can I ever praise it?

To those further to the right, I am a frequent disappointment: Why don't I state clearly my love for Israel? Why am I all the time criticizing it? Why do I spend so much time on the rights of Palestinians when I should be concerned with Israeli victims of suicide bombings? Why don't I ever praise it?

And those in the center fear they have no voice and wish I would raise my voice with their point of view. They too are frequently disappointed. Tonight, standing here before all of you, I raise my own voice, which leans a little to the left, a little to the right, and often stops at Kolot's center. I feel sort of like the kid who caught the ball and now has to run with it. I have established that you are all going to be disappointed, so relax, sit back, and listen.

I supported Israel's response to Hezbollah at first, fearing and hating Hezbollah as I do and agreeing that they couldn't just cross the border to kill and kidnap without a strong response. I still believed in Israel's military strength and its vaunted intelligence and thought the response would be swift and clear and right. Soon, I watched in horror as that reasonable response turned unreasonable, too focused on air strikes and bombs, too murderous of civilians. And, from where I stand, it also didn't work: Israel did not get back its kidnapped soldiers in Lebanon or Gaza, it did not defeat Hezbollah. It didn't even seem to know, with that famous Israeli intelligence, the extent of Hezbollah's strength. Hamas is looking a little more defeated in Gaza, due to lack of funds, and may even enter a unity government with the PLO, though that is iffy. And they too still have their kidnapped Israeli soldier. The Palestinian people are the biggest losers, I think—so many of those killed in Israel were Arabs, there is less attention given to them now, they are suffering more, and it is not clear when there may be any kind of agreement between their leaders and Israel's.

Later this summer, I began to think and then read enough to feel confirmed that Israel had allowed itself to be used as what one Kolot member called the United States' cat's-paw and what writer Seymour Hersh called its stalking horse, with Israel and Hezbollah as stand-ins for the United States and Iran. Now Hezbollah is the darling of those who wish to defeat Israel and probably has a slew of new recruits to its murderous ways. It also has huge supplies of funds and weapons from Iran and Syria, no real opposition in Lebanon, and great cachet in the Middle East and beyond. And the United States government seems to be thinking about attacking Iran, in spite of the failure of its stalking horse expedition. Here, though, there are questions being raised about the arms we send to Israel, notably cluster bombs whose use or misuse some in Congress are questioning. That is where my head is.

My heart weeps for the loss of life, for the children everywhere caught in a fight not of their making. On Monday, August 14, the same day we had our discussion at Kolot, we learned that twenty-year-old Israeli soldier Uri Grossman, son of well-known and often controversial writer David Grossman, had been killed in action a few days before that day's ceasefire between Israel and Hezbollah. I wept when I read it. I have no family members in Israel to worry about, and David Grossman became my family that day in a way I would never have expected. I cried for his loss of a son, the sacrifice even this left-leaning writer ended up making.

It was David Grossman who let so many Israeli and American Jews—including this one—hear the voices of Palestinians in his books *Yellow Wind* and *Sleeping on a Wire*. He is solidly against the Israeli occupation of the Palestinian lands and sparked controversy and discussion in Israel with his words. So it was David Grossman, among others, whom I watched in July and August to see how he would respond when Hezbollah attacked an Israeli army patrol and began raining rockets down on civilians in the north. He supported Israel's retaliation. By mid-August, Grossman and fellow writers Amos Oz and A. B. Yehoshua held a press conference to call for a ceasefire and to denounce the Israeli plan to inflict a more devastating blow to Hezbollah and thus even more death and pain to Lebanese civilians. In that press conference, David Grossman said, "Now we must look three steps ahead and not to the regular direction, not to the familiar, instinctive reaction of the Israeli way of fighting—that is, what doesn't work with force will work with much more force. Force, in this case, will fan the flames of hatred to Israel in the region and the entire world, and may even, heaven forbid, create the situation that will . . . push the Middle East to an all-out, regional war." Two days later his son was killed.

My colleague Rabbi Maya Leibovich officiated at the funeral. Another rabbi said to me, "Maya Leibovich is sort of like the Ellen Lippmann of Israel [meaning mostly that she began her own congregation], and now she has had to do this hard thing." I tried to imagine being an Israeli rabbi and doing all those hard funerals for twenty-year-olds. I weep for these deaths and I mourn other losses: The "we can't even pretend any more" loss of the early Zionist dream that Israel would act according to the best of Jewish values, would in fact become a light to the nations. The loss of Israel's feisty independence, as we realized what a strong role the United States had in this summer's fighting. The final loss of the image of the strong, beautiful Israeli soldier—those strong, beautiful soldiers have spent too much time stopping Palestinians at checkpoints, so, for a moment, fighting against Hezbollah looked like a right and moral war, an antidote to the years of upholding oppression . . . but only for a moment.

On Rosh HaShanah, when we will read the *Akeidah*, the story of the near sacrifice of Isaac, I wonder about sons and sacrifices. The late great Israeli poet Yehuda Amichai once wrote, "A child is a missile into the coming generations. I launched him: I'm still trembling." In this summer of missiles, how could the Israelis, the Lebanese, the Palestinians launch their sons and daughters? I weep as I hear more and more people wondering about Israel's own survival.

Many, like me, were afraid this summer that somehow this fight showed that Israel might not survive. And now there is another kind of talk, a questioning of whether Israel should exist or, in an odd replay of the early Zionist arguments, whether Israel should exist there. Maybe Argentina looks good, someone said to me— Argentina! Where early Zionists thought of putting their new state and where bombs apparently orchestrated by Hezbollah ripped apart a Jewish Community Center in 1992 and 1994. Part of me is angry at these questions: Sudan kills hundreds of thousands of its people and no one suggests Sudan should cease to exist or move somewhere else. The United States right now is doing several things that I find wrong or even abhorrent, yet no one speaks of the U.S. not existing. What internal and external antisemitism raises the questions so quickly about Israel? These questions are not asked by crackpots, but by reasonable people who are showing their fear.

Here in New York, here at Kolot Chayeinu as the new year begins, it looks like Israel's actions—maybe even its existence— makes it harder to be safe as a Jew elsewhere. How ironic, that the place created as a haven for Jews facing pogroms and regular discrimination has come to be seen as a creator of insecurity and fear. We here know that fear. We also know the joys of living in the biggest Jewish city in the world mostly without fear. I always say that God did not know America yet when instructing Moses to take us Hebrew slaves out of Egypt and move us toward the land of promise. In 1987 I came up out of Egypt and arrived back in Jerusalem in time for the Passover seder, at the end of which I said with gusto, "Next year in New York!"

This city is my Jewish home. But something stirs in me when I arrive in Jerusalem, something born of ancient longing and recent experience, of evening light on marble walls and breathing desert air. How can I not love the place that inspires Amos Oz and A. B. Yehoshua and David Grossman to write as they do? How can I not love the place that—major threats and canceled parade and all—

hosted World Gay and Lesbian Pride this summer? How can I not love the place that thrives on loud, vehement, passionate public debate, perhaps never more so than now?

I asked a few people what they would say if they were speaking about Israel tonight. A carpenter and home repair contractor—a Jewish Red diaper baby—said he would remind us all that the damage done by the Holocaust is still very much alive. A rabbi friend who doesn't work in a congregation said, "I would say that we have a choice, we have chosen to pretend that we don't have a partner for peace. We have always had a partner for peace and we do now." A friend, a secular Jew who studies history, said, "I thought we were chosen to be the moral conscience of the countries we lived in and we lost that role when we got our own country. . . . We were much better off when we did not have an Israel. But we do and it is. There is no going back."

Right now, I love and hate Israel, feel betrayed by it, rage at the gaps between its people, gaps imposed by leaders a little drunk on fear and power. Do you know that in the midst of all the fighting this summer Jerusalem's mayor decided to demolish again the home of the Dari family that I went to rebuild last November after its first demolition? Why is that necessary, if not just as a show of power? And this is mild compared to what else Israel does to Palestinians. But I love and hate Israel the way one loves and hates family. Should Israel exist and exist there?! It has to. Not only because it remains a haven for Jews when they need it—I think of fleeing there if need be, but I also think of fleeing to Canada. No, Israel must exist because it is in so many ways the focus of Jewish yearning and passion and confusion. Without it, how would we focus? Where turn our hopes and fears and doubts and rage?

I am not someone who thinks all Jews have to live in Israel, though I hope many will visit and use those visits to help shape thinking. But I do think we can't be fully Jews unless we are grappling with Israel. It is Israel that makes us question, "What does it mean to be a Jew?" It is Israel that makes us cringe or sigh at the sight of a Jewish army. It is Israel that helps us hone our values, too often in the breach. And it is Israel that shows that Jews, having founded a nation like other nations, acts a lot like other nations.

Amichai wrote, "What are we doing in this dark land with its yellow shadows that pierce the eyes? . . . Spilled blood is not the roots of trees but it's the closest thing to roots we have." I am tired of an Israel whose roots grow too much in spilled blood. I am tired of knowing that Israel has to defend itself but doesn't know when to stop. I am tired of wishing that someone would take up the hope David Grossman expressed two days before his son was killed, his wish for leaders to talk before killing more sons.

Abraham Joshua Heschel taught that despair is a great sin. I am trying not to despair. I wish that Israel and the Palestinians would arrive at a real plan, would become two states that can live peacefully with one another. I wish they would talk to each other— and I wish the United States would intervene to help make that happen—as David Grossman once said to Bill Moyers, "There is a proverb in Hebrew, 'the prisoner cannot set himself free from prison.' We need someone from the outside to bring us out of this prison, because we are prisoners of our history, of our trauma, of our psychology."

God, I pray that the Israelis and the Palestinians can be set free from the prison in which they are locked together and can create states of peace. First of all because it is right, and second of all because perhaps without the issue of the Palestinians to use as distraction, other nations who could truly care less about them would be forced to look inward and help their own people in need. I wish that Israel's neighborhood was not as tough as it is and that Israel did not contribute to its toughness. I wish that instead, true peace could be achieved between Israel and all its neighbors, and that the region could become a beacon of hope—truly *hatikvah*— for the world, rather than a model of militaristic misery. I wish that sacrificing sons and daughters were not the modus operandi of the region and that suicide bombing, missile launching, cluster bombing, and every other sort of way to kill children would cease in favor of education, jobs, home-building, and the overcoming of despair with hope. I wish that the land could be quiet for forty years, as it says over and over again in the Book of Judges, every time a new leader takes over. I used to think this was low expectation. Now I wish for it: Imagine! Quiet for forty years. I wish for new leaders to create that quiet, a quiet of justice and right. Where are the strong leaders we need here and in Jerusalem and Ramallah and Gaza and Beirut, leaders who do not turn to violence and war at any offense, but who are able to move past that impulse to higher achievement?

And I wish that the American Jewish community, whose loudest voices often brook no criticism of Israel, would take a good look at Kolot's Values Statement: "We believe that Jews have an obligation to grapple with the many issues and emotions connected to our historic attachment to Israel and the current political situation in Israel and Palestine. While we join Jews everywhere in facing Jerusalem while we pray, we have no consensus on political solutions nor their philosophical underpinnings." I love that we have no consensus, because the issues are so big and so complex and so scary that we are right to be confused, to hold off, to argue. It shows our strength. When we first formed Kolot Chayeinu, with our dream of a café that could hold prayer and art and learning and discussion, an early model was the great New York Jewish cafeterias. My strongest memory of sitting in the old Garden cafeteria on East Broadway is of the intense arguments that went on between sips of soup or tea, arguments over literature, over politics, and certainly, though I was less aware of it then, over Israel.

The Garden cafeteria and its arguments are still much on my mind when I think about Kolot's future. Such arguments do not divide; rather, they strengthen connection. They are at the heart of Kolot's non-consensus about Israel, and here too, they need not divide but rather help clarify, create new bonds, forge real *kesher*—connection. My hope lies in the strength of arguments and connections. *HaTikvah* says, *Od lo avdah tikvateinu*—"Our hope is not yet lost." Much of the time it is hard to hold onto that hope, to know how to change with it. In a recent *New Yorker* article, Bill Clinton quotes Seamus Heany's poem "The Cure at Troy" in honor of Nelson Mandela and Walter Sisulu. I leave you with his hope:

> History says, Don't hope
> On this side of the grave.
> But then, once in a lifetime
> The longed-for tidal wave
> Of justice can rise up,
> And hope and history rhyme.

Israel/Palestine

Yom HaZikaron and Yom HaAtzma-ut

Seeking Redemptive Peace

April 2007

Tonight sirens will sound across Israel calling the nation to a moment of collective reflection and sorrow for Yom HaZikaron, Israel's Memorial Day. When the country was established, Israel's leaders were determined to link Yom HaZikaron to Yom HaAtzma-ut; as the sun sets on Yom HaZikaron, Yom HaAtzma-ut begins, and slowly, Israelis begin their Independence Day celebrations.

I love counting the Omer. This simple ritual that helps us count from Pesach to Shavuot—from freedom to responsibility—grounds me in those intervening weeks, reminding me that while Pesach and Shavuot are peak moments in our calendar, each and every day, each and every effort, counts. I am struck that the Omer count is the umbrella under which so much else takes place: ordinary days aplenty, but also most of Pesach, Yom HaShoah, Yom HaZikaron, and Yom HaAtzma-ut. Throughout these days in which we celebrate freedom, mourn our people's greatest tragedy, remember fallen soldiers, and celebrate the independence of the State of Israel, we are also counting, night after night, day after day. As we count, we can imagine the Shoah's victims counting the days to deportation or barely imaginable freedom; the families of fallen Israeli soldiers counting the minutes after hearing the news of their loved one's death; the Israelis of 1948 counting the seconds until they heard the good news of independence.

As we move toward Yom HaZikaron and Yom HaAtzma-ut this year, we have so much sorrow to count: the numbers injured and killed in last year's war with Lebanon; the young women harmed in what became the Israeli presidential sex scandal; victims of official corruption; victims of rockets and bombs. And as we count, we can't ignore the mounting suffering of Palestinians having their homes demolished, watching their olive groves—and livelihoods—uprooted by the route of the security barrier, experiencing lengthy checkpoint waits, struggling with growing poverty, and more. How will we find hope or joy as we count to this year's Yom HaAtzma-ut?

Significantly, at Yom HaAtzma-ut, many greet friends and family with the words *mo-adim l'simchah* (happy season), the greeting traditionally given during the intermediate days of Pesach and Sukkot. Expressed at Yom HaAtzma-ut, it seems to imply that this day—despite much joy—is no full festival, whose appropriate greeting would be *chag samei-ach* (happy holiday). Further, the traditional response to this Yom HaAtzma-ut greeting is *l'geulah sh'leimah* (to a complete redemption)—surely the joy of Yom HaAtzma-ut cannot be complete until the hoped-for *g'ulah sh'leimah* has arrived. Can it arrive when so much is so wrong in the state we love so well? How many changes would have to take place to bring about that time of true redemption, a time when the dual observances of Yom HaAtzma-ut and al-Nakba (the Palestinian Catastrophe) are blended into a harmonious end, a joint tale of two independent and secure states? How many days and nights would we have to count to move from this isolated happy, not-quite-a-festival season, to that longed-for complete redemption?

I suggest we let the Omer counting serve as a reminder and a model: even in our most desperate moments, we must not forget that there is still hope, that there are many who continue to make the enormous effort that peace requires. Perhaps we should begin on Yom HaAtzma-ut this year, the fifth of Iyar, counting not measures of grain as with the Omer, but efforts toward redemptive peace. We can begin by counting from the first day of Iyar, Rosh Chodesh and count—along with our Omer—to the fifth day, Yom HaAtzma-ut: Count one for the first round of talks between Israeli Prime Minister Ehud Olmert and Palestinian Authority President Mahmoud Abbas with a second round already planned during the second half of May with Secretary of State Condoleeza Rice. Count two for H Res. 143 introduced by congressional rep. Susan Davis (D-CA), calling on President Bush to appoint a special envoy for Middle East peace in order to return Israelis and Palestinians to the negotiating table. Count three for the Arab League's unanimous endorsement of the Saudi Arabian peace initiative at their March meeting, which proposes a general Arab peace agreement with Israel in exchange for a two-state solution to the Israeli-Palestinian conflict. Just this week, Israeli Prime Minister Olmert said, "I'm ready to accept the Saudi initiative as a basis for discussions with the Palestinians, together with the Saudis." Count four for Syrian peace overtures, diplomatic indication that the Syrians themselves are willing to take the first step toward peace with Israel.

And finally, count five for Brit Tzedek, which celebrates its fifth anniversary this month. Five years of hard work and dedicated hearts have made an enormous impact on the Jewish American scene. In 2002, those of us who would seek peace with the Palestinians felt isolated and silenced, but in no small part due to the efforts of Brit Tzedek, we now know that we are part of a growing group of Jewish Americans who have understood that to be pro-peace is to truly be pro-Israel. Congratulations to Brit Tzedek, and to all of us who are involved. *Yeshar koach!*

Surely we can all think of more signs of hope and keep this count going. How should we count? Begin by reading or singing

Psalm 122:6–7 in English or Hebrew: "Pray for the well-being of Jerusalem; / May those who love you be at peace. / May there be peace within your walls, / Equanimity within your enclosures." Add this prayer, adapted from *The Book of Blessings*, by Marcia Falk: "*Nish'al mei-ein hashalom*—Let us request of the source of peace / For nothing is whole that is not first rent and out of the torn we make whole again. May we live with promise in creation's lap, redemption budding in our hands." Then say, "This is the first (second, third . . .) night of the count toward *g'ulah sh'leimah*, complete redemption in Israel. May redemption bud in my (our) hands." To make that last phrase real, make a donation to and/or volunteer your time for an organization working for peace.

> *Od yavo shalom aleinu*
> *Salaam, aleinu v'al kol haolam*
> *Salaam, shalom*
> Peace will yet come to us
> Peace: on us and on the entire world
> Peace, peace.

Israel, Exceptionalism, Human Rights

Responding to Peter Beinart

Rabbis for Human Rights–North America Conference,
December 7, 2010 / 30 Kislev 5771

Thank you, thank you, Jane Eisner, and my friends the conference planners who suggested I speak today. And thank you to Peter Beinart, who shook up the established Jewish world with his critique, coming as it did from someone who looked more like an insider than an expected critic. Peter, I want to say welcome to denunciation from the right! And also to express my gratitude: we need more openings to discussion these days.

I am speaking as co-chair of Rabbis for Human Rights–North America[37] and as the rabbi of a congregation in Brooklyn, a liberal, even left-leaning congregation that nevertheless has as much trouble talking about Israel as any other. We are trying to remedy that. Our Values Statement says, "We believe that Jews have an obligation to grapple with the many issues and emotions connected to our historic attachment to Israel and the current political situation in Israel and Palestine. While we join Jews everywhere in facing

---

37. Now known as T'ruah.

Jerusalem while we pray, we have no consensus on political solutions nor their philosophical underpinnings." Not exactly a Jewish establishment view.

Peter, when I first read your essay I had two thoughts. One was, "What took you so long?" Rabbis for Human Rights, which I will talk more about in a moment, was founded more than twenty years ago, and our North American group has been around for at least eight, to do exactly what you suggest is missing in American Jewish talk about Israel. So I am going to be wanting to ask you to tell us a little about what brought you to this place and where you came from.

But first, a story: A member of my congregation died a couple of years ago, way too young. His daughter, a young woman who had grown up in our congregation, was in her early twenties and was angry and bereft after his death. I met with her and suggested she come to shul to say *Kaddish* with us. She said, "I don't want to have anything to do with anything Jewish, because of Israel." When an Israeli friend wrote me after reading your article last spring and asked if it was true that young people were distancing themselves from Israel and from Judaism, I thought of this young woman. "Yes, it's true," I wrote.

But . . . about a month ago, I had the honor of speaking to a group of about forty-five college students who had come from all up and down the East Coast to protest the Hebron Fund's "Hebron Aid Flotilla" fundraiser. J-Street U organized these students, but other organizations also work with Jewish college students on issues related to Israel. They are not distanced from Israel. They may not be Zionists, but they are not distanced from Israel. The young people who disrupted Netanyahu's speech at the GA are not disengaged. In fact, they are deeply engaged. They are not embracing the old message about Israel that you deplored in your article; the American Jewish establishment surely does not speak for them. But these young people argue, urge action, bust up meetings, study, travel, and otherwise make known their connection to Israel—and to Palestine.

I think that some young Jews are distancing from Israel and some are not. Some are embracing Israel while leaving their liberal American values here. Some are embracing it with more fervor than they give to any cause here or anywhere else. Either way, it is exceptional.

I was in Israel and Palestine in late October on a Rabbis for Human Rights–North America human rights mission. Among other things, I stood in the walled-in, walled-out city of Hebron, where I confess my love for Israel was hard to find. I have been many times in the past decade and find that I can no longer go just as a friend or just as a tourist. I must engage in protest, see human rights abuses with my own eyes, plant or harvest or rebuild with my own hands. I don't feel like that about traveling to New Mexico or to Spain, both of which remind me of Israel. Conversely, I don't want to travel to Sudan or China or Iran at all. Israel is exceptional. It is not just another lovely or historical place, and it is not the worst human rights abuser in the world.

What it is, is *our* human rights abuser, for those of us who see it as ours because we are Jews and it is a Jewish state. Israel is also exceptional because it bills itself as a Western-style democracy, and therefore, it calls to us to judge it by Western democratic standards, by its standards, the standards of its Declaration of Independence, which says, "The state of Israel . . . will ensure complete equality of social and political rights to all its inhabitants, irrespective of religion, race or sex" and more. The U.S. too strays far from our Declaration of Independence. But we have to be clear that so does Israel.

We who connect to Israel and criticize and protest its actions do so from an understanding of, as you have written, "the defining values of American Jewish political culture: a belief in open debate, a skepticism about military force, a commitment to human rights."

But many of us also do so from what we understand to be the defining values of Judaism: *tzelem Elohim*, the belief that all people are created in the image of God; *tzedek tzedek tirdof*, the understanding that we are urged to pursue justice using just means; *laasot tzedekah u'mishpat*, the understanding that we are to honor our heritage by doing what is just and right. Those of us who engage in the work of Rabbis for Human Rights do so precisely because we want to bring together our American values and our Jewish ones and support what you describe as "a Zionism that challenges Israel's behavior in the West Bank and Gaza Strip and toward its own Arab citizens."

RHR was founded as that kind of Zionist organization, espousing Zionism—again quoting from your article—"that recognized Palestinians as deserving of dignity and capable of peace." We wanted those values in our work for Israel, and we wanted them in our work for rights and justice here in North America as well.

We have also always thought that Jewish values—not just American values—mean a belief in open debate. Events of recent years have taught us that in fact the Jewish community is afraid of open debate when it comes to Israel. Over and over again we have watched and often protested as scholars, artists, writers, students, and rabbis who told the truth as they saw it have been scorned, vilified, and occasionally physically attacked.

I went to two protests during my recent trip. First, I joined friends in Tel Aviv for a two-thousand-people demonstration against this ridiculous insidious government loyalty oath. And second, I joined the dedicated young people who go each Friday to Sheikh Jarrah to protest the evacuation there of Palestinians from their homes so that Jewish settlers can move in. They have coined a phrase that still rings in my ears: *Ein k'dushah b'ir k'vushah*, "There is no holiness in an occupied city."

I was struck by the phrase—by the use of the word *k'dushah*— "holiness." It did not say "there is no justice in an occupied city" or "there is no peace in an occupied city." To use the word *k'dushah* connects to a deep religious sensibility, that of the settlers they hope to address, surely, but also that of people like me, people who find a home with Rabbis for Human Rights. For us, it is a religious motivation that underlies our actions in and about Israel. I would hate to live with a defined split that sees religious and conservative together, secular and liberal together, with no room for liberal and religious.

I would suggest that liberal or left and religious might be a place that would attract more young Jews, those who are flocking to Yiddish and *musar* classes, those who want to protest Israel's human rights abuses and also learn Jewish and pray Jewish.

Having said all this, I have two questions for you, in addition to "What took you so long and how did you come to this place?" which is my first question. Also:

1. I see from the piece in last week's *Jewish Week* that one reason for your concern now is that you want your own children to grow up differently, to be able to blend liberal American values and profound Jewish connections. I am curious as to how you think we can or should teach our children about Israel now. How do we teach them to connect to Israel and to abhor what Israel does to Palestinians within Israel and in the occupied territories? We are trying in my congregation and in others headed by rabbis here, but it is tough.

2. At some point the questions of what the Jewish establishment or disaffected young people think or do is beside the point when serious human rights abuses are taking place in an Israel in which the very bases of democracy are being eroded, as we heard Naomi Chazan say the other night. So what do we do? Specifically, can you address the new "edge" question, the one that keeps coming up and that I think we need to take seriously, the question of divestment or boycott as a strategy? Several people at the conference have decried it. I am uncertain, but I am sure that many of those who espouse it care deeply about trying to get Israel to live up to its Declaration of Independence.

What do you think?

Kolot Chayeinu as an Open Tent

I have regularly been asked, "What does Kolot Chayeinu think or feel about Israel and Palestine?"

Well, in 2005, the community ratified what was then a new Mission and a Values Statement. The "value" about Israel reads:

> *"We believe that Jews have an obligation to grapple with the many issues and emotions connected to our historic attachment to Israel and the current political situation in Israel and Palestine. While we join Jews everywhere in facing Jerusalem while we pray, we have no consensus on political solutions nor their philosophical underpinnings."*

That Value statement led to a way of operating we refer to as the Open Tent: We accept a wide range of opinions, have held a variety of programs, and co-sponsored others, while deciding not to co-sponsor some that might upset a fragile balance that allows us to move forward together in community. That Open Tent has also sometimes had a stifling effect.

Kolot's Values Statement was a consensus about no-consensus. A new 2018 Israel-Palestine Working Group is currently digging into both the Values Statement and the idea of the Open Tent, to explore possible changes in language, and new ways to for the community to approach the myriad issues that arise when American Jews look at Israel and Palestine.

Dreaming in the Night

March 27, 2010 / 12 Nisan 5770

It is Shabbat HaGadol, the great Shabbat before Pesach, so let's go back to Exodus.

Come dream with me: It is darkest night. You cower in your home as the wails and weeping of the Egyptians grow louder. You cover your ears, hide under a bed, anything to get away from that terrible sound as they find their firstborn children dead. But then—what?!?!—you hear your leaders' voices rising in joy: "Pharaoh has let us go free. He wants us out now!" The Egyptian voices stop weeping for a moment and urge you on, saying, "Go! If you stay we shall all be dead."

And so the Israelites left Egypt, left slavery, left the narrow place that was Mitzrayim, the constriction of soul and body. That was a night of vigil, of watching, for God; "that same night is *Adonai's*, one of vigil for all the children of Israel throughout the ages" (Exodus 12:42).

But wait! Is it a night of vigil or a night of Exodus? Or is it a night of seder and dreaming, preparing to leave?

God said to Moses and Aaron: "This is the law of the Passover offering: . . . It shall be eaten in one house. . . . The whole community of Israel shall offer it. . . . And all the Israelites did so. . . . That very day [*b'etzem hayom*] the Eternal freed the Israelites from the land of Egypt" (Exodus 12:43–51). So they left during the day?

Return with me for a moment to the night, a night of vigil, of watching, a *leil sh'murim*, a night of vigil to bring them out of the land of Egypt. Return to the night. Night is terror, strange sounds, people appearing and disappearing, demons appearing and disappearing, nightmares rising, sleep interrupted. "To leave by night," Aviva Zornberg reminds us, "is to be surreptitious, unsure of one's claims."[38] No way the people left at night; they refused Pharaoh's demands, sure of themselves, waiting to walk out in full daylight, with arms raised, defiant. At night, they prepared. For them too, it was a night of watching, of readying, of opening hearts and souls, of dreaming themselves into freedom.

Former Zen priest Clark Strand writes about what seems to be the normal human impulse to alternate sleep and wakeful rest during the night; he suggests that the expectation of a full night of sleep is a modern aberration. This waking restfulness is the time for dreaming and imagining, undistracted by artificial light or by human engagement. Rebbe Nachman of Bratslav said, "The best time for meditation is at night, when everyone is asleep."

This liminal time—a time between waking and sleeping—offers us the real possibility of our own night of watching: the seder night, a night of watching and opened awareness, a night of revelation and imagination.

Dream with me: Pharaoh has issued his orders—Out! But with Moses in the lead, the people—us!—refuse. We are emboldened by our refusal and insist on staying a night, to leave in the daylight. Some say that is when we raided the Egyptian homes for gold and silver, torches in hand. Some say we went searching for Pharaoh himself, the defeated king, groveling in defeat like a dog in the dirt. But I say we slept and dreamed, slept and dreamed. Could we have a dream as glorious as Jacob's night dream of that ladder? By sleeping and dreaming, owning our natural rhythm, we pre-

38. Aviva Gottlieb Zornberg, *The Particulars of Rapture: Reflections on Exodus* (New York: Schocken, 2001), 164.

pared our minds and hearts for freedom. We dreamed: First step. Arm raised. Flat bread. A vast sea we might swim across. And in all our dreams, somehow we knew, God was with us. *Hayinu k'cholmim*: We were as dreamers, yet were awake; sleepers, stoking the fire of imagination.

And now? What of our seders? Can they offer us the symbols and foods to stoke imagination, so that the night that follows is a time for dreaming freedom? Can we dream and imagine our own freedom from the narrow places that constrict us? Can we be expansive in our dreams, ready for the broad *midbar* to come? Can our seders not celebrate freedom so much as prepare for it?

John Ruskay, CEO of UJA-Federation of New York, writes:

> *At its core, the seder is an act of imagination. The curriculum of the seder assumes if we enact the rituals of oppression, if we taste the foods associated with slavery, then we will be able to experience bondage as if we were actually in Egypt. And if we can imagine ourselves slaves on these nights of Passover—as we are commanded to—then we will be able to better understand and experience what it feels like to be unemployed and scared. Or homeless and hungry. Or elderly and alone . . . Passover is about looking out. It's about stretching and strengthening our empathetic muscles, which can atrophy from excessive fear, anxiety, and self-involvement.*[39]

So what is freedom? Our haftarah, the text from the prophet Malachi, offers us a vision: That the night of watching, our night of dreaming, may yet lead to *yom Adonai, hagadol v'hanora*, "the great and awesome day of God," when families will be reconciled, Elijah appear, and in that unity we prevent destruction (Exodus 3:23–24). "The sun of victory will rise to bring healing" (Exodus 3:20).

Malachi is the last prophet. The dreams are up to us now, and we need preparation. This is Shabbat HaGadol, the Great Shab-

---

39. John Ruskay, "Passover: Imagine, Empathize, and Act," https://www.ujafedny.org/news/passover-imagine-empathize-and-act/.

bat, because it gives us a chance to envision the sun that brings healing, but not without the night that gives us time and space to dream. We look ahead as well as past. *Karev yom asher hu lo yom v'lo lailah.* The day is coming that is not day nor night, but in fact is both: the night of dreaming, the day of freedom, the night of terror, the day of redemption.

Hope

These Things I Remember
and I Pour Out My Heart

Yom Kippur 2006 / 5766

A painful Rabbinic story:

When they led Rabbi Akiva to the executioner, it was time for recit-
ing the Sh'ma. *With iron combs they scraped away his skin as he*
recited Sh'ma Yisrael, *freely accepting the yoke of God's sover-*
eignty. "Even now?!" his disciples asked. He said to them, "All my
life I have been troubled by the verse: 'Love the Eternal your God...
with all your soul,' which means even if God takes your life. I often
wondered when I would be able to fulfill that obligation. And now that
I have the opportunity, should I not do so?!" He left the world while
uttering Echad—*God is one. (Babylonian Talmud,* B'rachot *61b)*

Eileh ezk'rah v'nafshi alai eshp'chah, "These things I remember
as I pour out my heart." After the Yom Kippur *Avodah* service
tomorrow we will read *Eileh Ezk'rah,* "These Things I Remember," a poem about ten martyrs who died under Roman persecu-
tion for teaching Torah. It entered the Ashkenazic liturgy in the
Middle Ages, a "cry of anguish and bewilderment at the savagery
of Jewish fate during the Crusades."[40] We Jews know about torture, by the Romans, the Crusaders, the Spanish Inquisitors, the
Nazis. *All of these we remember and pour out our hearts.*

40. Jonathan Magonet, in *Hadeish Yameinu,* ed. by Ronald Aigen (Montreal: Congregation Dorshei Emet, 1996), 621.

So if we know and remember what it is to be victims of torture, why am I talking about torture tonight? I am talking about it because as a member of the Executive Committee of Rabbis for Human Rights–North America, I have been in on the Rabbis Campaign Against Torture from the beginning and have had a chance to hear from experts, learn from rabbinic sources, and advocate with those in Washington who are finally beginning to work against it. But mostly, I am talking about it because I wept when I realized how far our country has fallen. This was in June, when I heard Josh Rubinstein, Northeast director, Amnesty International, say, "We have always worked with centers for treatment of torture victims from countries around the world, *but never in thirty years of my work in this field have we had to look at victims of torture committed by our own country.*"

I startled myself by weeping, but after his talk I broke down. I wept for my country and how far we have come from the ideals I learned to love as a child. I wept for shame. When I told this to friends, some said, "How naïve can you get?! The United States has been involved in torture and abuse the world over for years!" I know that. And yet . . . We have crossed a line here, damaging further our reputation abroad and our safety there and here, and pouring out a little more of our hearts with each incident, each humiliation, each conviction of a Pvt. Lyndie England while higher level officials remain at large. Kolot member Elizabeth Holtzman, writing in *The Nation* in July, said, "President Bush likes to blame a few 'bad apples' for the serious mistreatment of Iraqi prisoners. But the problem is not limited to a few bad apples at the bottom of the barrel."[41] She strongly advocated holding senior officials accountable and urged congressional action: a special prosecutor, legislation, hearings, press conferences, and more. It is gratifying that the Senate, led by Senator John McCain (who knows of torture

41. Elizabeth Holtzman, "Torture and Accountability," *The Nation*, June 28, 2005, https://www.thenation.com/article/torture-and-accountability/.

firsthand), has finally voted—decisively—to bring military prison camps under the rule of law, banning the use of cruel, inhumane, or degrading treatment (which was already illegal). Two weeks ago a delegation of rabbis met with Senator McCain and presented him with our "Rabbinic Letter against Torture," signed by close to six hundred rabbis. He told them how much he appreciated our efforts and how important public opinion is in the success of his initiative. The rabbis made a commitment to him to do all we can to support his efforts and other similar initiatives aimed at ending torture. I was not at that meeting but was at a meeting the next day with a leading staff person in Senator Carl Levin's office, where we also presented our letter. It felt hopeful to be doing something, to do what we as rabbis—and Jews—can do. We have developed a Jewish Campaign Against Torture, too, which will amass thousands of signatures on a letter to use in similar advocacy. Some of you have a brochure in your *machzors* that allows you to sign on, to join activists like Tony Kushner on this important list. Please do so, or ask me how if you don't have the brochure.

Yet while six hundred rabbis and Senator John McCain and Bob Herbert are doing all they can to bring torture into the public eye, it remains largely unspoken, ignored even as we read other news of the war in Iraq, march in protest of the war, question the U.S. administration for other lapses and errors. Why? Before we at RHR began this Campaign Against Torture, I was—maybe like you—someone who either read about sexually charged torture with creepy fascination or turned the page as fast as I could. In either case, I certainly didn't feel I was reading or thinking about human beings being tortured. Yet torture, like terror, is about human abuse of other humans, and I think we ought to pay more attention. "Hayder Sabbar Abd reported that seven men were all placed in hoods . . . and the beating began. 'They beat our heads on the walls and the doors. . . . He said his jaw had been broken . . . . He received 50 blows in two hours. . . . When we refused to take off our clothes, they beat us and tore our clothes off with a blade.' He saw himself in the photos from Abu Ghraib, naked, his hand on his genitals, a female soldier pointing and smiling with a cigarette in her mouth."[42]

The abuses at Abu Ghraib were perfected at Guantanamo and are seen in Afghanistan as well. And we know that the United States has been practicing extraordinary rendition, which means sending people they want to torture to serve sentences in countries where torture is less constrained.[43] It is painful to face these truths, yet it is a painful honor, as my friend Rabbi Margaret Holub has said. It is painful to realize that President Bush appears likely to veto the Senate bill, and as the *New York Times* reports, "continues to block any serious investigation of the abuse, torture and murder of prisoners."[44] The *Times* urges the creation of a bipartisan and independent commission, armed with subpoena power, to investigate. It may be a long wait. Yet it is an honor to be part of a group that has gotten six hundred rabbis and untold numbers of other Jews to sign onto letters against torture, which has been able to meet with the key legislators, which is getting out a Jewish voice that has been largely silent about torture. And it is an honor to realize that one place we can look to for support is Israel and a landmark 1999 decision by the Israeli Supreme Court. I and many of you have been critical of much of Israel's behavior in the last many years, and we are often fearful as Jews because of how Israel's behavior is perceived by the rest of the world. In the case of torture, we can now—since 1999—hold Israel up as an example. Would that the U.S. government would adopt a ruling as clear and important as that of the Israeli Supreme Court! We should be proclaiming it from the rooftops!

The background: In 1988, the Landau Commission there authorized the use of "moderate physical pressure" in what they

42. *Washington Post*, January 2002.
43. Melissa Weintraub, "A Rabbinic Resource on Jewish Values and the Issue of Torture" (Rabbis for Human Rights–North America).
44. *New York Times*, October 9, 2005.

called "ticking bomb" situations, in which a suspect is thought to know of an immediate threat. Soon, though, most or all Palestinian detainees were treated as potential "ticking bombs." In 1999, the Supreme Court in Israel, recognizing that most Palestinians were being tortured in some way, ruled that torture and other cruel, degrading, and inhumane means of interrogation are illegal. The ruling states, in part, that "although a democracy must fight with one hand tied behind its back, it nonetheless has the upper hand. The rule of law and the liberty of an individual constitute important components in its understanding of security. At the end of the day, they strengthen its spirit and this strength allows it to overcome its difficulties."

A couple of years ago I had the chance, thanks to [congregant] Russ Pearce, to hear Israeli Chief Justice Barak speak about this decision. Many members of the audience were furious! They accosted him afterward, shaking fingers and raising voices: How could he decide that someone's—in their eyes, a potential Palestinian terrorist's—human rights were more important than the threat of security?! Yet that is exactly what he and the court decided, and the United States should be looking to that decision. I asked Ken Roth, executive director of Human Rights Watch, what the effect on the ground had been after the decision. He replied that it had made a huge difference: that the use of torture by Israel since 1999 has been nothing like it had been before the ruling; not that there is no torture, but that it is enormously reduced. *These things I remember and my heart grows strong.* Jewish sources abound that can help us. Jewish Theological Seminary rabbinical student Melissa Weintraub, doing groundbreaking work, has written four articles about four categories in Jewish law that stand against torture. The categories are:

1. **The ban against self-incrimination**, seen in the Talmud, *Sanhedrin* 9b, as "A person may not incriminate himself," since he/she is his own kinsman. The Rambam later suggests that one

would have to be in deep misery to offer a confession of one's own guilt. Modern scholars have suggested that the ban's purpose was to repudiate the kind of justice system that depends on brutality and violations of privacy and human dignity.

2. ***K'vod HaB'riyot*: dignity of human beings**, seen in the Talmud, *Bava M'tzia* 58b, which states that "anyone who shames his fellow in public, it is as if he spilled blood." Human dignity derives from the understanding that all human beings are created *b'tzelem Elohim*, "in the image of God"; to dishonor a human being, therefore, is somehow to dishonor God.

3. **Balancing the *rodeif* defense**: Restrictions on the use of force even when being pursued or defending oneself. There is a Talmudic story of one who came before Rabah and said to him, "The governor of my town has ordered me, 'Go and kill so-and-so; if not, I will kill you.' Rabah answered him, 'Let him rather kill you than that you should commit murder; why do you think your blood is redder? Perhaps his blood is redder'" (Babylonian Talmud, *Sanhedrin* 74a; *P'sachim* 25b). Rashi, reading this, elaborates, "Who says your life is more beloved by God than his? Perhaps his life is more beloved" (Rashi on *P'sachim* 25b). Weintraub teaches us that from a Jewish legal perspective, to be able to use violence when being pursued, the danger has to be imminent and spontaneous; you must be certain that it is so; you cannot harm third-party suspects; and if permitted to use some violence, you must do the minimum possible harm. These requirements are rarely, if ever, being met in United States military detention facilities.

4. **Knowing the heart of the stranger**, as we are taught in Exodus, "You shall not oppress a stranger, for you know the heart of the stranger, having yourselves been strangers in the land of Egypt" (Exodus 23:9). We know from the inside what it can mean to be abandoned to powerful governments. The Geneva Conventions, which ban torture as a war crime, were drafted and adopted by the nations of the world in response to the

atrocities of Nazi Germany. As Jews, we have or could have a special sensitivity to the immorality and costs of torture.

These things we remember and pour out our hearts.

So what is the matter, the heart of the matter? Why haven't Americans, Jews or not, responded in full voice to the outrageous abuses and torture by our government? Is it just that it is all so far away, and we can barely manage to get through our days as it is? Or is it that we are ambivalent? The people being tortured are almost all Muslim prisoners, and as Jews and New Yorkers we have been given reason to fear Muslim terror. Too many Muslims across the world express the basest antisemitism, and some have engaged in outrageous violence, sometimes against Jews particularly, sometimes against Muslims and others. Others perpetuate myths from the Protocols of the Elders of Zion to the four thousand Jews absent from the World Trade Center on September 11. We have reason to fear. Yet our fear is precisely why we must take extra precaution, remember the words of Israeli Chief Justice Barak, and maintain the democratic ideals that should keep this country and us Jews safer. Torture does not succeed in getting accurate information, and outrage against U.S. torture practices will only add fuel to terrorists' fire. Just as we are to know the heart of the stranger, so too we know what it is to see our tortured leaders made martyrs.

Shall we watch as the United States becomes like ancient Rome, creating martyrs from "religious fanatics"? Shall we become like the Crusaders or the Spanish Inquisitors?

The inquisitors ordered Maria Lopez a Jewish prisoner of the Spanish Inquisition, to be taken to the torture chamber and to be undressed and placed on the rack of torment and to be tied with some hemp ropes. She was . . . admonished by the . . . inquisitors to tell the truth: who were those persons whom she had seen commit those heretical crimes of which she is accused? . . . The order was

made to pour water with a pitcher and to put something additional
upon her face on top of the silk headdress that she had on her face.
It was ordered for the ropes to be tightened with a tourniquet and it
was tightened with two tourniquets.[45]

One form of torture currently being used by the United
States against its detainees is called waterboarding: the prisoner
is strapped to a board and lowered under water until the prisoner thinks he or she will drown. I cannot see how it differs
from the torture imposed on Maria Lopez. All the methods,
all the sadism, were perfected long ago: the water, the focus on
sexual organs, the humiliation, the abuse of religious items and
principles, the face coverings, the hanging by one's feet or fingers or bent arms, the small spaces, the use of fear of death. A
researcher named John Conroy—no relation—found that studies
of bystanders suggest that dehumanization tends to accompany
feelings of powerlessness to help. Torture heralds the breakdown
of empathy, in other words; we fail to see the one tortured as a
human being. That is certainly true for the torturer, who long
ago stopped seeing the victim as human. Yet Conroy suggests
that it is true for us, as well. We too see "torture victim" when
we ought to see human being. Seeing "torture victim" allows
us to stop seeing, to turn away, to turn the page, to turn to the
needs of everyday life.

Yet on this day, when our task is to turn, to ask God to turn
us, we cannot turn away. Part of our *t'shuvah*, our turn, on this
Yom Kippur, must be to turn toward hope. Signing onto the Jewish Campaign Against Torture letter is a small step that will take
a few minutes, as I said earlier. Yet the many small steps added
together, even from just this one gathered community, will add
weight to the understanding of human dignity, of Jewish memory,

---

45. Renee Levine Melammed, *Heretics or Daughters of Israel: The Crypto-Jewish*
Women of Castille (New York: Oxford University Press, 2001), 136–37.

of empathy and compassion. Write to Senators McCain and Levin and others who are going to try to keep this issue alive even in the face of a presidential veto, or write to the president, write to the press.

But is there something we can do that comes first, something to remind us of humanity, of *k'vod hab'riyot*, the dignity of a human being who was created in the image of God? What can we do to ensure that every time we see someone being degraded in a military prison camp, we see "human being"? What must we do to make that turn, that slight shift of mind that changes every-thing? The Chasidic teacher Zeev Wolf of Zhitomer taught that *t'shuvah* happens in an instant and happens all the time. Let's us try to make those instant shifts every time we read the paper, every time we see a disturbing photograph, every time we hear about the kind of gruesome torture that makes us want to flinch and turn away instead. Let that shift to seeing "human being" be our *t'shuvah* on this Yom Kippur.

Akiva, flayed to the bone, understood the words of the *Sh'ma* as he never had before. It gave him hope even in death, hope that he was fulfilling the desire of his God. Can we on this Yom Kippur find the hope to answer the call to love God with all our hearts, with all our souls, with all our strength, without having to be tortured? Can we find hope in the letters we sign, the calls we make, the shifts that will form our *t'shuvah*? The Senate is finally awake and public opinion may be following. There is room to hope for the results of our actions. Can we then muster enough memory and heart to respond to God's words, Akiva's words, with our actions? If God on this day is called by the name He told Moses—*El Rachum v'Chanun*—then we must rise to meet that challenge and ourselves be compassionate and loving, with all our hearts, all our souls, all our strength. *These things I remember as I pour out my heart.* Lisa sing: Lamentations 2:19: "Pour out your heart like water / And remember."

Soul-Shattering

Rosh HaShanah 2007 / 5768

I used to think Rosh HaShanah was mainly a holiday of reunion. When I was a kid we ate apples and honey and honey cake, dressed up in new clothes, wished each other a sweet year, and prepared to get serious at Yom Kippur. Rosh HaShanah for me is still reunion time, a time—as at a Pesach seder—to look around and see who is here and who is not. Rosh HaShanah is also the time when we return to God: *Hashiveinu Adonai eilecha v'nashuvah*—We ask God to return us and we pledge to return. We stand at the gate hoping to find a way in.

In the parlance of the nineteenth-century Chasidim, God has now left the field of the month of Elul, when we all had easy access to the Divine Presence, and has reentered the palace and ascended the throne. How do we connect to God now? How do we open the gate, walk up to the throne? What is the point of Rosh HaShanah in a time and place far from kings and queens and the prayers of farmers and shepherds? An answer came to me a few weeks ago, as I met with Rosie Silber-Marker as she began to prepare a *d'var Torah* for her upcoming bat mitzvah. In the *Chumash Etz Hayim*, Rosie and I found a comment that has stayed with me: Commenting on the fact that Jacob is shaken or afraid after awakening from his dream of the ladder and God standing by him, it says, "We tend to speak casually of coming into God's presence. Jacob's response here reminds us that to truly encounter God in our lives is a soul-shattering experience. We are shaken to the core of our souls, and we are never the same person afterward."

On Rosh HaShanah our encounter with God is not casual. We dare to hope that it will be soul-shattering. *Avinu Malkeinu*, we sing yearningly, have mercy on us, answer us. We want to feel Your presence to the core of our souls. That yearning, that encounter is the reason for Rosh HaShanah's continuing power, after the apples and honey are gone and the new clothes get a little limp in the heat, as they always did. The dictionary (*Webster's Unabridged*) tells me that to shatter is to break something into pieces, as by a blow; to damage; to destroy or impair; to weaken or refute; or to be broken into fragments. I am reminded by writer Ellen Frankel that "the Baal Shem Tov taught that there are many keys to unlock the gates of repentance, but that the ax—that is, the sincere prayer of the broken heart—is the mightiest key of all, capable of shattering even the strongest gate. Similarly, Nachman of Bratslav taught that nothing is as whole as a broken heart."

In some way, we all know that soul-shattering: I look around this room tonight and see the faces that reveal so many stories. Soul-shattering is your aging mother losing her mind and memory. Soul-shattering is a diagnosis of cancer or Parkinson's, forever changing your future. Soul-shattering is hitting bottom with drink or drugs or gambling. Soul-shattering is the loss of a baby or a young daughter or a dear friend or a nearly grown son.

We also know the joyful way our souls can shatter and open. I remember a moment a few years ago when I felt so lucky to be in my life—when many things came together at once—so lucky that I wept and wished my meager words of prayer could come close to the life-changing joy I felt. Looking around the room again, I know that soul-shattering may be a baby coming into the world, or falling into the love of your life, or living when you had thought you might die. We are shaken to the core of our souls, and we are never the same person afterward.

When I was a senior in college, my mother tried very seriously to commit suicide. My family was in Virginia, I was in Boston, and I have never prayed as hard as I did in the hours between hearing she was missing and learning that, somewhat miraculously, she had been found and revived. I was shaken to the core of my soul; in some ways I am still recovering. Only now am I able to wonder about her shattered soul, beyond what I have known for years about the ravages of clinical depression. When I think of her despair—the hopelessness that must have so consumed her—I am deeply saddened and wish I had a way to reach out to her now. I do know that she was always glad she did not succeed in killing herself.

I was twenty when my mother tried to kill herself. She lived another twenty-seven years, full of pain and joy. At Rosh HaShanah, I don't visit her grave. I don't look at photographs of her. It holds no meaning. Instead, I visit her life. I sing the songs she loved to sing, enter the holiday saying the prayers I learned from her, gather friends and family as she so often did. And this year, for what combination of reasons I am not sure, I can recognize that her near suicide was soul-shattering for me. It was terrifying, and I carry the memory of that terror with me.

I think the reason we read about Abraham on Rosh HaShanah is because his story shows us two kinds of shattering—the stunning, transforming joy of having a child when he had given up on the idea altogether, and the unfathomable agony of being asked to give up—to kill!—the child he loves and has waited so long for. He and Sarah both laugh when they learn they are to have a child; Abraham falls on his face! The Torah reports no response from him to God's stunning request to sacrifice that child. The midrash shows him holding it off, step by step. As we begin the year, each year, we are asked to take in this story, to try to imagine Abraham's joy and his agony, his embrace of Isaac, his unwilling expulsion of Ishmael, his horror as he lifts his own hand grasping the consuming knife. Jewish tradition says God tested Abraham ten times.

The tenth test is the *Akeidah*, the binding—the agreement to sacrifice—Isaac, his hard-won son. After it is over, after Abraham has found another way, a ram in place of his son, God finally says, "Now I know that you are in awe of God, in fear of God."

Soul-shattering is Abraham's encounter with God, God saying, "Understand at the first and the last that life lived fully includes the highest joys and the deepest pain, heartbreaking love and soul-shattering agony." Our task on Rosh HaShanah is to confront that reality, over and over again, year after year. The king is on the throne and we stand at the gate, trying to decide whether to push to enter or not. As the poet Muriel Rukeyser has written:

> To be a Jew in the twentieth century
> Is to be offered a gift.   If you refuse,
> Wishing to be invisible, you choose
> Death of the spirit, the stone insanity.
> Accepting, take full life.   Full agonies . . .
> The gift is torment. . . .
> But the accepting wish,
> The whole and fertile spirit as guarantee
> For every human freedom, suffering to be free,
> Daring to live for the impossible.[46]

Abraham dared to live for the impossible. Let's be truthful: We sitting here live mostly pleasant lives. We have great joys, I hope. And I hope we have few agonies. We can watch on television or read in the newspaper or online any time of day or night the most horrifying stories and images we can think of, yet they rarely touch us in a way that reaches our souls. Otherwise, as Kathryn said to me last week, we would all be at the White House right now or on a plane to Darfur or Iraq. I cannot get out of my head Nina Berman's photo of the Marine wedding (you may have seen it too)—

---

46. Muriel Rukeyser, *Collected Poems of Muriel Rukeyser*, ed. by Janet Kaufman and Anne Herzog (Pittsburgh, PA: University of Pittsburgh Press, 2005).

that young man whose head and face were reconstructed beyond recognition, yet here he is getting married to a young woman who sent him off to war with the promise of love in both their hearts, a promise that transcends the intervening horrors. It shakes me, and I cannot shake off the memory. Yet I see it from a distance; it is a photograph, after all.

Even the Shoah is becoming a series of photographs to our children, and soon that will be true of 9/11. What was once shattering fades in memory. But Rosh HaShanah is Yom HaZikaron—the day of memory, of remembrance. And it is the day we remember Abraham, and remember risk, and remember death, and life. Remembering, facing what may shatter our souls, we become whole again for another year. Last summer at my last retreat with the Institute for Jewish Spirituality, we were introduced to a practice called *hitbod'dut*, being alone with yourself. In this mode, borrowed from Chasidic Judaism, we were to walk outside alone—to wherever we wanted at the center we were at—and talk out loud to God, continually, without stopping, for half an hour. We could say we were stuck, we could say we didn't know what to say, but we had to keep talking.

I started walking up a hill to an abandoned campsite and began talking. Within a minute or two I was weeping as my shyness at actually talking out loud to God without printed prayer gave way to actually talking out loud to God. I poured out my heart, including things I didn't even know I was thinking about, grief I thought had long dissipated, hopes I had not yet spoken. I cried and cried and talked and talked, walking and talking and crying until I was spent, my shell of poise or calm or capability shattered. I felt drained and open: able to move on in ways I did not even know I needed to.

It took Abraham and Isaac three days to go a very short distance, a long journey of the soul up to Har HaMoriah: the mountain of God's teaching, of God's appearance. My life's troubles, my little walk up that hill, seem puny by comparison. But I have known great joy and great sorrow and strive on Rosh HaShanah to encounter God in a way that truly touches God and transforms me. The opposite of the shattered soul is not the hard shell of denial, but indifference, *sh'veih nefesh*, the overbalanced soul. I would rather have the shattering, the imbalance we live with, the tears this life can provoke, the extraordinary joys that are still possible. Otherwise, we live as though looking at a photograph.

Rabbi Margaret Holub wrote once about being the person chosen to sit with a dead body overnight, guarding it in the traditional way. This was the body of someone she had known in life, and Margaret said looking at her body was like looking at a photograph of her: It looked like her but was not her. The soul had left, the breath had left, the life had left. That is what Abraham came to know and what we Jews confront this and every Rosh HaShanah.

A new year has arrived with who knows what joys and horrors yet to come. Abraham's story reminds us that we can't escape. The new year brings new life, and life is soul-shattering. With shattered souls and broken hearts, we are open to life, to God. It can hurt like hell or break us open in joy. Each of you sitting here has to know what will enable you to live life most fully and avoid indifference. What I mean to say is that Rosh HaShanah is a time to begin. Our society likes to be happy, likes to avoid aging and sorrow and pain and death. Judaism likes to be happy too and wants us to know sorrow and pain and even death as the parts of life that they are. Life can shatter the soul. But it is all we have. The only other choice is death, or indifference.

In Hope,
Rabbi Ellen Lippmann

CPSIA information can be obtained
at www.ICGtesting.com
Printed in the USA
FFOW02n1710220518
46821543-49004FF